# JESUS, PAUL, *and* POWER

# JESUS, PAUL, *and* POWER

◆　◆　◆

Rhetoric, Ritual, and Metaphor
in Ancient Mediterranean Christianity

## Rick F. Talbott

Foreword by S. Scott Bartchy

CASCADE *Books* · Eugene, Oregon

JESUS, PAUL, AND POWER
Rhetoric, Ritual, and Metaphor in Ancient Mediterranean Christianity

Cascade Books
A Division of Wipf and Stock Publishers
199 W. 8th Ave., Suite 3
Eugene, OR 97401
www.wipfandstock.com

ISBN 13: 978-1-59752-448-3

*Cataloging-in-Publication data*

Talbott, Rick Franklin, 1949–.
Jesus, Paul, and power : rhetoric, ritual, and metaphor in ancient Mediterranean Christianity / Rick F. Talbott ; foreword by S. Scott Bartchy.

xviii + 194 p.; 23 cm. Includes bibliographical references and index.

ISBN 13: 978-1-59752-448-3

1. Jesus Christ. 2. Paul, the Apostle, Saint. 3. Church history—Primitive and early church, ca. 30–600. 4. Bible. N.T. Matthew—Criticism, interpretation, etc. 5. Bible. N.T. Corinthians—Criticism, interpretation, etc. 6. Bible. N.T.—Social scientific criticism. 7. Ritual. 8. Rites and ceremonies. I. Bartchy, S. Scott. II. Title.

BS2653 T35 2010

Manufactured in the USA.

Dedicated to Kees W. Bolle,
master teacher, indelible spirit, faithful friend

"If it is true that we no longer regard other nations and traditions as mentally inferior, it is still not enough to recognize their equality in a purely formal and abstract way."

—Kees W. Bolle

# Contents

# Foreword

An apparent paradox that has vexed many scholars of the early history of the Christ-movement is the fact that, while Paul of Tarsus became the earliest and most prolific writer in this movement, he appears to pay little attention to the historical Jesus of Nazareth. In his letters, Paul quotes Jesus fewer than five times, when it would seem to have made his admonitions more persuasive had he frequently reinforced his judgments with "a command from the Lord." To the contrary, at one point after citing Jesus' teaching on divorce, he then makes an exception to it—on his own authority (see 1 Cor 7:10).

The scholarly emphasis on the undeniable differences between Jesus and Paul apparently began with Ferdinand Christian Baur at the University of Tübingen, Germany, during the middle of the nineteenth century. By the end of that century, Wilhelm Wrede at the university in Breslau had opened the chasm even wider between the "morally religious" Jesus and the "dogmatic" Paul.[1] Wrede claimed that the differences between them were so great that Paul, not Jesus, was the real "founder of Christianity."

During the twentieth century, various influential attempts to bridge this chasm notably failed to persuade most western scholars and thus kept alive the questions: Did Paul, after all, really know anything substantial about the historical Jesus apart from his execution at the hands of the governing authorities? And did Paul value whatever he may have known about Jesus' life to be significant? Had he not written these words: "We regard no one according to the flesh, even though we once knew Christ according to the flesh" (2 Cor 5:16)?

1. See Victor Paul Furnish's comprehensive and reliable survey of this discussion: "The Jesus-Paul Debate: From Baur to Bultmann," originally published in the *Bulletin of the John Rylands Library* 47 (1964/65) 342–81, and now slightly revised and easily accessible in *Paul and Jesus*, ed. A. J. M. Wedderburn, JSNTSup 37 (Sheffield: JSOT Press, 1989) 17–50.

The scholarly discussion remained focused on comparing the respective "theologies" of Jesus and Paul, leading Rudolf Bultmann to make the astonishing claim that discontinuity between Paul and Jesus was actually a good thing. Was not Paul the theological genius who rightly concluded that knowledge about the historical Jesus was neither necessary nor even helpful to anyone's authentic faith in the saving action of God through the "Christ event"?

Bultmann knew many pious Christians who claimed to know much about Jesus but who had not made the critical existential decisions to accept Jesus as the eschatological in-breaking of God's kingdom and then order their own existence accordingly. The liberal theology of that era shined the spotlight on Jesus and his moral teaching and pushed the theological Paul off into the wings. In contrast, Bultmann invited Paul out of the shadows back to center stage to function as the key to reading the New Testament, without worrying about what could be known or not about the historical Jesus. Paul's theology rose again (following Martin Luther's emphasis) as "die Mitte der Schrift" (the theological center of the Christian Scriptures).

Note that the entire discussion focused on theological issues, with an ongoing emphasis on difference and discontinuity. In the meantime, various scholars initiated the "third quest of the historical Jesus" ca. 1980 with a fresh emphasis on sifting the traditions about Jesus through the sieve of the dominant culture and economic realities of the early Roman Empire. In the view that emerged from this reassessment, the historical Jesus was clearly a social prophet, even a social radical, as were those among his followers who created the Gospel genre which focuses on what Jesus did and said prior to his execution, i.e., the historical Jesus.

This perspective soon made the question regarding the continuity/ discontinuity of the Jesus tradition with Paul all the more acute. Where was Paul in all this? In light of the sordid history of the later use of Paul's words by persons in power to support the divine right of kings, the oppression of women at home and in church, and the institution of slavery, how could anyone regarded him in any way as a "social radical"? Answers began to come in from those scholars who initiated what might be called the "quest for the historical Paul." Now the fact that Paul carried out his mission in the context of Roman culture, economics, and military power became a central focus. As scholars constructed a thick description of that context, Paul looked more and more like a social radical himself. After all, had not Roman authorities executed him as they had Jesus?

At the same time, however, influential feminist scholars were publishing a very different response to Paul's words because of the divine authority ascribed to Paul's words in the New Testament. Moving past the rant heard in the 1970s that "Paul is a male chauvinist pig," these scholars did important work by focusing their unswerving attention on the multiple ways various defenders of the status quo frequently quoted sentences from Paul's letters to give divine sanction to oppressive patriarchal social systems, to justify male dominance in all areas of life, and to reinforce claims that hierarchy in human relationships is inevitable. For such interpreters, the simple fact that Paul's letters became a central part of the Christian Bible has been sufficient for them to blend the historical Paul out of the picture and to think of each sentence as an expression of the will of God.

While some feminist scholars continued efforts to interpret Paul's words by focusing on the specific historical circumstances that provoked him to write his letters, many other feminist scholars concentrated their attention on the consequences of the fact that millions of people regard his words as revealed words from God. This way of reading Paul's letters has been facilitated by the ease of isolating the meaning of each sentence from its context by reference to its chapter and verse number. For many readers, this citation system has apparently functioned as an open invitation to read Paul's words as timeless and context-free. Constrained neither by any serious interest in these words' historical context nor even by their rhetorical function within a specific letter, these interpreters assume that Paul's words, as God's inspired words, must be directly applicable to all times, places, and cultures.

It is this contextless reading of Paul's words and the widespread use of them to support relationships of domination that have increasingly attracted the attention of the feminist scholars with whom Talbott interacts in this book. These scholars employ an analytical method that draws robustly on the deep insights into human behavior proposed by the cultural critic Michel Foucault and other philosophers regarding the quality of power-relationships. Their approach analyzes the ways in which those who have occupied "power up" positions sought and seek to justify and maintain their control of others. This is the framework that these feminists use for their analysis of Paul's letters, with particular attention to how Paul crafted his rhetoric for the purpose, as they see it, of securing for himself a position of dominance over his converts.

In this book, Talbott has chosen to meet these scholars on their own ground and to insist that even there they have told only one-half of the story. He insists—rightly I think—that the many passages in which Paul presents himself as a servant, really a "slave," of his converts must be brought into any fair-minded analysis of his relationship with those to whom he sent his letters. To that end, building on Elisabeth Schuessler Fiorenza's neologism for relationships of domination, "kyriarchy," Talbott has coined his own new word "kyridoularchy" (dominating/serving) to incorporate in one complex term the tension he finds in Paul's fluctuation between giving strong commands and yet clearly also using his power to serve his converts.

In a fascinating comparison of Paul to Jesus as presented in the canonical Gospels, Talbott concludes that Jesus consistently put aside the privileges and power that he enjoyed as a male in his society, that he thereby made himself "a eunuch for the sake of the kingdom of God," while Paul did not. To that extent, Talbott agrees with many of the feminist scholars he references while arguing that they have overlooked evidence that he finds critically important.

Talbott has carried forward in a very productive way the historical and comparative sensitivities that he developed to a high level in his doctoral dissertation. In this book, he displays both a truly extraordinary range of reading across disciplines and the mental dexterity to integrate many of the contesting views that circulate in contemporary scholarship, with special attention to the contributions of many feminist scholars. Then he proposes original solutions to some of the most vexing problems related to understanding Jesus and Paul in the context of ancient Mediterranean religion and culture. His powerful key to unlocking the door to deeper understanding of these ancient documents is his close analysis of how Paul's letters describe and apply power when compared with the evidence in the Jesus tradition.

A few years ago, Prof. Talbott made an enthusiastically received presentation to my advanced seminar at UCLA dealing with sexuality and spirituality in early Christianity. His original analysis of the significance of Jesus' perplexing saying about "becoming eunuchs for the kingdom's sake" made excellent sense to all the participants, including myself. At that point, we encouraged him to expand these insights into a book, which he has done, and which you now have in your hands.

Shortly after Talbott sent his manuscript to the publisher, both he and I were invited by two colleagues who are also very interested in the interpretation of Paul's letters to join them for a series of long and lively discussions about the issues that Talbott treats in this book. The most extensive debate was provoked by Talbott's statement: "Paul comes off as very authoritative with a typical form of kyriarchal (i.e., dominating) rhetoric that required submission and obedience—especially for those who opposed him." Here Talbott agrees with many other feminist scholars. Indeed, even a casual reader of Paul's letters quickly observes that Paul wrote to his converts using strong, authoritative rhetoric and stressing his own status as an apostle of Christ as his basis for his exhortations.

Here are some of the questions that these discussions provoked.

- What other option did Paul have than using authoritative rhetoric, if he hoped to gain and keep the attention of the males in his culture who had been raised to dominate all persons they could? As at least his letters to the Corinthians and the Galatians frankly reveal, some of those who responded well to his authority at first were now resisting both his leadership and his message of new life in Christ.

- Was it not his converts' own vacillation in this regard that provoked his repeated assertions of his authority?

- Was his own "doularchy"-type behavior so contrary to what was expected from "real men" and conventional male leadership that he created serious confusion among his converts?

- In response, did some of the Corinthians simply choose to leave this new and radical community when Paul wrote such challenging words to them, rather than to accept his unfamiliar and, in their judgment, weak style of leadership while with them?

- Did Paul intend to create a permanent structure of control over his converts? If not, why did he write to them with strong words, sometimes even sarcastically ("I wish that you had become kings!" 1 Cor 4:8)?

- How could Paul insist that his new way of understanding reality was right and that the dominant and violent culture in the Roman Empire was on a trajectory of death without re-inscribing the very patterns of power-relationships he seems to be trying to deconstruct?

- In the context of his cultural constraints, were there any options for Paul but to use "anti-language" to undermine the dominant discourse? How could he depose fathers, husbands, and emperors as "lords" without putting Jesus, the Christ who did not please himself, in their places? And how could he encourage his converts to accept Jesus as their paradoxical "lord" without claiming to have Jesus' authority for his message?

- Once Paul's words became treasured as Christian Scripture, with the implication of their timeless authority, how can the strongest case be made for insisting that knowledge about the historical Paul's specific cultural context is essential for any adequate interpretation of his meaning?

Talbott suggests that Paul's attempts to deconstruct conventional patterns of authority while stressing his own God-given authority resulted in his becoming a "bifurcated" communicator. Thus Talbott challenges his readers to reflect on some of the most pressing issues in today's New Testament scholarship: the degree of Paul's continuity with the historical Jesus, Paul's own historical situation and cultural constraints, and the serious consequences of the fact that Paul's occasion-specific letters became regarded as God's revelation in Christian Scripture.

Keeping in mind the title of this challenging, creative, and informative book, I invite you to follow Talbott and decide for yourself about the extent to which Paul followed Jesus in the non-hierarchal use of power.

S. Scott Bartchy
Professor of Christian Origins and the History of Religion
Department of History, UCLA
June 2010

# Preface

This book assumes that Jesus of Nazareth and Paul of Tarsus, like all ancient Mediterranean peoples, were products of powerful intersecting cultural and social systems.[1] Jesus and Paul responded to a set of specific circumstances in ways that can also be considered typical according to ancient Mediterranean standards and social structures. Their responses had corresponding religious, political, and economic ramifications for themselves and their respective communities. The Second Testament Gospels[2] along with Paul's surviving letters give the modern reader some indication how Jesus and Paul—along with certain members of these early communities—responded. But this is possible only after careful analysis informed by current scholarship from several fields. Insights about these intriguing ancient texts and the figures they refer to require literary analysis and reconstruction of the texts' historical, cultural, and social contexts. No small task, but doable thanks to decades of serious scholarship. Chapter 1 summarizes several different critical approaches that are used collaboratively in this book.

The modern reader need also realize that these ancient texts reflect a dynamic interaction between both their authors and the targeted audiences. This suggests that the communities who heard these texts read around their shared meal also had influenced the texts' authors. Subsequently, one should also imagine other "voices" within the texts as one reads say-

1. Cultural systems that include accepted values, standards of behavior, roles based on gender and one's status, which translated into honor—power and privilege. Social systems included religion (expressed through symbolic texts, rituals, places, and artifacts) embedded in politics (found in institutions like kinship, government-legal agencies, and education) and the economy (linked to production of goods, control of labor and land, taxation, and debt). See Hanson and Oakman 2008, 12–14, 124.

2. I will use the terms *First Testament* and *Second Testament* instead of *Old Testament* and *New Testament* throughout this book. I also include the saying source Q and the *Gospel of Thomas* as important sources in this regard.

ings ascribed to Jesus and letters written by Paul. Additionally, one must come to terms with the sobering recognition that we as modern readers have also been conditioned by our own cultural assumptions. Based on these premises, I proceed to examine how Jesus and Paul responded to and used power—taking note that their responses involved using power in the form of ancient rhetoric, rituals, and metaphors. Recent scholarship on religious rituals and Jesus's and Paul's communities' meals will be used as one way to analyze their power relations. We now understand that such ancient meals represented ways of negotiating power relations—especially when bringing different social and ethnic factions together represented tension and an almost-certain probability of conflict. This book analyzes and seeks to understand the nature of Jesus's and Paul's responses to and uses of power as both conditioned (and therefore typical) as well as creative (and therefore innovative) for the time.

Chapter 2 suggests that Jesus and his Galilean movement began as a response to conflict Jesus encountered with his own kyriarchal[3] village authorities. Jesus challenged the traditional powers at Nazareth over issues that impacted peasants economically—such as debt and honor-shame values. This conflict precipitated the emergence of new fictive kinship groups throughout lower Galilee. Jesus's fictive kinship groups were based on an antikyriarchal structure and were forced to develop economic support for themselves. As we shall see in chapter 2, the formation of these new fictive kinship groups actually caused poverty among some families that lost sons or daughters to the Jesus movement.

Chapter 3 challenges the idea that Jesus repudiated marriage in favor of celibacy based on the eunuch metaphor in Matt 19:12. I base this interpretation on reading the eunuch saying as a metaphor about male power. This saying should be understood as part of Matthew's text about marriage, divorce, and remarriage (19:3–11), and against the ancient Mediterranean concept and treatment of eunuchs. Subsequently, Jesus did not oppose marriage but kyriarchal marriage, divorce, and remarriage that privileged males while oppressing women. The eunuch saying

---

3. Throughout this book I will use Elizabeth Schüssler Fiorenza's neologism *kyriarchy* in place of *patriarchy*. Taken from two Greek words—*kyrios* for "lord," and *archē* for "rule," *kyriarchy* refers to any person, male or female, who uses his or her power over others in concert with the prevailing and intersecting social systems. More detailed definitions and justifications for this term are addressed along the way.

in this passage should be understood as a metaphor that repudiated male power enshrined in the kyriarchal twin institutions of households and marriage-divorce-remarriage that were generally also supported by religion (Deut 24:1).

Chapter 4 engages modern theories on Paul's use of power and suggests that none of the current treatments of Paul on the subject adequately accounts for the complexities and inconsistencies found in Paul's writings. Paul must be viewed as responding to an interconnected web of conflicts created by Roman imperial ideology and a variety of issues within his own Christ communities, including issues Paul addressed involving Christ communities at Rome. Chapter 4 notes Paul's ambivalent and inconsistent responses to and uses of power as bifurcated between traditional kyriarchy and "kyridoularchy"—a neologism referring to Paul's appeal for community members to use any form of power to serve others after his example and the paradigmatic example of Christ himself.

Chapter 5 examines parts of 1 Corinthians and especially passages where Paul fluctuates between power over others (kyriarchy) and empowerment for others (kyridoularchy). This analysis likewise maintains that Paul did not demand Christ-community members to choose celibacy over marriage. Rather, Paul provided advice for the married that reveals a restructured, nonkyriarchal marriage along with progressive liberties for wives, singles, and widows, based on mutual kyridoularchy. Similarly, Paul's advice to the Corinthians' practice of the Lord's Supper also reveals his preference for nonkyriarchal relationships based again on Christ's own example of kyridoularchy. However, Paul also comes off as very authoritative with a typical form of kyriarchal rhetoric that required submission and obedience—especially for those who opposed him. The book concludes by comparing Jesus's and Paul's uses of power, finding basic similarities based on social and cultural conditions. However, it also contrasts Jesus and Paul in the final analysis, comparing Jesus's consistent repudiation of kyriarchy with Paul's vacillation between kyriarchy and kyridoularchy.

# Acknowledgments

I am indebted to a host of friends and helpers that have helped to make this book possible by their critical suggestions and friendly encouragement. First, I wish to thank the editor in chief of Wipf and Stock Publishers, Dr. K. C. Hanson. His scholarship and professionalism have guided me from the inception of this project. Readers will notice that many references and quotes in this book have been taken from Dr. Hanson's own articles and books. Chapter 2, "Nazareth's Rebellious Son: Deviance and Downward Mobility in the Galilean Jesus Movement," was originally published in *Biblical Theology Bulletin* 38 (2008). It appears here with permission from *BTB* and with my gratitude to the editor, Dr. David M. Bossman. Some revisions have been made to the original article. Chapter 3, "Imaging the Matthean Eunuch Community: Kyriarchy on the Chopping Block," was originally published in the *Journal for the Feminist Study of Religion* 22 (2006). I am indebted to the editor in chief, Elizabeth Schüssler Fiorenza, for permission to use the article here and for her gracious encouragement during its first publication. Some revisions to the original have been made.

Dr. S. Scott Bartchy served as one of my mentors in the graduate program at UCLA in the Department of History. His scholarship is internationally known. His career at UCLA has been formally recognized with awards for exceptional teaching and as the head of the Center for the Study of Religion. I am one of his many students indebted to his incredible devotion to us—and now privileged by his devotion as a faithful friend with his lovely wife, Nancy. Several references from Dr. Bartchy's works also appear prominently throughout this book. I very much appreciate Dr. Bartchy taking the time to discuss various issues regarding my book and then agreeing to write the Foreword. Closer to home, Dean Elizabeth Say has always taken time to inquire and to encourage my work—this book in particular. This is remarkable given her duties and workload managing the College of Humanities at California State University, Northridge. I am particularly grateful to Dr. Patrick Nichelson who recently retired after forty years of extraordinary service. Patrick served as Chair of the Department of Religious Studies and was President of the statewide California Faculty Association—holding several other positions of leadership at the University. Patrick has been a great source of support in all my university responsibilities and a great dialogue partner about historical Jesus research. He often covered for me to free time for writing. His good humor and gracious leadership have made teaching and those nonteaching responsibilities at the university a more rewarding experience. My friend and colleague Dr. Crerar Douglas remains unsurpassed in erudition and wisdom. His example of devotion to scholarship and teaching inspires colleagues and students alike. He too has been a tremendous encourager throughout my university career and naturally in the writing of this book. Dr. Linda Lam Easton has the capacity to energize and lift up everyone fortunate enough to be in her presence; her students continue to praise her innovative and impassioned teaching. She provides balance and a sense of sanity when it's needed most. Her efforts certainly helped advance the publication of this book. Dr. James Goss remains one of the most knowledgeable scholars on religion, Jesus, and early Christianity. It was always a privilege and joy to discuss these topics with him over lunch. He provided insight and encouragement that contributed to this book. Jim was an exceptional chair for our department for many years, always engaging faculty and staff with wisdom and good cheer. Upon his retirement, I was a recipient of hundreds of books from his rich personal library—many used for researching and writing this book. Our department administrator, Linda Jones, has made life easier for all of us. She has been instrumental in helping me with my duties at the university, which also helped to facilitate the research and writing of this book. My thanks to Dr. Elaine Goodfriend for helping me translate sections of *Qiddushin* and *Sifre Devarim*.

Dr. Amir Hussain and his partner Joan Becker have been great friends and now indispensable sources of edifying companionship. Dr. Hussain has always acted on my behalf to help advance my university career. I am also a better person for knowing him and Joan. Professor Randal Cummings and I have been friends from junior high school through graduate school at UCLA, and now as colleagues at CSUN. Over these many years now, I have benefited from his exceptional scholarship and especially his comradeship. His suggestions were likewise exceptional. Robert Mason's helpful criticisms aided with the chapters on Paul. I appreciated his efforts, knowing of his demands as a PhD candidate at Claremont School of Religion. Mark Grover, tried-and-true friend if there ever was one, gave me feedback necessary to clarify several points for the nonspecialist reader. Scott Van Antwerp and Matthew Sagen also gave me invaluable help by going over the introduction and chapters 4 and 5. This in the midst of administrating a youth center in San Fernando and ministering to over fifty inner-city youths five days a week. I thank Alvin Durham, Danny Mares, and Geoff Bottenfield—along with all the good people at San Fernando for their gracious support and inspiration. James "Skip" Stock continues to inspire many who seek to be truly human with his wisdom and tenacity. Skip's courage is contagious, and his concern for all "others" is humbling. Everyone experiencing the demands and trials of book writing or of life in general should have a friend like Skip.

Finally, I get to thank my wonderful wife, Anne. She typed the bibliography, a chore only genuine love could endure. Most important, she has been the source of my healing and the rejuvenation of my appreciation of human relationships built on mutual concern and love.

# Abbreviations

## ANCIENT SOURCES

| | |
|---|---|
| *Ant.* | *Antiquities of the Judeans* (Josephus) |
| *b.* | Babylonian Talmud (*Babli*) |
| *CD* | *Damascus Document* (Qumran) |
| *Contempl. Life* | *On the Contemplative Life* (Philo) |
| *Creation* | *On the Creation of the World* (Philo) |
| *1 En.* | *1 Enoch* |
| *Jub.* | *Jubilees* |
| *Laws* | *On the Special Laws* (Philo) |

## MODERN SOURCES

| | |
|---|---|
| AB | Anchor Bible |
| *ABD* | *Anchor Bible Dictionary*. 6 vols. Edited by David Noel Freeman. New York: Doubleday, 1992 |
| *ANRW* | *Aufstieg und Niedergang der römischen Welt* |
| *BTB* | *Biblical Theology Bulletin* |
| HTS | Harvard Theological Studies |
| *JAAR* | *Journal of the American Academy of Religion* |
| *JBL* | *Journal of Biblical Literature* |
| *JFSR* | *Journal of Feminist Studies in Religion* |
| *JSOT* | *Journal for the Study of the Old Testament* |
| JSNTSup | Journal for the Study of the New Testament: Supplement Series |
| *NTS* | *New Testament Studies* |
| OBT | Overtures to Biblical Theology |
| SBEC | Studies in the Bible and Early Christianity |
| SBLDS | Society of Biblical Literature Dissertation Series |

| | |
|---|---|
| SBLSS | Society of Biblical Literature Symposium Series |
| SNTSMS | Society for New Testament Studies Monograph Series |
| WMANT | Wissenschaftliche Monographien zum Alten und Neuen Testament |

# 1

## Analyzing Ancient Power
## with Intersecting Modern Methods

Ancient Mediterranean patrons and their institutionalized patron-client structures impacted every aspect of society from economics to gender relationships (see Hanson and Oakman 2008, 57–91). The modern reader has been conditioned by theological and devotional readings of the Second Testament Gospels to view "scribes," "Pharisees," and "priests" as exclusively religious figures who sometimes argued with Jesus over spiritual matters. But such persons in ancient Palestine functioned both as religious authorities and power brokers for peasants, with veritable economic consequences. The same Gospels portray Jesus in power struggles with his village elders, his own family, temple-state authorities from Jerusalem, and indirectly with Roman policies facilitated by the Roman-appointed ruler (*tetrarch*) of Galilee and Perea, Herod Antipas. As we shall see, these conflicts had to do largely with political and economic issues (see chapter 2).[1] Such conflicts determined power relations and continued to surface within the Jesus movements themselves (Mark 10:35–45//Matt 20:20–28).

Paul also operated under the ominous shadow of Roman imperial power and its ubiquitous institutions. He also dealt with religious and civil authorities in ancient colonized Greco-Roman cities, and—like Jesus—became a victim of Rome's institutionalized violence by being incarcerated and perhaps even executed (2 Cor 11:23b; Phlm 1). One can

---

1. "Those who ruled and taxed the Galileans would have been based in a temple-state, a Roman client-state, or a city with jurisdiction over the villages and towns" (Horsley 1995, 9).

1

likewise observe similar conflict over power in Paul's writings within his own Christ communities (see chapters 4 and 5).

Ancient rulers and power brokers represented and were extensions of powerful patron-client institutions like the temple-state in Jerusalem, and the Roman Empire—all legitimized by religious authority. Rome's imperial power took on many forms that impacted villages and cities throughout the ancient Mediterranean world through its policies of colonization, taxation, and urbanization. These policies were enforced with official policies of intimidation through a combination of imperial rhetoric and violence (Horsley 1987). The temple in Jerusalem, functioning as a temple-state, also wielded its own economic power over Judean peasants in concert with Rome. Colonized Roman cities like Thessalonica, Philippi, and Corinth, where Paul established Christ communities, reflected imperial power and propaganda like suburbs of Rome itself. Even in lower-Galilean villages like Nazareth, where Israelite peasants resisted Roman domination, one could still find oppressive manifestations of Roman imperialistic policies, the encroachment of Hellenism, and local examples of patron-client power relations among its village elders. Both Jesus and Paul sharply criticized and challenged such oppressive demonstrations of power over others. They responded in part by establishing communities based on an alternative polity of power relations (Horsley 2003a). As mentioned above, these very communities in the early Jesus movements exhibited their own problems with power relations. This book explores how Jesus and Paul responded to and used power to address various issues of conflict in their own communities. The book concludes with a brief comparison based on my critical analysis.

It may seem ironic, but Jesus and Paul responded to their communities' internal power relations with an authoritative rhetoric of their own. This raises questions about their own use of power and its impact on their respective communities. Since both Jesus and Paul exercised power to resocialize and to address issues involving power among their communities, how can we assess their use of this power in the process? Were they simply operating from the same type of dominating power that Roman officials, temple elites, and village elders used? If Jesus and Paul repudiated this type of oppressive power in the name of Israel's God, is it also possible that they reinscribed it with their own authoritative rhetoric of obedience? Could Jesus or Paul, as ancient males with self-proclaimed authority, completely avoid using their power in dominating or ambivalent ways? Or can Jesus or Paul be understood as basing the respective "kingdom of God" and "gospel of Christ" agendas on a different type of nondominating power—a type of empowerment for others? I will argue that neither a dominating "power-over" nor an empowering "power-with" model adequately captures this complex set of circumstances for Jesus's and Paul's use of power (see Ehrensperger 2007).

## WHY POWER?

My strategy to address these questions is based on a critical and contextualized reading of relevant Second Testament texts and an analysis of various modern theories of power. While the question of power involves a rather complex methodological scheme and raises controversial issues that challenge traditional interpretations, I would contend that neither Jesus nor Paul can be adequately understood without engaging the current scholarly discourse on power. As mentioned above, this is necessary because multifarious forms and manifestations of power in ancient Mediterranean culture shaped the lives of Jesus and Paul as well as the communities they established. Simply put, ancient Mediterranean societies rested on patronage-clientage "pyramids of power."[2]

The power I refer to has to do with the prevailing ancient political and economic systemic forces that began to condition one's life at birth and continued to construct one's material and symbolic worlds to the grave. It will be vital for readers to remember that Jesus and Paul not only lived in a different time but were also products of a culture that was structurally, functionally, and ideologically different from our modern, Western culture to the degree that we cannot glibly impose our cultural assumptions on the texts (see Hanson and Oakman 2008, 3–8).[3] The fail-

2. See Hanson and Oakman 2008 (chap. 3) for a detailed breakdown of patronage-clientage power relations in ancient Palestine with helpful charts.

3. The contention that ancient Mediterranean culture was "totally different from our own" has been challenged by feminist biblical scholars like Elizabeth Schüssler Fiorenza (2001, 100). I will address this in more detail below. Note Hanson and Oakman's characteristics of societies like ancient Roman Palestine and their similarities to Two-Thirds-World cultures. Advanced agrarian societies: 1. use horticulture, plow farming, viticulture, herding, and fishing; 2. are composed predominantly of peasant populations; 3. include household slaves but are not "slave economies"; 4. have clearly demarcated so-

ure on the part of so many modern readers to recognize the differences leads to anachronistic and therefore misinformed assumptions. For example, even highly-educated modern readers often assume that Jesus and Paul had little to say about the political and economic matters of their day. This stems from another misleading notion that assumes both Jesus and Paul dealt solely with religious or spiritual matters.[4] Modern people in Western culture separate religion from politics and emphasize a personal, introspective approach to religion that results in an exclusively theological or devotional reading of the Bible (Stendahl, 1976, 78–96; Hanson and Oakman 2008, 7).[5] Most modern Christians in Western culture find it unfathomable to think of Jesus in political terms, or the concept of faith as inseparable from one's community. However, religion played an indispensable role in the politics, economy, and social formation of Jesus's and Paul's ancient Mediterranean world. We may think of religion and economics as being embedded in political institutions and kinship groups in this ancient culture. Acknowledging this hybrid relationship between religion and its social world enables us to further recognize the connection between religion and power. As we shall see, this embedded view of religion accounts for the diverse role of religion that functioned both to legitimize and challenge political powers. But power, in its various social institutions, was always part of the equation—always operating behind the text. I do not, therefore, begin with the uncritical theological position that accepts both Jesus and Paul as divinely inspired human agents called to accomplish God's will on the earth. This scenario justifies any use of their power as ultimately good, for the sake of the kingdom of God, and requires unfettered obedience to their authority by those who wished to do God's will.

---

cial boundaries set within aristocratic empires; and 5. are based on honor-shame values (2008, 8).

4. While it is popular in our culture to differentiate religion from spirituality, I believe this represents a confusing and false dichotomy. Generally speaking, people who consider themselves spiritual but not religious do so in order to distinguish institutionalized religion from their personal beliefs and practices. Most of this group maintain a belief in God, pray or practice meditation, and continue to adhere to an ethical code based on religious teachings or ideology. See Ellwood and McGraw on new religious movements (2009).

5. Stendahl (1976) was one of the first to challenge the notion that Paul rejected Judaism for its parochial and legalistic understanding of God's salvation.

Developing the skill to resist anachronistic and theological readings represents only part of the challenge for the modern reader. Even after careful historical reconstruction and nuanced readings based on current scholarly critical methods and theories that sensitize us to the machinations of power relations inscribed in the texts, our readings are still susceptible to reinscribing the very forms of oppressive power our careful scholarship has exposed. Both feminist and postcolonial biblical critics have made this quite clear by pointing out how the Bible has functioned as colonial literature with antiwomen, anti-Jewish, and antisubaltern imperial agendas (Sugirtharajah 2006, 69). Schüssler Fiorenza warns that "if one does not deliberately deconstruct the language of imperial domination in which scriptural texts remain caught up, one cannot help but valorize and re-inscribe it" (2007, 6).

So our diversified task involves not only methodological and hermeneutical challenges but also ethical ones these days. This brings us back to the question about Jesus's and Paul's use of power. Should Jesus and Paul be exempt from the charge of reinscribing any form of dominating power over others because of their lofty places in Christian history? Have biblical scholars ignored critical questions with regard to Jesus's and Paul's exercise of power because of political pressure from within the field to rehabilitate and defend either Jesus or Paul?[6] Schüssler Fiorenza poignantly sums up this dilemma with the following extended quote:

> These new Christian Testament studies of the Roman Empire have often sought to rehabilitate Christian writings, rather than proceeding in a self-critical fashion. Studies of the gospels, the Pauline literature, or other writings, which examine their attitude toward the Roman Empire, have tended to argue that these were critical of Roman imperial power and resisted its structures of domination because they were written by subordinate and marginalized people. However, such historical arguments overlook that even resistance literature will re-inscribe the structures of domination against which it seeks to argue. A historical reading, which places the Roman Empire and early Christian writings alongside each other, ends up using the Roman Empire and its power as a foil, in order to underscore the non-imperial meaning of the lordship

6. Schüssler Fiorenza (2007, 4 n17) makes this charge against Richard Horsley. Elizabeth Castelli (1991, 24–33) and Joseph Marchal (2008, 116) make similar criticisms of biblical scholars.

of Christ and the rulership of G*d. By claiming that the gospel of
Paul is counter-imperial, such a reading is no longer compelled to
inquire as to how such inscribed imperial language functioned in
the past, and still functions today, and what this type of language
does to readers who submit to its world of vision. (2007, 4)

Schüssler Fiorenza's point must be acknowledged in the current
discussion among biblical scholars on power relations. The rhetoric of
imperial power was inscribed at the very heart of early Christian theology
with its own politicized "kingdom of God" and "lordship of Jesus Christ"
language, which requires critical analysis of power relations, not just exegesis on the theology of Jesus and Paul. Historical reconstruction, insights
from social-scientific criticism, Empire studies, rhetorical criticism, feminist analysis, and postcolonial biblical criticisms avail the serious modern
reader with the tools for such careful and critical readings. The array of
such challenging issues involved in examining power relations from the
early Christian texts both situated in the ancient Mediterranean world
and yet still highly influential demands such methodological collaboration. The question of Jesus's and Paul's responses to and uses of power in
this context has become a matter of historical, social, theological, and
ethical significance in our modern world.

## APPROACHES AND METHODS USED

I rely on interdisciplinary, cross-cultural methodological approaches that
emphasize a collaborative and complementary relationship between various fields of study. By using this intersection of approaches I intend to rely
on the expertise that has developed in each field. This is necessary for interdisciplinary and cross-cultural approaches that have been developing
since the nineteenth century in biblical and religious studies. The early
developments of higher criticism or historical criticism among biblical
scholars helped shape methodologies in the fields of anthropology, phi-
lology, history, and the comparative study of religion (phenomenology).[7]

---

7. Ivan Strenski has written about this: "A consistent theme of this book has been that
much of the progress in the study of religion has been due to questions about religion
arising in connection with the study of the Bible" (2006, 115; see also 33–59; 118–22).
He also notes—with some regret—the present alienation between the fields of religious
studies and biblical scholarship (2006, 115).

Although the fields of biblical scholarship and religious studies have since migrated apart,[8] both disciplines have been using forms of literary and social-scientific theories, methods, and models for some time now. I use cross-cultural approaches taken from religious studies throughout the book to complement the overall task of analyzing religious phenomena in their social contexts. This stems from the recognition that religion also animates social life along with political and economic forces. The fact that religion was embedded in political institutions and kinship groups in the ancient Mediterranean world and should not be separated from this social context does not mean that religion played a simply superfluous role. On the contrary, the hybrid relationship between religion and its social matrix acknowledges that religious phenomena were not simply dominated by the more salient, concrete, and real underlying political and economic powers. No doubt politics and economics shaped religion. But the reverse was also true at times: Religion can and did contribute to the formation and adaptation of social structures as an embedded phenomenon. Only through critical analysis that does not isolate religion from its social-cultural context can we determine which aspect in this hybrid, symbiotic relationship may have been the more relevant factor in any given social situation.

The Judean temple-state based in Jerusalem exemplifies a case in point. Here the political and economic factors appear more central to understanding how the temple's policies and collaboration with Rome impacted Judean peasants during the first century. Religion played an important role legitimizing the entire enterprise. In the following chapter, I will argue that Jesus of Nazareth came into conflict with the traditional power brokers at his village, including his own father. This precipitated a response that gave birth to communities based on Jesus's interpretation of ancient Israel's religious tradition—which included both its domestic and political economy.[9] Jesus's vision of the kingdom of God had a discernable economic impact not only on his followers but also their families and vil-

8. I cannot attend to the reasons for this alienation here. But I join Strenski and others who bemoan this separation because of the ways each field could benefit from each other methodologically.

9. "Domestic economy was concerned with provisioning the household, and its basic goal was consumption." "Political economy, managed by political kin, was concerned with what was produced and its major goal was to control the distribution of what was produced" (Hanson and Oakman 2008, 13, 14).

lages. A social-scientific analysis of this phenomenon helps to explain how
Jesus used power based on religious ideology and ritual to challenge and
modify patron-client structures, which in turn disrupted village economic
life. Peter Oakes, beginning with a quote from Karl Polanyi, reminds us
that "all ancient economies were 'embedded economies.' Financial decisions in such economies were *rarely taken for financial reasons alone*. For
example, the nature of patron-client relationships ensured constant dis-
tortion of what we might expect to be market interaction. Distribution of
resources was dependent much more on *power relationships than on the
market*" (2009, 11; italics added).

I will elaborate and draw attention to the various intersecting
methods and approaches utilized in the following chapters when such
elaboration serves to help readers better understand various aspects of
my critical analysis of Jesus's and Paul's use of power. Methods not only
help us gather information to study and interpret our subject matter
but also partially condition the entire process. Although based primarily on social-scientific methodology and its assumptions, this work does
not elevate any one approach over another but views all as having the
potential to serve as helpful tools. But every scholarly method also has
certain limitations, which makes each subject to criticism. I acknowledge
at the outset that the argument that follows has been conditioned by my
selection and use of scholarly methods and theories as well as by my own
presuppositions as a white, male scholar of biblical and religious studies
employed by a secular state university. The same critical apparatuses used
to analyze the texts and ancient figures in this book have also sensitized
me to be aware of my own social conditioning and limitations. In spite
of these caveats, the following critical methodologies have provided the
parameters that guided my research and influenced my conclusions. I remain confident in the process—even though it remains part of a dynamic
process itself.

## Social-Scientific Criticism

Social-scientific criticism is a relatively new discipline that has stimulated
great interest among biblical scholars because of its innovative use of the
social sciences to interpret the Bible. Social-scientific criticism emerged
in the 1970s when certain scholars sought to expand cross-cultural and

exegetical approaches to the Bible by incorporating the social sciences with traditional historical-critical methods.[10] By 1986 an international group of scholars committed to a social-scientific approach to biblical exegesis began to meet; these meetings eventually led to the now well-known organization called the Context Group (formally established in 1990). The Context Group has been most prolific in advancing a social-scientific agenda with meetings, conferences, and publications. Virtually every current work dealing with the First and Second Testaments, Jesus movements, and early Christianity includes either some reference to specific publications by Context Group members or engagement with particular social-scientific models or with social-scientific criticism in general.[11] The journal *Biblical Theology Bulletin* publishes articles based on social-scientific approaches and regularly features scholars from the Context Group.

Perhaps no one was more influential in the early formation of the social-scientific method applied to biblical studies than the German scholar Gerd Theissen. His social-scientific approach of the Second Testament Gospels analyzed Jesus's sayings and their transmission from the perspective of the sociology of literature. "Itinerant Radicalism: The Tradition of Jesus Sayings from the Perspective of the Sociology of Literature" made a direct connection between the Gospels and human behavior (1976, 84–93). Theissen's approach drew attention to social forces that conditioned the texts and their "transmitters," which departed from a strictly theological interpretation. Jesus's sayings took on new significance under Theissen's sociological perspective and inspired several other scholars to incorporate his social-scientific method with historical criticism. John H. Elliott adroitly sums up Theissen's work: "Theissen's studies range widely in their subject matter but in general demonstrate how fresh questions concerning the correlation of belief and behavior, ideas and material con-

10. These same scholars think historical criticism is inadequate for the task of interpreting the Bible and its world without the aid of social-scientific criticism. It does not seek to replace the historical-critical method but to expand and improve it (see Elliott 1993, 13). They also distinguish between "social history" and anthropology and related social sciences. The former attempts to describe historical phenomena through sociological concepts while social sciences attempt to explain human behavior based on models representative of generalities of a specific social group (Malina 1982, 232, 241).

11. This would include those who criticize social-scientific criticism. I address this below.

ditions, theological symbols and social relations can generate new per-spectives on old texts and revisions of previously 'assured results'" (1993, 22–23).

Elliott is not only a member of the Context Group but one of the ar-chitects behind the method now referred to as social-scientific criticism. Elliott defines this approach to the Bible as "that phase of the exegetical task which analyses the social and cultural dimensions of the text and of its environmental context through the utilization of the perspectives, theory, models, and research of the social sciences" (1993, 7). General social-analytical approaches to the Bible recognize that its writings, the original audiences hearing texts read in their respective communities, and our modern readings are all social acts and therefore in need of social analysis. The essential use of social-scientific criticism, however, has remained committed to providing exegetical tools to explore the "meaning(s) explicit and implicit in the text," which are studied as "both a reflection of and a response to the social and cultural settings" that originally produced the texts (Elliott 1993, 8). Social-scientific criticism offers several methods through the use of theories and models for biblical interpretation. Bruce J. Malina lists the following six features of social-science models that he suggests most enhance biblical interpretation: (1) They should be cross-cultural models. (2) The model needs to provide a "sufficient level of abstraction to allow for the surfacing of similarities that facilitates comparison." (3) The model should comply with sociolinguistic paradigms for interpreting texts. (4) A model for biblical interpretation should be based on experiences known from the original biblical world. (5) Models' meaning need not be relevant to the modern readers' society. (6) Social scientists must accept the application of such models (1982, 241).

Elliott characterizes models by their capacity to denote similari-ties for clarification through comparison, to "stimulate imagination," to serve as a "link between theories and observations," to provide a simpli-fied framework for examining data, to test theories, and to "analyze the properties of social behavior, social structures and social process" (1986, 3–26). Theory, by contrast, "is based on axiomatic laws and states general principles. It is a basic proposition through which a variety of observa-tions or statements become explicable" (4–5).

Conceptual models make up part of the process of social–scientific criticism. The researcher must select an appropriate model and then use it for making comparisons. For example, Elliott has employed the sociological model of the sect to study early Christianity. He borrowed a messianic-sect model from John Gager and applied it to his interpretation of 1 Peter, which yielded innovative and insightful perspectives not only on the text itself but on how the ancient household functioned as a social basis for early Christianity (2007). Context Group scholars also find sociologically based theories like conflict theory, structural-functionalism, sociological ambivalence, and cognitive dissonance useful methodological tools. Scholars evaluate such theories against the available data and either criticize and discard them or put them to use as an interpretive method (Malina 1986b).[12]

Conflict theory represents one of the general approaches used and assumed throughout this book. The Second Testament Gospels and Paul's writings illustrate constant tensions and multiple conflicts between Jesus and his opponents and Paul and his opponents. Jesus began his Galilean mission after conflict broke out between him and the authorities in his own village (Luke 4:20–29). Jesus challenged Roman rule through its clients, and confronted representatives of the Jerusalem temple-state aligned with Rome (Luke-Q 13:34–35; Mark 11:15–17). Jesus's practice of exorcism can be understood metaphorically as "God's kingdom defeating Roman rule" (Horsley 2003, 99). Jesus is even portrayed having conflict with his own disciples (Mark 8).

Paul confronted opponents outside and within his Christ communities (1 Cor 4:19–21; 2 Cor 10–13; Gal 1:7; 3:1; Phil 3:2). Conflict theory accounts for the production of power in the interplay with central social domains in the ancient Mediterranean world: "kinship, politics, economics and religion" (Hanson and Oakman 2008, 6). Power is always operative when one social faction attempts to dominate and control another for its own good. "Conflict theory seeks to understand who benefits from the social structures and how conflict is managed: 'lumping it,' avoidance, coercion, negotiation, mediation, arbitration, or adjudication. This approach is identified closely with the materialist tradition, mindful that

---

12. Malina criticizes Gager's theory of cognitive dissonance because it fails to stand up to the data from Mediterranean society (1986).

adaptive and economic pressures have shaped social relations" (Hanson and Oakman 2008, 7).

I utilize social-scientific criticism to analyze Jesus's and Paul's use of power. Social-scientific criticism makes for a particularly fruitful dialogue partner with the various disciplines used in this book to examine power relations. First of all, we observe power in all relations as a social phenomenon contingent on the institutionalized dynamics of politics, economics, class, status, gender, age, race, ethnicity, sex, occupation, slavery, and religion. Second, using models and theories based on the social sciences have become particularly helpful to organize and compare the structures of power relations in early Jesus movements with typical social institutions in the ancient Mediterranean world. Since religious rituals and meals played an important part of shaping these social institutions and encoding cultural values, they too have become subject to the scrutiny of social-scientific analysis.

In the following chapters I will argue that both Jesus and Paul used meals to resocialize their respective communities especially with regard to power relations. The fact that meals in the early Jesus movements were typical of all meals in ancient Mediterranean culture facilitates making basic comparisons to analyze the parameters of how such meals functioned as devices of socialization and social change (Taussig 2009, 6, 21, 23). This comparison will also provide specific examples of how Jesus and Paul used their respective communities' meals for such transformative social maneuvering.[13] Meals functioned as powerful social tools that could simultaneously convey and construct a whole set of complex cultural values: "When people gathered in the first-century Mediterranean cultures, the event was laden with meaning. Meals were highly stylized occasions that carried significant social coding, identity formation, and meaning making. Participating in a meal entailed entering into a social dynamic that confirmed, challenged, and negotiated both who the group as a whole was and who the individuals within it were" (22).

Ritual studies confirm the capacity of religious ritual to transform social reality based on the rituals' perceived power to change the initi-

13. I rely on current ritual studies and works that deal specifically with meals in the ancient Mediterranean world. See Catherine Bell 1992, 1997; Mary Douglas 1966; Matthias Klinghardt 1996; Dennis E. Smith 2003; Jonathan Z. Smith 1987; Hal Taussig 2009; Victor Turner 1967, 1969; *Semeia* 68 (1994).

ate's religious status. For example, religious rituals such as initiation rites enable the uninitiated participants to successfully transition from their profane, marginalized status before the sacred to a corresponding new status within their communities (van Gennep 1961). "In other words, rituals per se may indeed have a great deal to do with social order and change" (Taussig 2009, 20). Jesus's and Paul's communities' meals most certainly did.

I also analyze honor and shame as central cultural concepts and values and as conditioning factors for social behavior in the world of Jesus and Paul. Honor and shame can be used to better understand how power relations operated within early Jesus movements. In ancient Mediterranean societies, where honor is perceived as a limited good, the concepts of honor and shame played one of the pivotal roles in conditioning human behavior and therefore served to reveal various dynamics in power relations.[14] Malina links honor and shame at the intersection of authority, gender, and respect, and defines the honor-shame dynamic as "the value of a person in his or her own eyes (that is, one's claim to worth) plus that person's value in the eyes of his or her social group" (2001, 26). "Ascribed honor" comes with birth and is relatively fixed by one's inherited ethnicity, gender, wealth, and family's status. "Acquired honor" results from benefaction and/or by taking it from another after winning honor or shaming another in a public form of challenge and riposte. Where honor is deemed to be limited, virtually all interactions with non–family members constitute a challenge to honor, forcing one to decide if either personal honor or family honor (particularly the honor of one's father or wife, mother, or sister) is threatened. If one determined that a challenge had been made, some type of riposte was expected in response. Public opinion judged who won. Malina stipulates that such challenges and ripostes could only occur between "social equals" (2001, 19).[15] According to Malina's scheme, gender determined the social expectations for men

14. Neither Malina nor any Context Group scholar to my knowledge has ever made the claim that the concept of honor and shame was the only meaningful value in ancient Mediterranean culture. Even those who criticize the exaggerated use of honor and shame as a heuristic device to interpret biblical texts do not deny its importance (see Schüssler Fiorenza 2001, 98; and F. Gerald Downing 1998, 55).

15. I disagree with this particular point and will illustrate it in chapter 4. For a fuller treatment and challenge to this aspect of Malina's concept of honor and shame see Crook (2009, 592–611).

and women, which public opinion confirmed based on local practices (2001, 44–51). Men embody honor. But even though women embody shame, a woman's honor resides in her sexual purity, passive behavior, and motherhood (2001, 51). Malina's characterization of the honor-and-shame dynamic as a "pivotal" value of Mediterranean culture, though challenged over the years, has essentially stood the test of time.[16]

### Feminist Criticism

Feminist biblical criticism represents an important methodological strategy in this book for several reasons. Feminist criticism's "hermeneutics of suspicion" has served to remind us that women played important roles in the early Jesus movements even while often elided from our androcentric texts and interpretations. Reading women back into the history of the Jesus movements and recognizing their central place in Jesus's and Paul's communities has required the development of a rigorous and critical methodology. No one has been more influential and prolific in this enterprise than Elizabeth Schüssler Fiorenza: "All critical inquiry that deserves to be called scientific has to start with a critical discussion of methodology before it is able to turn to a social-historical reconstruction of the Jesus movement" (2001, 84). *In Memory of Her: A Feminist Theological Reconstruction of Christian Origins*, first published in 1983, not only demonstrated Schüssler Fiorenza's erudition but also the innovative and

16. See Zeba Crook, who has recently made this point based on "more than enough evidence to defend" honor and shame as pivotal (2009, 591). In this excellent article, Crook also claims that male subordinates and women could challenge those deemed to have more honor. I agree with him on this completely. Yet, the examples he gives for women challenging men in public places and besting them with their ripostes all reveal that the women who took honor or who shamed men acted like men—that is, they took on masculine roles and exhibited masculine behavior. He concludes from this that "power, wealth, and gender" are secondary in determining the rules of honor and shame to the "public court of reputation" (594). This does eliminate the binary model of honor and shame. But examples of women's winning honor from men by typical masculine behavior suggest that power, wealth, and especially gender remain central. If women essentially have to act like men by demonstrating masculine traits and behavior (aggression, physical strength, bravery, wit, wisdom, rhetorical skills, leadership, self-control), how was gender not still a factor in ancient Mediterranean honor-shame? Women could not challenge men and win honor with feminine behavior and traits. The public court of reputation "distributed" honor to those women who proved to be the better man. This makes sense because gender with masculine and feminine traits is a social construction.

insightful interpretations based on feminist criticism and theology. Her additional publications evidence the growing sophistication, complexity, and usefulness of feminist critical analysis with regard to biblical interpretation and the politics of interpreters. Schüssler Fiorenza's influence and feminist biblical criticism in general constitute part of the collaborative methodological approach of this book; her influence is especially notable in chapters 3 and 4.

Feminist criticism's analysis of the social formation of gender provides a cogent theoretical basis to examine power relations: "If one conceptualizes the reality of wo/men not in terms of gender dualism, but in terms of a socially constructed web of interactive systems of power structured as pyramids of domination and subordination, then one is able to understand societal oppression as engendered by a variegated social, interactive, and multiplicative structures of exploitation and dehumanization" (Schüssler Fiorenza 2001, 98). Biblical scholarship has traditionally tended—and in some cases continues—to ignore the social factors that construct male and female gender.[17] But if one acknowledges that gender is a social construction based on biological sex, which determines masculine roles for men, feminine roles for women, and requirements for how men and women relate to one another, then one must also recognize that the constructed nature of gender directly impacts the use of power. In patriarchal cultures like the ancient Mediterranean world, gender socialization was rooted in the father's power and therefore privileged males over females, sons over daughters, husbands over wives. But this simple categorization does not adequately address the more complex and subtle aspects of gender relations and power. Here again I turn to Schüssler Fiorenza's feminist analysis for clarification.

Schüssler Fiorenza coined the term *kyriarchy*[18] to illuminate and expand the concept of patriarchy to include other social dimensions in addition to gender. Since patriarchy literally means the "rule of father," it tends to portray power and authority in a simplified, dualistic manner in which men—by nature and with divine sanction—ruled over women and children. However, men dominate not only women but other men through several institutionalized mechanisms like kinship groups, reli-

17. See Janice Chapel Anderson (2008, 115).

18. Literally from two Greek words: *kyrios*, meaning "lord," and *archē* meaning "rule." Emperors and all those with elevated status over others were given the title of *kyrios*.

gion, colonialism, imperialism, economics, race, class, status, age, honor-shame, and other factors. Schüssler Fiorenza describes these multiple systems of domination and subordination as an interlocking pyramid in which an elite woman may have power over a non-elite man. This highly nuanced understanding of power relations evoked by the term *kyriarchy* advances the discussion of gender and our inquiry into Jesus's and Paul's use of power as a social, feminist heuristic model. This more-comprehensive approach to power through the interpretive lens of kyriarchy also suggests that patriarchy must be problematized and gender reevaluated as having a more central role in the social formation of power relations in the early Jesus movements. A methodologically and ethically necessary question to ask becomes: Did Jesus and Paul rely on kyriarchy, or did they repudiate it?

Schüssler Fiorenza has addressed the issues she feels stand in the way of collaboration between the two. Her solution would require that social-scientific historical-Jesus studies "engage feminist critical questions and methodologies" (2001, 114). According to Schüssler Fiorenza, feminist scholars incorporate social-scientific Jesus research, but the reverse is not true, because of different "hermeneutical goals"—not methods. She believes that feminist criticism would sensitize social-scientific histori-cal-Jesus scholars to reflect critically on their work to ensure that it does not "perpetuate ideologies of domination and thereby reif[y] structures of oppression" (2001, 84). Based on the following statement by Malina, this type of critical self-reflection already composes part of the social-scientific task for biblical scholars: "Perhaps the most significant feature of the use of social-scientific models in biblical interpretations is the way social science models of the cross-cultural sort constantly require the interpreter to articulate and account for his or her own social location" (1982, 238).[19] Critically analyzing heuristic models used to explain the social conditions behind biblical texts should also include a conscious ef-fort to ferret out even subtle legitimizing forms of abusive power that our models expose through the texts' social context or rhetoric. For example, the interpreter must not simply conclude that ancient forms of kyriarchy justified male domination over women and subaltern men as part of the "natural order" of things without also identifying this as a machination

19. See a similar comment by Schüssler Fiorenza (2001, 88).

still employed to marginalize and subordinate those not recognized as part of the dominant culture.[20]

Social-scientific criticism has also been charged with an epistemologically weak and indefensible type of "positivism" that claims to reconstruct the "real" world of Jesus and Paul while describing "what actually happened."[21] According to Schüssler Fiorenza, "both social-scientific and social-historical historical Jesus research tend to understand androcentric—or, better, kyriocentric—language as a window to the world of the Historical-Jesus and to presuppose that texts reflect and represent reality objectively" (2001, 91). Unless one analyzes and deconstructs kyriocentric language through feminist criticism, this "outdated notion of language" has the potential to reinscribe dominating hierarchies based on gender.[22] Mary Ann Tolbert faults social-scientific critics for essentially constructing ancient Mediterranean society as "fact," which they in turn impose on the Christian texts, thereby "inverting the social-scientific method" (1993, 266ff).[23] Schüssler Fiorenza has also criticized social-scientific criticism for its gender "dualism," and says, "honor-shame is only one, though an important," aspect of ancient Mediterranean culture. She suggests that honor and shame would become more useful by including "patriarchy/kyriarchy" as a social model (2001, 98).

In spite of these poignant criticisms, Schüssler Fiorenza maintains that if social-scientific historical-Jesus research would incorporate the "analytic concept of kyriarchy," it could avoid the above-mentioned criticisms (2001, 98).[24] Following Schüssler Fiorenza's scholarship, postcolonial feminist scholars like Kwok Pui-lan (1995) and Joseph Marchal (2008) have also appealed to biblical scholars to recognize through feminist analyses that "read against the grain" of "malestream biblical scholarship"

20. The Context Group scholar S. Scott Bartchy continues to reveal ancient forms male domination based on gender as well as to expose and critique its modern manifestation (see 2003).

21. This criticism is also made against anthropology and sociology (Schüssler Fiorenza, 2001, 91–93).

22. Schüssler Fiorenza defines *kyriocentrism* as "naturalizing and legitimating not just gender but all forms of domination" in both the ancient and modern periods (2001, 95).

23. See Hanson and Oakman (2008, xxi–xxii) on those who criticize social-scientific approaches.

24. I have taken her advice with regard to the use of *kyriarchy* in this book.

(Marchal 2008) the central role gender relations play. Because gender is a social construct that participates in a nexus of other power systems it enables us to explore its ramifications for power relations without resorting to facile gender dualism.

## Rhetorical Criticism

Both Jesus and Paul used rhetoric to persuade their audiences. The focus on how rhetoric functioned in the ancient Mediterranean world and in biblical texts has gained great support from many biblical scholars. Rhetorical criticism enables scholars to better understand how Jesus's sayings and Paul's arguments would have been received by their particular audiences. Some rhetorical critics have shown more interest in how a text can have meaning rather than in what either Jesus or Paul originally meant. This type of rhetorical criticism understands biblical texts as dynamic, as still generating new meanings for modern readers rather than as static and fixed meanings from the past. Others look at the process of modern scholarly interpretation as its own form of rhetoric and as capable of perpetuating dominating and oppressive kyriocentric and kyriarchal language. Nonetheless, the manifold types and uses of rhetorical criticism reveal the important connection between rhetoric and power.

Rhetorical criticism stems from literary studies and criticism, and has more recently become part of the biblical interpreter's repertoire of methodological approaches (Wendland 2002, 169–95).[25] One encounters both basic and complex forms of rhetorical criticism that include "virtually any type of semiotic social interaction" (170). Rhetorical criticism draws attention to the fact that biblical authors also used ancient forms of rhetorical devices to address specific audiences with specific issues.[26] This fundamental observation includes the recognition that the texts' authors did not simply set out to record what really happened or merely to de-

25. This is especially true of reader-response criticism.

26. Wendland calls this "the Greco-Roman model" by which one examines the entire "rhetorical unit" in its contextual setting, then moving on to determine the "specific problem, question, or issue." Next the critic analyzes the *invention* or various proofs; the *disposito*, or compositional structure composed of *exordium* (introduction), *narratio* (statement of case), *probatio* (main argument), and *perpratio* (conclusion); and finally the *elocution*, or arrangement and style (2002, 173–74). See also Christopher Forbes for Paul's use of classical Greco-Roman rhetoric (2003, 134–71).

scribe what was taking place among their original audiences. Rhetorical criticism discloses that the biblical authors were attempting to persuade and influence their target audiences. However, careful analysis of an author's rhetoric does help the interpreter to reconstruct or get some sense of the historical situation that the author addressed. Feminist and postcolonial biblical criticisms extend the canopy of rhetorical criticism to cover the biblical interpreter's own set of influencing hermeneutical factors and assumptions.[27]

Rhetorical criticism has taken on many forms that the biblical critic can choose to incorporate along with various other hermeneutical approaches. This selective employment of rhetorical criticism (like other methodological devices) predisposes the scholar to focus on certain dynamics of the text under investigation.

Not surprisingly, one finds scholars deploying rhetorical criticism in concert with social-scientific and feminist biblical criticism. "The combination of situation and setting (or 'rhetorical exigency') with reference to the original context has been the focus of much analysis by the prominent social scientific school of biblical criticism" (Wendland 2002, 184–85). Elliott identifies a text's "rhetorical strategy as a vehicle of meaningful persuasive discourse in its original historical, social, and cultural context and as a medium of social interaction" (1993, 69). Typical of rhetorical critics in general, Elliott also highlights the function of rhetoric as a medium of communication and social interaction in the biblical text. He and other Context Group members are more interested in the text's original meaning than in a noncontextual, contemporary meaning derived from the modern reader's own experience. But the significance of rhetorical criticism as complementing and completing the task of social-scientific criticism is evident among Context Group scholars.

The following summary of the correlation between the text's social situation and the author's rhetoric illustrates the methodological similarity between social-scientific criticism and rhetorical criticism. Elliott lists eight questions abbreviated or summarized as follows.

27. "A feminist sociocritical rhetoric concurs with postmodern discourse analysis that all texts, interpretations, and historical reconstructions are relative and perspectival. If what one sees depends on where one stands, social-ideological location and rhetorical context are as decisive as text for how one re-constructs historical reality or interprets biblical texts." (Schüssler Fiorenza 1999, 138)

1. Who are the text's *readers-hearers*, explicitly mentioned or implied? And what is their relationship to the author?

2. Who is the *author-sender*, explicitly mentioned or implied?

3. "How is the *social situation* described in the text?"

4. "How does the author(s) *diagnose and evaluate* the situation?" What is approved, commended, disapproved, condemned, and or need to be changed?

5. How is the text's *strategy* related to its style, organization, and ideological point of view?

6. "What *response* does the author(s) seek from the targeted audience?" What are the modes and means of rhetorical argument employed?

7. "How does the author(s) attempt to *motivate and persuade* the audience?" Are there dominate root metaphors or symbols that express collective identity and action?

8. "What is the nature of the situation and strategy of this text as seen from social-scientific *etic perspective* with the aid of historical and comparative social-scientific research?" Can a cross-cultural comparison be made with comparable groups in comparable situations? (1993, 72–73).[28]

Just as social-scientific biblical criticism has its nuanced versions of rhetorical criticism, so does feminist biblical criticism. Feminist biblical critics also chide rhetorical biblical criticism with what Schüssler Fiorenza calls "a critical rhetoric of inquiry" (1999 85). This "critical rhetoric of inquiry" directed at rhetorical criticism in biblical studies continues along the same line as the charge against biblical scholars' "empiricist-positivist" claims of historical reality and their reinscribing kyriocentric language. Therefore, rhetorical biblical criticism also fails to engage feminist criticism that exposes and challenges to all forms of kyriarchy (1999, 97). Schüssler Fiorenza provides four insights suggesting how a critical feminist rhetoric of inquiry could contribute to biblical studies and rhetorical studies. I summarize or abbreviate them as follows.

28. Elliott based these points on the text of 1 Peter as an example of a social-scientific reading of a biblical text (italics original).

1. "Grammatically androcentric language is not reflective or descriptive of reality, but it is regulative and constructive."

2. "Language is not just performative; it is political." "Kyriocentric language serves kyriarchal interests and kyriarchal interest shape kyriocentric texts."

3. "Hence a critical intratextual analysis of the language and rhetoric of the texts does not suffice. It must be complemented by a critical systemic analysis of sociopolitical and religious structures of domination and exclusion."

4. Language and knowledge of the world are rhetorical, that is, they shape the political landscape. The task is not just to know the world as it is but to transform and change it (1999, 93).

Based on the feminist critique of rhetorical biblical criticism, feminist biblical criticism offers an approach that reflects both methodological collaboration and innovative hermeneutics for all biblical scholars. Here again, Schüssler Fiorenza has been instrumental (1987, 386–403; 1999, 105–48). But first a clarification must be made about feminist rhetorical criticism. One might assume that the feminist critique of positivistic claims to reconstruct the actual historical situation behind biblical texts has led feminist biblical scholars to abandon any attempt to uncover the text's social and historical backgrounds. Schüssler Fiorenza contends that feminist biblical critics take reconstructing history seriously and endeavor to provide a "more adequate account of the historical world."[29] How do feminist biblical critics like Schüssler Fiorenza suggest one access the text's historical situation in order to reconstruct the best possible history?

Schüssler Fiorenza's has applied her method for using rhetorical analysis mostly to Paul's writings, and 1 Corinthians in particular (1987, 386–403; 1999, 105–28).[30] She first distinguishes the "rhetorical situation" from the "historical situation" as a more reliable means to reconstruct the possible historical situation. The "rhetorical situation" in 1 Corinthians represents what Paul has inscribed in the text to persuade the Christ

29. She makes this claim while criticizing any postmodern criticism that "eschews all historical diachronic reconstruction" (1999, 138–39).

30. See Cynthia Briggs Kittredge for an example of Schüssler Fiorenza's influence on her rhetorical analysis of the Pauline tradition (1998).

communities in Corinth to act in accordance with the values he shares in common with them. The rhetorical situation functions to evoke such a response from the Corinthians. To accomplish this, Paul inscribes himself as a "called apostle of Christ Jesus" who exhorts the Corinthians to "imitate" him; Paul also inscribes the controversies and tensions between themselves and Paul (1:1; 4:17, 21; 11:16). Paul as the "inscribed author" portrays himself as a model for his inscribed audience to follow in order to resolve the problems as Paul has inscribed them, according to Paul's perspective, and based on Paul's authority. Rhetorical criticism seeks to complete the hermeneutical chain by linking the audience's possible responses to this rhetorical situation (determined by their own expectations). In this way, the rhetorical situation sheds light on the historical situation. One must analyze the inscribed author's rhetoric and imagine the inscribed audience's response (one must hear their voices, as it were) and must not seek to hear merely Paul's voice in isolation.[31] Feminist biblical critics also incorporate extrinsic historical and social information with the above-mentioned rhetorical analysis to reconstruct the possible historical situation.

## From Postcolonial Criticism to Postcolonial Biblical Criticism

Postcolonial criticism surfaced in the latter part of the twentieth century, having developed from literary criticism. It became prevalent in English departments where literatures of Commonwealth nations were observed against the background of European colonization. It is also associated with postmodernism and poststructuralist theory, postcolonial theory, and struggles against neocolonialism—understood as continuing colonization with or without actual occupation through imperial policies of globalization and other types of domination.[32] Postcolonial criticism de-

31. Schüssler Fiorenza writes, "Rhetorical criticism of the Bible must distinguish between the historical argumentative situation, the implied or inscribed rhetorical situation, and the rhetorical situation of contemporary interpretations, which can be either actual or textualized" (1999, 109).

32. R. S. Sugirtharajah distinguishes between "postcolonial theory" and "postcolonial criticism" by noting that Two-thirds–World scholars like Edward Said, Gaytri Chakravorty Spivak, and Homi Bhabha used poststructuralist theory to analyze the link between Western systems of knowledge and the brandishing of Western imperialism without taking up a postcolonial ideology. Postcolonial theory itself followed "the dis-

constructs what is deemed to be the heart of Western colonial and imperial power: its discourses and metanarratives. Its critique of colonial and postcolonial literatures in colonial and imperialistic contexts shows "how cultural texts are central means in both the imposition of and resistance to imperialism" (Dube 2000, 47). Such deconstruction of dominant discourses reveals what Edward Said described with the term "orientalism": the capacity of Western discursive power to create an "other" (1985). The power to otherize is essential for colonialism and imperialism. Western conquest can be exemplified by a simple label like, "Orient." Following Foucault, Said used the concept of discourse as a nexus of knowledge and power to illustrate how the West constructed the "Orient" as an object of study. Colonialism usurped non-European cultures and reduced them to Enlightenment categories of information, facilitating their marginalization as inferior to the West. Said's "Orientalism is a misrepresentation and falsification of other peoples by the West, which slots them into separate and distinct ethnic extractions or essences so that they become controllable and assessable" (Sugirtharajah 2006, 66–67). Postcolonialism addresses the interests of the "other" victimized by Western hegemony and its legacy of imperialistic self-interest by retrieving, preserving, and resourcing the cultural productions of the colonized.[33]

Postcolonialism has both parallels with and distinctions from liberation theology. Both criticize Western domination and acknowledge the value of marginalized cultures while articulating concern for the "other." But whereas liberation theology takes its inspiration directly from its own biblical hermeneutics, postcolonialism questions the authority of the biblical texts and their interpretations. For example, Sugirtharajah points out that liberation interpreters use the biblical motif of the exodus paradigm to express the "oppressed point of view," but they fail to mention the "ambivalent nature of the Exodus narrative" itself (2006, 78–79). The exodus story also includes the death of the Egyptians' innocent first-born children (Exod 11:5) as well as instructions for Israelites in the buying

---

course of resistance in nationalist movements," and "creative literary production in the form of novels, poems, and art" (2006, 66). Eventually, the above-mentioned scholars began to see their theoretical models could also address the interests of the colonized other.

33. See Tat-Siong Benny Liew for an excellent summary of postcolonial criticism and its application to the Gospel of Mark (2008, 211–32).

and selling of slaves after their liberation (21:1–11). Sugirtharajah thinks that liberation hermeneutics should at least raise the question, "what sort of God is it who sides with one set of people and neglects the rights of the other by such a liberative act" (2006, 78)?

Liberation theology also places great emphasis on the poor as economically disadvantaged while postcolonialism cites several types of oppression. This difference can be seen in Sugirtharajah's postcolonial reading of the widow in Mark's Gospel, who gave all the money she had to the temple treasury (12:41–44). Liberation theologians interpret the widow's act of sacrificial giving as a demonstration of "ideal piety" while postcolonialists use this story to draw attention to the corrupt temple system that "maneuvered and tricked" the lower classes out of their resources (2006, 79). One can easily imagine such differences, given liberation theology's beginnings in Roman Catholic Latin America. Its exclusively Christian approach and biblical worldview have served to place both Christianity and its Bible in a privileged position that some secular, university-based postcolonial critics find highly problematic. A robust postcolonial biblical criticism has ensued in part because of these differences along with a poignant critique of traditional biblical scholarship. However, this criticism has not resulted in the abandonment of the Bible by postcolonial biblical critics.

Postcolonial biblical criticism challenges both the Bible's privileged, authoritative status and hegemonic biblical interpretations. It probes the "gaps, silences, ambiguities, and complexities embedded within biblical narratives" and sees "the Bible as both a problem and a solution" (Sugirtharajah 2006, 78). According to Sugirtharajah, the Bible is a "text of both emancipation and enervation," so it must itself be emancipated from "its implication in dominant ideologies at the level both of text and of interpretation" (2006, 78). Sugirtharajah was the first to introduce postcolonial criticism to biblical studies in an article in the *Asia Journal of Theology* in which he attributed colonialist tendencies to biblical studies (1996). He contends that the fundamental theoretical features of postcolonial criticism have "clear biblical applications" (2006a, 67). Homi Bhabha's original concepts of "hybridity" and "mimicry" continue to be incorporated, but by only a few biblical scholars.[34] Musa Dube, Fernando Segovia, Stephen Moore, Richard Horsley, Havlor Moxnes, Elizabeth Schüssler Fiorenza, Kwok Pui-lan, Joseph Marchal, Laura Donaldson, Elsa Tamez, Tat-siong Benny Liew, and of course R. S. Sugirtharajah are scholars who incorporate certain aspects of postcolonial biblical criticism in their works to different degrees.[35] The postcolonial feminist theologian Kwok Pui-lan actually maintains that "postcolonial criticism has the potential to open up the interpretive process, making the Bible a highly relevant and invaluable resource for our postcolonial situation" (2005, 79).

Sugirtharajah has elaborated on three goals of postcolonial biblical criticism that I abbreviate or summarize as follows: First, postcolonial biblical criticism "seeks to situate colonialism at the center of the Bible and biblical interpretation" (2006a, 73). Since the Bible comes from various colonial contexts, postcolonial biblical criticism examines biblical narratives for "colonial assumptions, imperial impulses, power relations, hegemonic intentions, the treatment of subalterns, stigmatization of women and the marginalized, land appropriation, and the violation of minority cultures" (2006a, 73). Only in this way can silenced voices be reclaimed. Second, postcolonial biblical criticism scrutinizes biblical interpretation to expose hidden ideologies behind claims of neutrality. Issues of expansion, domination, and imperialism are assumed to define both biblical narratives and interpretation. Third, postcolonial biblical critics "re-read the Bible in light of postcolonial concerns and conditions—plurality, hybridity, multiculturalism, nationalism, diaspora, refugees, and asylum seeking" (2006a, 73). According to Sugirtharajah, the Bible does not have

34. See Joseph Marchal (2008), whose work appears in chapter 4, and David Sánchez's award-winning book (2008). Hybridity is not the same as syncretism, which carries the idea that a more dominant culture overtakes a weaker one, as in the case of Western cultures in the modern period. Hybridity refers to the mixing of different cultures due to colonization resulting in a new transcultural form that allows for the subaltern's voice to be heard (Spivak, 2009). Musa Dube says, "Hybridity becomes a form of resistance, for it dispenses with dualistic and hierarchal constructions of cultures, which are used to claim the superiority of colonizing cultures, and shows that cultures grow and are dependent on borrowing from each other" (2000, 51). Mimicry describes the ambivalent relationship between the colonizer and the colonized. The colonized never measure up to the colonizer's cultural standards, only a "blurred copy." Mimicry turns into a type of mockery when the colonized distort or satirize the dominant culture in a form of resistance.

35. See R. S. Sugirtharajah 2006 for articles using postcolonial biblical criticism.

solutions to problems that colonialism created. The question raised has to do with whether or not the Bible can "evolve as an appropriate Word of God in response to issues which were not the primary concern of these narratives." Concerns for personal salvation and piety derived from the Protestant Reformation and the Western Enlightenment's bent on historical reality have impeded the capacity of the Bible to function as a vehicle for emancipation and decolonization (2006a, 67).[36]

In spite of these valid critiques, observations, and goals, western biblical scholarship has generally trivialized or completely ignored postcolonial biblical criticism. This continues to be the case in light of the obvious colonial and imperialistic context of the Bible and its historical connections to Western expansion and hegemony. Note Sugirtharajah's comments.

> Talking about colonialism, one of the notable features of biblical scholarship is its failure to address the relation between European expansion and the emergence of the field. Biblical scholarship thrived in nations at a time when they were strong and domineering. Perhaps the flourishing of biblical studies in Europe should be seen not only in the intellectual context of the time but also as propelled by the colonial ethos and the political realignments of the period. Similarly, one wonders whether the current boom of the discipline in the United States is due to the country's status as a neocolonial power. This link between the burgeoning of the discipline and the political predominance of the nations in which it is practiced needs to be investigated (2003, 135).

Sugirtharajah has also written about the "remarkable reluctance on the part of Western biblical scholarship to address imperialism as an inherent component both in biblical narratives or biblical interpretation" (2006, 68). He blames Western biblical scholarship's heavy emphasis on the religious, theological, and socioeconomic background of biblical texts for the propensity to ignore the presence of imperialism in them. According to Sugirtharajah, this must be "overturned" by recognizing colonialism "at the heart of biblical material and scholarship" (2006, 68).[37]

36. It should be pointed out that postcolonial biblical criticism does not follow postmodernism's disinterest in history.

37. Joseph Marchal says the feminist, postcolonial analysis that focuses on "the dynamics of gender, sexuality, ethnicity, and empire is not only appropriate for the study of Paul, but that it might also revitalize biblical scholarship by reformulating our tasks for

As mentioned above, not all biblical scholars ignore postcolonial biblical criticism. Richard Horsley says, "Postcolonial theory's resistance to colonial metanarratives and deconstruction of dominant discourses, of course, may well assist biblical studies' current struggles to mount a more crucial analysis of the Roman imperial context of the Jesus movements and the New Testament literature and to allow previously obscured histories of Jesus movements to emerge into historical view" (2003, 94). Horsley also admits to the connection between European biblical studies and colonization (2003, 95). But his predilection toward analyzing the Gospels and Pauline letters as historical cases of resistance to imperial rule without scrutinizing the imperial-kyriarchal rhetoric inscribed in these very texts does not reflect a central strategy of postcolonial biblical criticism.[38] Subsequently, Horsley has been accused of defending Paul for not criticizing his rhetoric of obedience and subordination that serves to marginalize other voices in Paul's communities (Schüssler Fiorenza 2007, 103).[39] It appears that Horsley's half-hearted use of postcolonial biblical criticism can be attributed to his open criticism of its "backward orientation to the era of European colonialism," its de-emphasis of capitalism because of an "adamant rejection of Marxism as a historical scheme," and its repudiation of all metanarratives (2003, 94–102).[40]

Some may challenge the notion that biblical criticism fails to engage postcolonialism or to use postcolonial biblical criticism, citing the two issues of the journal *Semeia: Postcolonialism and Scriptural Reading* (1996) and *A Vanishing Mediator? The Presence/Absence of the Bible in Postcolonialism* (2001). One could argue that Sheffield Academic Press's series of four volumes, called The Bible and Postcolonialism, also evidences serious attention by biblical scholars to postcolonialism (1998, 1999, 2000, 2001). And what of a major session devoted specifically to "New Testament Studies and Postcolonial Studies" for consultation at the 1999 national conference for the Society of Biblical Literature? But where did these publications and key conference meetings lead? Postcolonial

---

the twenty-first century" (2008, 111).

38. Schüssler Fiorenza says: "such historical arguments overlook that even resistance literature will re-inscribe the structures of domination against which it seeks to argue" (2007, 4).

39. For a more detailed discussion of this issue, refer to chapter 4 below.

40. See also Anne McClintock's criticisms of postcolonial theory (1992, 85–86).

biblical criticism remains a small subfield carried by only a few prolific scholars such as R. S. Sugirtharajah and Fernando Segovia in particular. Postcolonial biblical scholars like Stephen D. Moore and Segovia refer to their subfield as a "leakage" from literary studies—not biblical studies— and admit that only a few biblical scholars collaborating with them show any interest in actually using the label "postcolonialism" (2005, 8). Moore and Segovia also comment on the fact that "some" collaborating biblical scholars were exclusively interested in the ancient imperial contexts and not "the contemporary contexts in which the biblical texts are appropriated" (2005, 8). The attempts at normalization and collaboration appear rather meager at this point. The traditional field of biblical studies continues to skirt postcolonial biblical criticism and feminist biblical criticism (Marchal 2008, 17; Dube 2000, 20).[41]

Postcolonial criticism has also been sharply challenged for its perceived myopic concentration on language, texts, and cultural representations that tend to obscure social relations, politics, economics—and for a time—even gender.[42] Of the many outspoken critics of postcolonial scholars' early neglect of gender as part of its analytical framework, none has been more incisive than Elizabeth Schüssler Fiorenza. Addressing early postcolonial biblical criticism she writes, "like all malestream studies, this new scholarship has seldom engaged or learned from critical feminist studies" (2007, 4). Just as she advocated an intersectional approach to the various systems of domination with her neologism kyriarchy for social-scientific criticism, she likewise has appealed to postcolonial biblical scholars (2007, 125). Postcolonial feminist biblical critics acknowledge her contributions even if they may not always thoroughly agree with her.[43] Postcolonial feminist biblical critics like Dube, Kwok, and Marchal

41. Roland Boer notes that hardly any working in postcolonial criticism have considered the Bible in their works. Most likely because of the perception that biblical studies deals primarily with religious matters and theology (2001, 6–9).

42. See Moore and Segovia 2005; and Kwok 2009, 191–97. Marchal discusses postcolonial theory's and anti-colonial struggles' neglect of women's agency (2008, 85).

43. Kwok has both great admiration for Schüssler Fiorenza's criticisms and suggestions for postcolonial feminist criticism but disagrees with her in principle on various issues (2009, 196). Pui-lan maintains that "postcolonial studies contribute to the feminist study of the Bible in significant ways," and that "postcolonial theorists have argued that gender inequalities are essential to the structure of colonial racism and imperial authority" (2005, 65–66). But a few pages later she clarifies that "postcolonial male critics may

have expanded the approaches of both postcolonial criticism and biblical criticism. The following methodological summary of Kwok illustrates this expanded approach for both fields. She characterizes this work as follows:

1. Postcolonial feminist biblical criticism investigates "how the symbolization of women and the deployment of gender in the text relate to class interests, modes of production, concentration of state power, and colonial domination."

2. Postcolonial feminist critics focus on biblical women in the "contact zone": the colonized place where two different cultures once separated geographically and historically meet and clash.[44] This includes the capacity for "reconstructive readings as counternarrative."

3. Postcolonial feminist biblical scholars must scrutinize what she calls "metropolitan interpretations." Have male or female interpreters legitimized colonial ideology by "glossing over the imperial context and agenda, or contribute[d] to decolonizing the imperializing texts for the sake of liberation?"

4. Postcolonial feminist biblical criticism emphasizes the "roles and contributions of ordinary readers" to "subvert the dominant Western patriarchal interpretations."

5. Postcolonial feminist biblical critics must practice the "politics and poetics of location."[45] Interpreters look at their own social background including gender, race, sexual orientation, national and institutional context, and economic and educational status (2005, 79–84).

---

include some discussion of women's scholarship, [but] gender remains a marginal issue in their overall analysis" (80).

44. See Dube for further description of the concept of the "contact zone" in postcolonial theory (2000, 67).

45. Kwok borrows this concept from Tolbert (2001, 84).

Biblical Studies and Postcolonial Biblical Criticism:
Hybridity or Mimicry?

Traditional biblical scholarship continues to marginalize both postcolonial
biblical criticism and postcolonial feminist biblical criticism. Both have
responded with a type of mimicry. One finds both postcolonial and feminist biblical critics using methods and findings from traditional biblical
scholarship, including social-scientific criticism (see Schüssler Fiorenza
1999). But at the same time, they continue to denounce "malestream
biblical scholarship" on several fronts (see Marchal 2008). Schüssler
Fiorenza has written about possible collaboration with traditional biblical scholarship, but only if these scholars address their own unchecked
tendencies to approach gender in simplistic and dualistic ways and avoid
kyriarchal rhetoric in their interpretations of biblical texts, as mentioned
above (1999, 2007). Sugirtharajah has acknowledged the contributions
of biblical scholars like Horsley and Moxnes, who practice postcolonial
biblical criticism (2006, 68–69). But it is clear from his own description of
the task of postcolonial biblical criticism above that neither Horsley nor
Moxnes makes any of these points central to his respective works. The
relationship between biblical scholarship and postcolonial and feminist
biblical criticism remains ambivalent.

I would suggest a collaborative relationship based on the postcolonial concept of hybridity, used for cultures that merge different aspects
together without one culture's dominating the other as in syncretism.[46]
Rather than a hierarchical relationship, both methodological approaches
would depend on certain aspects of each other. An obvious starting
point would be for biblical scholars to acknowledge the tragic connection between European expansion and biblical scholarship. The politics
of collaboration are important. For the colonized and marginalized, this
is not a mere return and focus on the past but part of daily reminders
accompanied by continued forces that shape and determine their present
struggles. Biblical scholars also need to analyze the Bible's colonial contexts and examine its narratives for "colonial assumptions" and "imperial
impulses," as Sugirtharajah has suggested (2006a, 67). And it would be
especially crucial for biblical scholars to scrutinize their own interpretations for "hidden ideologies" when making claims of neutrality. Biblical

46. A similar use of this term has been suggested by Moore and Segovia 2005.

scholars' claim to neutrality and their insistence on using descriptive methodologies instead of interpretations based on normative categories marginalize postcolonial and feminist biblical scholars for their openly theological and ethical positions. The hesitancy to acknowledge or advocate normative agendas for the field of biblical studies is viewed as politically risky at the university. Biblical studies still raises suspicion because of Christian hegemony and the Bible's privileged status in the West. While this has resulted in some significant strides toward innovative and cutting-edge methodologies, biblical scholars remain under the purview of nonbiblical specialists at the university; this situation is exemplified by the need to distinguish the field from theology.[47] This collaborative strategy with postcolonial biblical criticism and postcolonial feminist biblical criticism with traditional biblical studies adds significantly to the entire discussion and analysis of power associated with the biblical texts and its interpreters.

POWER AS THEORY

The critical analysis of power has become pervasive and ubiquitous these days across several academic fields, which now include social-scientific, rhetorical, feminist, and postcolonial biblical criticism.[48] But it has just begun to surface in traditional biblical studies.[49] The emerging interest in power relations among biblical scholars is due in large part to the above-mentioned use of modern scientific rubrics to investigate social phenomena and literature in current biblical studies. In turn, many biblical scholars have also been sensitized by various social and political theorists who deal with power. For example, some biblical scholars fully engage and incorporate various aspects of Marx, Lenski, Scott, Weber, Arendt, Lukes, and Foucault. This exigency among biblical scholars to study power also

47. See Ivan Strenski for a historical discussion of the relationship between the early critical study of the Bible (historical-criticism) and the critical study of religion/s in general (2006, 33–59).

48. As stipulated earlier, I will use Schüssler Fiorenza's neologism, *kyriarchy*, to discuss power relations. Her concept of kyriarchy has parallels with postcolonial criticism's analysis of multiple structures of domination and subordination.

49. Horsley says that biblical studies "have tended to ignore power relations in both texts and history" (2008a, 169).

stems from the realization that religion, the production of its texts, the texts' rhetoric, the communities that read them, and scholarly interpretations of these phenomena all involve power.[50] Although we still speak of power abstractly when using models and theories, the process takes us beyond dogmatic theological abstractions to a structured discourse on social forces behind the texts. This should in no way minimize the text's theological dimensions but should actually clarify the text's theological significance in light of its social matrix.

Horsley has utilized the political scientist James C. Scott to explore power relations in the early Jesus movements. Horsley feels that aspects of Scott's works on "domination and resistance" can help biblical scholars better understand these power relations (2008, 169): "Scott not only insists that religion and culture operate in close interrelationship with politics and economics, but presents subtle and sophisticated ways of dealing with that interrelationship" (171). Horsley has used Scott's concept of subordinated peoples' resistance to dominate elites to analyze Jesus among Palestinian peasants and Paul's urban-based mission involving master-slave and patron-client relations. Horsley characterizes "the Jesus movements in Galilee and beyond" as types of resistance movements who use what Scott calls a "hidden transcript." According to Scott, "hidden transcripts" express opposition to dominant powers behind their backs; that is, out of the dominant's purview and control (Horsley 2008a, 175). The emotional trauma from material deprivation and control by the dominating elites, which generates the "hidden transcript" among the subordinated, can be found in the Gospel texts and Paul's writings. Jesus calls Herod Antipas a "fox" (Luke 13:32), and religious elites are "the blind leading the blind" (Matt 15:14). Paul chides the unenlightened "rulers of this age" for "crucifying the Lord of glory" (1 Cor 2:8). Both Jesus and Paul use counterimperial language by using the phrase "kingdom of God" against "kingdom of Caesar." I shall draw attention to this type of analysis of power relations later in the book.[51]

The following summaries are based on a few scholars whose works and theories on power have influenced biblical scholars who appear in

50. Said notes that the production of texts involves power (Sugirtharaja 2006b, 138), and Kittredge says interpretation involves power (1998, 4).

51. Scott has been criticized by other political scientists, and I think appropriately, for "romanticizing the peasantry" (see Weller and Guggenheim 1989, 4–5).

this book. These brief summaries are not meant to be fully representative of the theorists' works. They merely provide a basis to better conceptualize the discourse on power relations found in the following chapters.[52]

## Weber, Arendt, Parsons, and Foucault

Max Weber defined power as "the probability that an actor in a social relationship will be in a position to carry out his own will despite resistance, regardless of the basis on which this probability rests" (Lukes 1986, 2). Weber stresses both the person's intention or "will" and overcoming any "resistance." But how important is the role of intentionality? One can exert power without intention if the system they operate from exercises power by virtue of the person's elevated class or male gender or kyriarchal language or privileged knowledge. The priest officiating at the temple offering sacrifices need not intend to exercise power over those required to submit to his elite office and special divine knowledge. Does resistance always necessarily play a role in cases like these? Or did people submit voluntarily because of the benefit they hoped to attain for themselves? And is Weber's power-over such resistant others an appropriate model of all power relations?

Hannah Arendt and others have rejected Weber's conceptualization of power for its focus on a "command-obedience relationship" (Lukes 1986, 65–66). For Arendt, "power corresponds to the human ability to not just to act but to act in concert. Power is never the property of an individual; it belongs to a group and remains in existence only so long as the group keeps together. When we say of somebody that he is 'in power' we actually refer to his being empowered by a certain number of people to act in their name" (1986, 64). Arendt concentrates on the manifestations of power in political institutions and isolates power in communicative action. Though criticized for separating power from its economic and social context, Arendt's communicative-power theory recognizes the limitations of reducing power to a "command-obedience relationship" model and stresses the more positive and empowering aspects of power

52. Readers can easily find the original works and discussions on these theorists for further study. See Arendt (1958, 1970), Steven Lukes (1986), Foucault (1980). See Ehrensperger for an excellent summary on contemporary power theorists (2007, 16–34).

(1986, 62).[53] As we shall see in chapter 4, Kathy Ehrensperger uses Arendt in her consideration of Paul to show that power need not be asymmetrical but can also be understood as empowering others. For now I suggest that Arendt's model is too simplistic and perhaps idealistic to represent either Jesus or Paul, especially because of its oblique references to economic factors. In the chapters ahead I will indicate why economic factors were central to power relations for Jesus and Paul.

The sociologist Talcott Parsons narrows the complex phenomenon of power to "having to do with the capacity of persons or collectivities 'to get things done' effectively, in particular when their goals are obstructed by some kind of human resistance or opposition" (Lukes 1986, 94). For Parsons, power functions as a resource in social systems that relies on the institutionalization of authority and has parallels to money as a medium of exchange. Both power and money have symbolic values that need to be enforced and legitimized (103). Subsequently power arises from coercion based on binding obligations and consensus derived from collective goals. Parsons's conceptualization of power further contributes to the modern discourse and becomes useful to compare with Weber and others. Parsons, like Arendt, emphasizes the role of power in advancing the collective interests but without adequately discerning how this use of power may also diminish the freedom of others and impact economic factors (see Lukes's critique [1986, 11–12] of Arendt and Parsons).[54]

So how should one proceed with discussions about the connection between power relations and economics in the early Jesus movements? Biblical scholarship is no stranger to Marxist theory in this regard, but non-Marxist social-scientific approaches appear to have netted better results about the social-economic life of the ancient Mediterranean world (see Crossley 2006, 5–18). For example, Gerd Theissen criticized Marxist theory because of its problematic concept of religion and for minimizing the role it played in the early Jesus movements; Theissen criticized Marxism's misleading characterization of slavery in the first century, its homogenized portrayal of the earliest members of Jesus communities as from the lowest classes, and its failure to capture the complex nature of conflict and distribution in the first century (1992, 244–56). With Theissen, I would

53. See Habermas's critique of Arendt (Lukes 1986, 75–89).
54. See Lukes's critique of Arendt and Parsons (1986, 11–12).

contend that some aspects Marxist analysis can be helpful for biblical scholars.[55] But again, non-Marxist social-scientific analyses have proven more valuable when analyzing the early Jesus movements. Perhaps the best approach to date on the economic issues surrounding the early Jesus movements as related to power relations comes from the social-scientific analyses of K. C. Hanson and Douglas E. Oakman (Hanson 1990, 1997; Oakman 1985, 1986, 1991, 1996; Hanson and Oakman 2008). Aspects of both these authors appear in chapter 2.

Michel Foucault seems to have replaced Weber as the paradigm for discourse on power relations. Foucault has influenced the works of several biblical scholars recently, some of whom appear later in this book.[56] Foucault conceptualized power as a coercive force in modern societies' machinations of normalization—a process that subjects our bodies to dominating control. Power for him operates in a network of interactions among people in social life, which sheds light on groups within a society and the entire society (Lukes 1986, 233). Foucault says, "power is not to be taken to be a phenomenon of one individual's consolidated and homogeneous domination over others, or that of some group or class over others" (233–34). Therefore, power must be exercised. "It is never localized here or there, never in anybody's hands, never appropriated as a commodity or piece of wealth" (234). But without the production of truth, there can be no exercise of power. Power requires a "system of right" to control, subjugate, and dominate (231). It does not require intention, only "techniques and tactics of domination" (237). Power is not necessarily a bad thing for Foucault but always has the potential to result in domination (Rabinow 1984, 18). In the final analysis, Ehrensperger notes that "Foucault's approach does not allow for a perception of power which has positive and empowering impacts on social relationships" (2007, 21). In chapter 4 I will explore and critique the ramifications of this power-over concept for biblical scholars who use Foucault to interpret Paul. Foucauldian analy-

55. For example, Scott's use of Gramsci to suggest that the proletariat's need to break the elite's control of the "ideological sectors" of society and not just to control the physical means of production could be applied to both Jesus's and Paul's rhetoric and practice (1985, 38–39). Also see Lenski's critique of Marxist theory (1984, 417–18).

56. Refer to chapter 4 and Elizabeth Castelli (1991), Cynthia Briggs Kittredge (1998), and Sandra Hack Polaski (1999). Each has given Foucault a prominent role in her assessment of Paul's use of power.

ses remain helpful for biblical scholars, especially if supplemented with social-scientific and feminist criticism.

## CONCLUSION

The above considerations of context and methodological approaches served to draw attention to the importance of power relationships in regard to any critical analysis of either Jesus of Nazareth or Paul of Tarsus. These remarks also indicate the necessity for intersecting disciplinary approaches because of the complexity inherent in the manifold operations of power in societies. This complexity is compounded by the ongoing scholarly discourse on power. I have attempted to familiarize readers with basic aspects of the approaches and methodologies used in this book, particularly with the intent of revealing how I deal with the question Jesus's and Paul's use of power. These brief summaries should also help to remind readers of the inherent subjectivity involved in selecting and using various methods as well as to recall that one's method also conditions one's interpretation; but method and meaning are always inextricably intertwined.

# 2

## Nazareth's Rebellious Son

Because his kingdom-of-God agenda threatened their domestic economy and the kyriarchal power relations that sustained it Jesus's family and village elders labeled him a "rebellious son." Consequently, Jesus left Nazareth and initiated a movement among Galilean fishing villages, which had marked economic impact on a variety of Galileans.[1] The Jesus movement fostered several economic dynamics: it exacerbated the downward mobility not only of peasants alienated from their families but also of these very families, and even of some wealthy persons associated with the movement. Passages from Q suggest that new fictive kin groups quickly emerged and developed their own patron-client economy. By meeting the basic needs of its members, this household-based domestic economy also created a safety net for its disenfranchised and honored poor. The Jesus movement represented one of the many subsystems within first-century Galilee, and with some modification it resembled later urban Christian households, especially those reflected in Paul's writings and Luke-Acts.

### INTRODUCTION

Most middle-class Americans would have a difficult time understanding the two passages (one each from Luke and Deuteronomy) juxtaposed below, let alone their significance for power relations in the early Jesus movement. Even those who read the Bible regularly may fail to see how

---

1. I am indebted to Hanson's insightful article on the fishing economy in Galilee (1997) and Oakman's classic book on the economics of Jesus's day (1986) to analyze Jesus and his Galilean movement.

such passages can provide modern readers with important insights about village life in ancient Palestine. Conditioned by middle-class values and the assertion that religion and politics must always be separated, the same contemporary readers would also overlook the economic implications these texts had for ancient Mediterranean individuals and families. Why, for example, would ancient Israelite parents turn their own son over to village authorities for "execution," according to Deut 21:18–21? What parent in our "no-child-left-behind" culture, with laws that protect children from such abuse, could fathom this archaic imbroglio? In the height of my own youthful rebellion, the most I could expect from my parents was a pedantic lecture and the temporary loss of driving privileges. As problematic as this passage is to contemporary North American readers, also problematic is the tendency for modern Christians to associate such baffling passages to a perceived inherent harshness found in the Jewish law, which Jesus came to repudiate with his gospel of love and mercy. The common flaw of modern readers to decontextualize biblical texts based on middle-class values and personal experiences further distances the text from it original social context and theological content.[2]

Based on these unwarranted assumptions, people read the First and Second Testaments looking for personal spiritual direction, not the social and cultural context behind these texts. No wonder middle-class American readers are mystified by Jesus's own village at Nazareth attempting to kill him (Luke 4:29). Consequently, valuable windows to the ancient Mediterranean world and Jesus of Nazareth remain obscure. And perhaps more tragically, such anachronistic approaches tend to project anti-Jewish interpretations onto both the First and Second Testaments.

I use Deut 21:18–21 and Luke 4:16–29 (with other passages) to expose a common ritual of social marginalization for "rebellious sons" in ancient Israelite villages. Such social ostracism and banning not only resulted in the loss of honor and economic support for individuals and their families but also served to bolster kyriarchal authority. Social-scientific criticism and models from cultural anthropology help the modern reader to reconstruct the social dynamics and economic ramifications that Jesus and his movement had on Galilean peasants. It works from the tested premise that both religion and economics are embedded in kin groups

---

2. See Malina (2002, 3–9), Theissen (1992, 231) for discussions on anachronisms and interpreting the gospels.

and political institutions in the ancient Mediterranean world (Oakman 1986).[3] I hope to shed additional light on Jesus and his early movement while avoiding inappropriate, anti-Jewish interpretations.

To begin with, Galileans who joined Jesus groups suffered economic loses and potential destitution. Their downward mobility started with one Jesus followers' being labeled deviants. This, in turn, negatively impacted a deviant's family and those village households that associated with this family in the production of goods and services, in cooperative fishing or trade. New fictive kin groups had to respond with their own domestic economy in order to help one another survive the consequences of losing family support in an economic environment already heavily burdened by Herodian-Roman policies in Galilee (Hanson 1997, 4–9). This emerging socioeconomic trend occurred especially among Galilean fishing villages in the Jesus movement and remained discernable in parts of the Synoptic Gospels. Again I rely on social-scientific criticism to imagine such a historical scenario.

Social-scientific criticism, which employs models from cultural and economic anthropology, helps one navigate through the dark shadows of ancient history with greater confidence while also shedding light on Jesus's theology and the Christology or Christologies developed by the authors of the Synoptics. Separating religious language from political structures and economic practices in first-century Palestine often results in a highly romanticized, oversimplified, though perhaps laudable, portrait of a global Jesus drawn from various decontextualized, modern theological constructs. But I suggest that the Jesus we are about to consider led many to a lower economic status rather than simply rescuing peasants from economic hardship. And those individuals in the early Jesus-movement groups who voluntarily experienced social marginalization, loss of families, and economic hardship can hardly be conceived of as religious fanatics who were merely seeking personal fulfillment apart from purposely attempting to realize the kingdom of Israel's God. Social-scientific analysis of Jesus and the early Galilean movement also makes a carte blanche restoration of the Mosaic covenant at the village level problematic; otherwise Mediterranean kyriarchy and the honor/shame dynamic go unchallenged.

3. See Malina for a summary of this concept (2002, 10).

Jesus's call for prophetic ideals of economic justice also had to target political and domestic economies that had been saturated by elitist patron-client exchange systems that reached all of the way down to peasant kyriarchal households. Here I contend that social-scientific analysis also captures Jesus's theological vision of a antikyriarchal, new order that transformed family loyalties and Mediterranean honor/shame values. Halvor Moxnes reminds us that "social and economic exchange [is] embedded in a highly meaningful context of cult and ritual, linking the mundane to the transcendental" (1988, 38).[4]

## Name Calling at Nazareth

Kyriarchal authorities in Nazareth marginalized Jesus through a social maneuver that cultural anthropologists refer to as "labeling." According to Malina and Neyrey "Labelling has as its purpose to cut off the rule-breaker from the rest of society by invoking the socially shared presumption that one thus labeled is essentially and qualitatively different from other members of society, an "outsider," a special kind of person" (1988, 49). Labeling Jesus, like the "outsiders' vituperation" in the Fourth Gospel, served to "shame and dishonor Jesus" (Neyrey 2007, 53—540). Perceived as a deviant, Jesus threatened the social values and the hierarchal power relations embraced by his kin group and village. "As a rule, we consider anyone defined as radically out of social place as a deviant" (Malina and Neyrey 1991, 100). The deviant Jesus came into conflict with his family and village. This also happened to his followers as their families and villages labeled them deviants for loyalty to Jesus. In the words of Malina and Neyrey:

> Becoming a member of the new Jesus faction itself produces boundaries. In the instructions that Jesus is said to have delivered to those who would promote his name, he states that he came to force people to cross boundaries and to shift allegiances. He does not bring "peace on earth . . . but a sword," "a man against his father, a daughter against her mother, a daughter-in-law against her mother-in-law" (Matt 10:34–35//Luke 12:53). Conversion to the new group, then, will split families and set members on differ-

4. This becomes essential when considering nonkyriarchal power relations in the early Jesus movements.

ent sides of the boundary. Converts cross family boundary lines—perhaps even expelled by their families ([Matt] 10:21)—and so become outsiders. But they become disciples in that they enter the new, fictive family of the Jesus-movement groups (Matt 12:46–50), and so boundaries are maintained all around. (1988, 13)[5]

In addition to causing social conflict, labeling for allegiance to Jesus also precipitated a costly economic domino effect that extended beyond these marginalized deviant members of the Jesus fictive kin groups.

## *Luke 4:16–29 and Deuteronomy 21:18–21*

The initial conflict occurred locally between Jesus's family and the village elders of Nazareth but soon spread to several fishing villages around Galilee. Luke's theological treatment of Jesus beginning his ministry still preserves the tradition's memory of Jesus's leaving his family and causing an uproar in his own village (4:16–29). After mentioning Nazareth as the place where Jesus grew up (4:16a), Luke's longer version of this event presents a literate Jesus reading from the prophet Isaiah as if it applies to himself! The passage reads, "The spirit of the Lord is upon me for the selected purpose to bring good news to the poor (*ptōchos*); he has sent me to proclaim release to the captives and renewed vision to the blind, to send the oppressed away free, and to proclaim the year of the Lord's favor" (4:18, 19).[6]

All three Synoptic Gospels vilify the folks at Nazareth for failing to recognize that their son is actually a great prophet among them. The original context behind this polemical episode most likely had to do with Nazareth's elders condemning Jesus as a rebellious son and banning him. No doubt the Synoptics generally attempt to reverse the labeling of Jesus as a deviant (Malina and Neyrey 1991, 108). Theological redaction in these passages tends to obfuscate crucial social-cultural items like labeling and banning that help one understand Jesus and his activities in the region. Malina and Neyrey's analysis of various passages in Matthew indicates

5. Cf. Horsley (2005, 39–45). Horsley's characterization of Jesus's activities among certain Galilean villages lacks the element of requiring poor peasants to oppose family members over his kingdom-of-God agenda. My assessment not only differs but draws attention to the internal conflict caused by Jesus at the village level.

6. Unless otherwise noted, all translations of biblical passages are mine.

several examples of social labeling prevalent in societies—social labeling that employs sorcery and accusations (1988).

Jesus's conflict with Nazareth can be understood in part because he helped other villages, Capernaum in particular (Matt 4:13; Mark 1:21; Luke 4:23). Villages tended to be independent of one another and also suspicious of other villages (Moxnes 1988, 51). Luke's version emphasizes the attention that Jesus gave to the poor and oppressed. But this raises the question why Jesus chose to tend to the poor and oppressed in Capernaum rather than Nazareth among his own people! Mark's account more vividly exposes the essential honor/shame problem with a son of Nazareth's forsaking home for another village by preserving the line "A prophet is not without *honor* (*atimos*) except among his own village, relatives, and his own house" (Mark 6:4; Matt 13:57). It was expected of Jesus to participate in his own household and village because "in ruralized societies, the kinship group was the economic and religious unit as well" (Malina 2001, 82); and "the family/household was the basic social-economy form of Israelite society" (Horsley 1995, 198). "If a son were banned or disinherited by his father, he would be hated by the family and 'outlawed' from the family house and land" (Neyrey 1995, 148). The Talmud stipulates that a son must honor his father in life and death (*b. Qiddushin* 31b).[7]

Jesus lost honor in the eyes of his village for abandoning his responsibility to his father's household and for showing loyalty to non–kin group members in other villages. "In Mediterranean culture of past and present, those in subordinate positions should subject themselves or be subjected to authority above them (Reese 1998, 142). "Sons are raised to be absolutely obedient to their fathers" and "were usually bound to their father's authority until he died" (Bartchy 2003, 137). Abandoning his home village meant rejecting and challenging the age-old social structure of the village, rooted in kyriarchy and traditional patron-client relationships. None of these social dynamics can be understood in isolation from one another or without penetrating beneath the Synoptics' theological redaction by means of social-scientific and rhetorical criticism.

---

7. Bartchy, commenting on the passage in Deut 21:18–21, says: "In the rhetoric of this passage, this son is not called 'stubborn and rebellious' because he was necessarily a literal glutton and a drunkard but because his demonstrated lack of filial piety shamed his parents similarly to a son known to be one" (2003, 136).

Jesus's deviant behavior set in motion the social punishment village elders orchestrated when Jesus returned home to the synagogue at Nazareth (Matt 13:54; Mark 6:1; Luke 4:16). All three synoptic versions of this status-degradation ritual at Nazareth still reflect typical features found in social-labeling theory. Labeling took place publicly and functioned ritually as a counterritual that removed the person's previous status ascribed through human life-cycle rituals. Degradation rituals like *aposynagogos* ("excluded from the synagogue"), which involved banning and shunning, particularly evident in Matthew and John, are similar to the ritual of labeling one a rebellious son, which included keeping the rebellious son "outside the camp." "Status degradation rituals publicly categorize, recast, and, assign a moral character to deviant actors. This results in a *total change of their identity* to that of a 'deviant'" (Malina and Neyrey 1991, 107).[8] The ritual stripped Jesus of his status as a member of Israel, his village, and his family. The status-degradation ritual at Nazareth's synagogue also followed the same labeling and status-degradation ritual found in Deuteronomy (21:15–21).

Deuteronomy's indictment against rebellious sons dramatizes the severity of sons' failing to honor their peasant families: the threat of death. Both Philo (*Laws* 2.232) and Josephus (*Ant.* 4.257–66) comment on this passage in Deuteronomy and justify its provision of capital punishment, but only if the son did not reform. Philo further stipulates that the severity of the punishment required mutual consent by both parents, which he thought would be rare unless the offense "is very grievous." In a similar fashion, *Sifre Devarim* conveyed a list of conditions that would make the actual execution highly improbable; it applied only to adult sons after their third offense, but the parents could always forgive him. It is noteworthy in regard to the economic factors, that *Sifre* identified one of the rebellious son's offenses as "eating from his father's money" (218–20).

This passage in Deuteronomy magnifies the actual social ramifications of expulsion from one's kin group and village. It is therefore important to note that the rhetorical language the Deuteronomist uses to label a son rebellious exposes this text's original economic context. The parents call him "a glutton and a drunkard" (Deut 21:20b), the very label Jesus received in the Synoptics for associating with "tax collectors and sinners":

8. Italics original.

that is, outsiders (Luke-Q 7:34; Matt 11:9). Peasants hardly had the resources to feed their own families, let alone to eat and drink excessively. A son's forsaking his family responsibilities and habitually sharing meals with those outside his kinship group would be subject to such accusations in the context of first-century Mediterranean culture (Malina 1993, 2–3). The labeling in Deuteronomy functioned as a prescriptive injunction and was aimed at legitimating kyriarchal authority since "the men of the village" adjudicated and carried out the rebellious son's "execution"— "outside the village"—in order to "purge the evil from your midst; and all will hear and be afraid" (Deut 21:21 NRSV). The deviant's behavior belongs in moral categories similar to moral categories typical of "witchcraft societies" (Malina and Neyrey 2004, 23–32). Individuals labeled evil and impure threatened the entire community and were banned with divine authority. In social-scientific terms, such cultural scripts functioned to strengthen the protocol for sons' honoring fathers and thereby to regulate fragile village economics and social status. This required kyriarchal power.

Male heads of households and community authorities took responsibility to uphold the standards of the honor system with full backing from the deviant's family. Even mothers participated in turning their own sons in for punishment (Deut 21:19). Similarly, we find Mary and Jesus's siblings were present at the synagogue and in two additional public labeling scenes in Mark. Mark 3:21 recounts that Jesus's family discovers him in a house where they attempt "to seize him, saying that he is out of his mind." The labeling here comes from people who know him best in the culture: his own family. This text illustrates how ritual labeling redefined the person as "being out of place as a personality trait, an essential quality of personhood" in order to condemn the deviant's behavior (Malina and Neyrey 1991, 100). Any son who challenged the honor of his own household, therefore, readily became a concern for all kyriarchal families and village leaders whose power was rooted in the values of honor and shame and dependent on the stability of peasant domestic economics. The family played an important role in social labeling—positive or negative: "Moreover, since the transgenerational household was the basic social form and the basis of participation in the wider community, pressures on and disintegration of the patriarchal family were the pressure points at which the wider social order would begin to break down" (Horsley

1995, 196). The entire village, then, had a vested interest in protecting social boundaries against perceived evil that in fact threatened traditional power brokers and their control of village economics.

Another curious aspect of Luke's status-degradation ritual at Nazareth also parallels Deuteronomy's rebellious-son passage. According to Luke, the entire synagogue grows enraged at Jesus so that they "bring him out of the city" just before attempting to kill him (4:29); this is once more reminiscent of the passage in Deuteronomy, where "they seize him and bring him outside the city gate" to kill him (21:19). These expulsions outside of the city/village symbolized the deviant's social marginalization that the labeling ritual accomplished. The metaphorical use of being out of place also appears when Jesus's mother, brothers, and sisters come to the house where Jesus is teaching. The family remains "standing outside" while "calling for Jesus" (Mark 3:31). Someone inside the house tells Jesus, "Your mother, brothers, and sisters are outside seeking you" (3:32). The family continues to stand outside, refusing to come into the house and join those sitting at Jesus's feet (indicative of becoming his disciples), and Jesus refused to go out to them (presumably to return home, becoming subject to kyriarchal authorities).

The charge against Jesus as a rebellious son expressed by calling him "a glutton and a drunkard" in Luke-Q 7:34 most likely originated with his parents and culminated in the status-degradation ritual in the synagogue at Nazareth after Jesus returned from Capernaum. This scene also suggests another reason that the elders labeled Jesus and banned him from their village. According to Luke, as some in the synagogue began to marvel at Jesus's words, others reminded the crowd that Jesus was "Joseph's son" (4:22). In other words, not only should everyone have remembered Jesus's ascribed status as Joseph's son, but they should have also recognized that he had left his father's village to do good things at Capernaum (4:23). Therefore he should not acquire higher honor and status! On the contrary, village authorities would have certainly seen Jesus's return and presence at the synagogue as a challenge to their honor, not as a gesture of conciliatory submission. And since honor was believed to be limited in the ancient Mediterranean world, their response to degrade his status should be recognized as very typical in an honor/shame culture. The rebellious son returned not to repent and reform his ways but to reassert his challenge to their honor. This provoked a familiar yet dangerous response by the village elders: envy.[9]

The perception that Jesus returned to Nazareth expecting to be honored would cause significant envy among the village elders, and according to the values of honor and shame they would be forced to defend their honor (Malina 2001, 118). The threat of losing honor in the ancient Mediterranean world also caused envy because of anxiety over social and economic instability. Malina writes, "Envy, in collective cultures, clearly presupposes the perception of *limited good* . . . [T]he perception of limited good is the socially shared conviction that the resources enabling a community to realize its range of needs are in finite supply and that any disruption of the social equilibrium can only be detrimental to community survival. Persons believe that in their social, economic, and natural universe—in sum, in their total environment—all goods exist in finite, limited quantity and are always in short supply" (2001, 112–13; italics original). Even Jesus's habit of moving from place to place could have evoked pejorative labels and envy, because it "symbolized a break with inherited social role and rank" (Malina and Neyrey 1988, 22). A rebellious son was perceived to disrupt the foundation of village social and economic life.

Accusations of rebellion and deviance were shared by those who left families to join Jesus's fictive kin groups and caused envy from those feeling threatened by inevitable economic shortfalls. Matthew suggests that family members who became part of the Jesus movement were subject to being labeled rebellious brothers, children, and parents by their own family members (10:21). The Lukan Jesus exhorts disciples to hold fast to their allegiance to him "whenever they bring you to the synagogues" (12:8–11). Labeling within families and by village male authorities at the synagogue over this allegiance suggests unraveling consanguineal relations in households and anxiety over a family's ability to produce food or goods, to exchange with other villagers, and to pay tax revenues (Luke-Q 12:49–53; Matt 10:34–37).

---

9. Envy played a central role in the Cain and Abel story as well as later in Genesis between Joseph and his brothers (Gen 4:4–8; 37:9–11).

## How Did Jesus Contribute to Downward Mobility?

Further information for speculation about the social impact and nature of Jesus's mission is now available thanks to an innovative study and analysis by Hanson (1997), which focuses on the Galilean fishing economy around the first century. Of first importance is Hanson's recognition of the central place that the Galilean fishing villages, especially Capernaum, played in the Jesus movement. Village names given in the gospels for places where Jesus lived and traveled correspond exactly with several known fishing harbors: Bethsaida, Capernaum, Gennesar, Magdala, Gadara, and Gergasa (1997, 7). Hanson also convincingly demonstrates that the local fishing economy and its peasant families remained stagnant at a "subsistence level" due in large part to exploitative taxes under Antipas, who ruled in Galilee and Perea from 4 BCE to 39 CE with his aristocratic family. Such aristocratic families served their Roman patrons and contributed to the emperor's fantastic wealth (1997, 3). These peasant families worked together as a "social sub-system" within a vastly larger political economy that reached all the way up to the emperor. And typical of advanced agrarian societies, the wealth accumulated at the top, leaving the peasant workers trying to fend off indebtedness or worse: that is, becoming landless and destitute.

Hanson's work takes exception to those who claim that fishing villages and fishing families were better off than peasant farmers because fishing families often owned their own boats, worked together as a cooperative business, and hired laborers. Those things do not mean that such fishing families should be considered "middle class." They, like other peasants, did not control the production of their labor. Fishing families had to work with fish sellers and processors: "The distribution of the catch was also controlled by government approved wholesalers" (Hanson 1997, 11). Such government officials were themselves in debt to local brokers who ran the harbors and who issued fishing leases. In addition, the fishing families were taxed with close scrutiny. Hanson suggests that the gospels and Josephus reveal two layers of tax bureaucracy, and notes that Levi's toll office was actually located in Capernaum (1997, 7).

We can now begin to consider the impact of Jesus's calling disciples away from their fishing families as represented in the Synoptics. Jesus recruited four fishermen, the brothers Peter and Andrew, and then James and John, the sons of Zebedee, while they were working with their families along the shore of the Sea of Galilee. Perhaps these two families worked cooperatively. Luke's account refers to workers in two boats as "partners" (*metachoi*) and the sons of Zebedee as "cooperative-members" (*koionoi*; Luke 5:7, 9–10a; Hanson 1997, 10). Mark adds that Zebedee's boat had hired laborers (*misthotoi*; 1:20b). Any impression that these two families might have been able to manage the loss of four sons without much hardship can be dismissed in light of Hanson's work and the discussion below about honor and economics among peasant families. In fact, Matthew's redaction of the Markan original heightens the anomaly for the first-century Mediterranean honor/shame-based culture by noting not only that Zebedee's sons immediately left their nets to follow Jesus, but they also left their father standing in the boat alone (4:22)! Matthew's version makes no mention of hired laborers who might have eased the shock of Zebedee's sons' abandoning him to prepare the heavy nets by himself. Luke's version includes a miraculous catch of a "great multitude of fish" that softens the stark abandonment scenes in Mark and Matthew (Luke 5:1–10). But Luke's account still ends with, "they left everything and followed him" (5:11b). These "rebellious sons" dishonor their fathers and would have been labeled "gluttons and drunkards" for helping outsiders while creating economic hardship for their families—families now short four strong backs.

No doubt the peasant fishermen who left to follow Jesus experienced the same loss of honor and became poor like Jesus. Peter's exclamation to Jesus in Mark 10:28 characterized the disciples' new, impoverished status: "Look, we have left everything and have followed you!" The "everything" listed in the following verse includes one's "household," "brothers," "sisters," "mothers," "fathers," "children," and "fields" (Mark 10:29). But if Jesus opposed the exploitive political economy of Roman Palestine while advocating economic values based on general reciprocity and redistribution, especially for the poor, how can we understand the hardship the Jesus movement would have created on families whose rebellious sons and daughters abandoned them (Luke 8:1–4)?

One scholar cannot imagine Jesus "addressing such a call primarily to people who are already marginal and under increasing economic pressure—that is already mired in poverty and struggling to keep their households and village communities from disintegrating any further" (Horsley and Draper 1999, 60). Horsley claims that "there is simply no evidence to support the romantic notion of the last generation that Jesus attracted primarily the marginalized members of society, such as 'sinners' and prostitutes or rootless individuals who had abandoned their lands and families" (2005, 35). I agree: Jesus did not require all disciples to become wandering, itinerant disciples who left their families to follow him in an ascetic life of poverty. Nor did Jesus concentrate on the marginalized or the destitute in general to make up the bulk of his movement.

However, a few were called to leave their families to help take the mission to other villages. The four fishermen are examples. Like others, they were not poor or landless until they answered Jesus's call, and likewise others were not considered deviants or destitute until their families labeled them so for loyalty to Jesus. Little evidence supports Horsley's idea that some of the principal leaders in the movement may have come from the poor: those already cut loose from the land and free to move from village to village, people with nothing left to lose (Horsley 2005, 38). First, we have several modern examples of people divesting themselves of family, homes, and careers to join religious sects—Jonestown and Waco among the more infamous. Second, Horsley also maintains that Jesus did not create new communities but worked among the Galilean villages (not with separate groups) restoring the Mosaic covenant of Israel, which would have collectively ameliorated the plight of disintegrating village life (1987, 211). But this conclusion depends on interpreting Jesus's call for the restoration of the Mosaic covenant based on speeches in Mark and Q as if these ideals became social reality for entire villages (Horsley 1999, 248–49). Additionally, Jesus's call for justice appears more characteristic of Amos than Moses. Horsley's vision of such villages returning to "Mosaic justice" sounds familiarly romantic itself: peasants coming together to peacefully resist their elitist oppressors and help one another. But this idealized reconstruction of an early restoration movement fails to account for family members' hostility toward one another over loyalty to Jesus as depicted in Q, or to account for the economic cost to families impacted by sons' and daughters' leaving fields, boats, and households to "seek the kingdom of God" (Luke-Q 9:1–6; 9:57–62; 10:1–12; 14:25–38; Matt 4:22; 6:25–34; Mark 10:28–30).

Gerhard Lenski recognized that religious founders whose "faith" in a "God of justice" leads to the emergence of a "new social group" in the context of peasant oppression (1984, 266). Jesus followed his Israelite tradition's prophetic call for justice. However, restoring Israel required something more than resistance to Herodian-Roman oppression and collective village cooperation. To establish the kingdom of God, followers of Jesus also had to challenge households and village authorities that were based on ancient Mediterranean honor/shame values embedded in kyriarchy and patron/client hierarchy. Jesus's religious vision of the God of Israel animated this so-called deviant behavior. How many fathers or male village leaders can we imagine were open to such a radical restructuring of their socioeconomic life at the expense of their honor, masculinity, and economic stability? What type of conflict ensued if sons and fathers came to disagree over forgiveness of a neighbor's debt? Realizing Jesus's vision of the kingdom of God not only came at the expense of his followers' social and economic status but also caused downward mobility for those peasant families left shorthanded. It also birthed new fictive-kinship groups.

## Honor: Economics and the Ancient Mediterranean World

Regardless of the particular scholarly constructions of Jesus of Nazareth (Jewish peasant [Crossan], prophet advocating the restoration of Israel [Horsley], apocalyptic-ascetic prophet [Ehrman]), most agree that Jesus initiated fictive kinship groups made up primarily of poor peasants, giving special attention to the poorest (Stegemann 1984, 23; Oakman 1992,120; Crossan 1998, 322). The poorest, as the plural Greek word *ptōchoi* suggests, were reduced to destitution, like beggars, in need of the material basics for survival: food, drink, shelter, health, land, and jobs (Hanks 1992, 415). The working poor, indicated by the Greek *penēs*, labored either in farming families on small plots of land or as landless peasants for landlords on large farms. Some also managed to survive as rural artisans or as peasant fishermen. Generally speaking, these working poor should not be considered destitute (*ptōchoi*) since they eked out sufficient resources as part of their family households or as day labors (Neyrey 1995, 139–40; Hanson 1997, 10). But all these working poor (*penēs*) in first-century Palestine lived under an ominous threat of joining the growing ranks of destitute peasants. Lenski reminds us: "*The fact is, unhappily, that in the long run, in all these societies, downward mobility was much more frequent that upward.* Failure to recognize this has led to most of the misleading assertions about the low rate of mobility in agrarian societies" (1984, 290; italics original).[10] Peasants' economic struggles could collapse into destitution by one or a combination of several possible circumstances that happen all too frequently in advanced agrarian societies like Palestine in the first century: a bad crop, a dying father or husband, a debilitating injury or disease, too much debt, higher taxes and tolls, nearby colonial urbanization and commercialization, a peasant revolt, loss of land, loss of job, and the loss of honor.

Modern readers in our postindustrial economy may have some difficulty conceptualizing the causal relationship between the loss of honor and becoming poor, because our culture tends to think of poverty in "purely economic terms" (Gans 2004, 104). Since the latter part of the twentieth century, many Americans have believed that unemployment, lack of education, low skills, and so-called bad neighborhoods cause poverty—not one's reputation in the community. Those who cannot escape poverty are not held in contempt by their neighborhood or family. In our individualistic culture, people who leave their families and neighborhood to "better themselves" receive praise from all, especially from the family. However, ancient Mediterranean cultures made a direct connection between one's honor and economic status. According to Neyrey, the ancient Mediterranean understanding of poverty differs from our modern conception in that for the ancient Mediterranean: "wealth is a component of honour, and both reside primarily in the family; second, if becoming poor (*ptōchos*) includes a corresponding loss of status, this could come about through actual loss of wealth (especially death of parents or husband); and, thirdly, such losses threaten one's honor rating, as well as one's economic situation. It would, then, be culturally myopic to consider 'poor' and 'poverty' merely in terms of economic levels" (1995, 144).[11]

A biting social stigma could also precipitate a decline into the lower stratum of begging poverty, making working peasants into destitute persons, especially if peasants were forced out of their household. Illness, impurity, sin, and being shamed represent similar forms of social marginalization in ancient Palestine that affected one's honor. Anthropologists distinguish "disease," a biomedical condition that afflicts one's body, from

10. See Lenski for an extended treatment of advanced agrarian societies (1984).

11. See Hanson (1997).

"illness," an abnormal sociocultural condition that undermines one's status in a community (Malina and Rohrbaugh 210–11). Likewise, impurity
symbolized something or someone beyond the bounds of divine and
social sanctions. For example, the "illness" of leprosy made one "ritually
unclean" (Lev 13:3b) and excluded one from community: "his dwelling
shall be outside the camp" (Lev 13:45b). Similar was the "stubborn and
rebellious son" who dishonored his father and mother and was seized
and taken outside of his village where "the village elders stoned him to
purge evil from their midst" (Deut 21:19b, 21b). Therefore one's illness
must be cured, impurity cleansed, or sin atoned in order for one to be
restored to family and to again become part of the network of kyriarchal
relationships rooted in honor and shame. The loss of honor due to such
marginalizing religiosocial stigmas also meant the loss of economic support from the person's kin group. Thus, honoring one's father combined a
religious duty with critical economic ramifications for the family and for
small villages in ancient Palestine, where "labeling is a serious challenge
to honor" (Malina and Neyrey 1988, 37).

Also unlike our modern society, the family or kin groups of the
ancient Mediterranean world "interpenetrated political, economic, and
religious institutions; power relations structured village, economic and
religious life" (Hanson and Oakman 2008, 5).[12] Consequently, it is also
crucial to recognize the interconnectedness between religion and economics within political and kinship systems in the ancient Mediterranean
world. Oakman's seminal work, *Jesus and the Economic Questions of His
Day*, demonstrates the inseparability of religion and economics with great
acumen, analyzing many of Jesus's parables and teachings. He concludes
that "religious and economic realities were bound up with social power
in that ancient context (207). This certainly holds true for temples and
shrines in the ancient Mediterranean world. The status-degradation ritual
in the synagogue at Nazareth illustrates the role of religious ideology to
protect honor and economic stability from threats deemed to be an af-
front to God. Jesus did not isolate economics from family households and
village honor/shame ratings while proclaiming his kingdom message.
For example, Jesus assured followers that God would provide for their
food and clothing needs if they would serve God and not "mammon"

12. Hanson and Oakman have an excellent chapter on power (2008, 63–98).

(Matt 6:24–33). These promises found fulfillment in the resocialization of Jesus's fictive kinship groups. In Mark's gospel, Jesus says that his followers would recover "houses, brothers, sisters, mothers, children and fields" in the new kingdom-of-God economy—already present in the Jesus groups (10:30).

## Addressing Downward Mobility and the Honored Poor

Imagine Jesus of Nazareth, himself a peasant whose activities cut across the political, kinship, economic, and religious life of Galilean peasant society in the late 20s (Oakman 1992, 120–21). Jesus's activities impacted a variety of families and individuals. I identify the following six groups: The first group consisted of the few itinerant disciples who traveled with Jesus (Matt 4:18–22; Mark 1:16–20; 10:28–29; Luke 5:1–11). Often neglected by modern scholarship, the second group represented those families who lost members to the Jesus movement, like Zebedee's family (Matt 4:21–22; Mark 1:19–20; Luke 5:10). The third group came from the honored poor: those who formed new fictive kin groups because their own families labeled and banned them for their allegiance to Jesus (Matt 5:3; 10:21–22; Luke 6:20; 9:57–62; 14:25–26). Fourth were patrons who gave economic support to various aspects of the movement (Luke 8:2–3; 19:8). Fifth were the working poor (*penēs*) and destitute (*ptōchos*) in general: those involuntarily made destitute by a variety of health, social, economic, political, and religious circumstances in Galilee—but nonmembers of the Jesus movement (Mark 3:7; 6:34). And the sixth group was made up from the same group of involuntary destitute as the fifth group, but these destitute became members of the Jesus movement (Luke 14:21).

I will be paying particular attention to the second, third, and fourth groups mentioned above. When considering the earliest stages of the Jesus movement in Galilee and its economic impact on peasant families, the second group (those who lost family members because of Jesus's activities) requires careful analysis. As noted above, loss of sons and daughters meant a concomitant depletion of a peasant family's ability to keep food on the table, and a corresponding loss of honor: "A son is the heir to his father's property, but as long as his father lives the son is supposed to share work on the land and to be obedient" (Moxnes 1988, 61). But the speculation only begins here. What about the debt such a family accrued to tax and toll collectors, to absentee elite landlords, or to other families in the village? For example, did Zebedee have to lay off his hired laborers after his sons James and John left him standing in the boat to follow Jesus (Mark 1:20)? Did his sons' abandonment mean that Zebedee now became indebted in order to feed his family? Would his neighbors have been willing to lend to a man whose own sons shamed him and whose prospects of economic recovery looked so bleak? Did Zebedee and his household become destitute as a result of James and John's joining the Jesus movement? How did this type of downward mobility caused by sons and daughters among previously stable peasant households affect the Herodian-Roman tax revenue? And why did Jesus appear to be so callously insouciant towards the plight of Zebedee and other families, including his own, left to endure such losses in honor and economic status?

Theissen, Mack, Crossan, Stegemann and Stegemann, Horsley and especially Oakman continue to speculate on the early Jesus movement and its social impact on those who associated with it, including the rich (*plousioi*), the working poor peasant (*penēs*), and the destitute poor (*ptōchos*). A variety of scholarly opinions persist with regard to the social dynamics of Jesus and the poor. For example, did Jesus actually require poverty (*ptōcheía*) of only a select group of radical itinerant charismatic preachers who left homes to follow him (Theissen 1978)? Or had the infusion of Hellenistic culture so transformed Galilee that peasant Israelite villagers began to envision individual freedom from Roman oppression and Jewish parochialism through unconventional attitudes and behavior modeled after a Cynic-style Jesus (Mack 1993)? As noted above, Horsley argues that it is "absurd" to think that Jesus would require "voluntary poverty" from Galilean peasants already marginalized under increasing economic pressures from Roman policies (1999, 60).[13] But how accurate is Horsley specifically with regard to those that Jesus and his Galilean movement directly impacted? He writes, "The downward spiral of indebtedness would have meant that many eventually either left their ancestral land or became tenants of their creditors. Literary sources from the first century CE, such as the Gospels, reflect the disintegration of the fundamental forms of social life that accompanied these economic burdens

13. Horsley's reliance on the political scientist James C. Scott for a moral economy among peasants has itself been challenged by others who claim Scott's work "romanticizes the peasantry." See Guggenheim and Weller (1989, 2–7).

on the people" (1995 221). Yet again the sayings source (Q) and Mark's gospel indicate not only that Jesus's activities fractured peasant families in Galilee (Luke 9:59–60//Matt 8:21–22; Luke 12:51–53//Matt 10:34–36; Luke 14:26–27//Matt 10:37–39), but also that his kingdom agenda disrupts the domestic economy of these hardworking village peasants (Mark 1:19), clearly resulting in poverty (*ptōcheia*) for those who left or were forced to leave their households (Luke-Q 6:20–22; Mark 10:28).[14] Except for those already destitute, downward mobility characterized the Jesus movement across the board. This was the case not simply because indebtedness weakened the domestic economy in Palestine generally. More specifically, downward mobility occurred as the result of a crisis within peasant families who became split over challenges to kyriarchal structured households and loyalty to Jesus's antikyriarchal vision of God's kingdom. Thus an analysis of Jesus and his early movement must include a more detailed investigation of the complex social and economic structures among the poor, the destitute, local retainers, and brokers appearing in the earliest sources.

Neyrey's insightful cultural analysis of the original context of the makarisms in Luke-Q 6:20–22 helps us recognize the direct correlation between the loss of honor and economic hardship for those experiencing alienation from their families over Jesus—group 3 above (1995, 139–58). His work also adds more details and refinement to our picture of the destitute in the early Jesus movement. Neyrey borrows from Hanson's pivotal article, "'How Honorable!' 'How Shameful!' A Cultural Analysis of Matthew's Markarisms and Reproaches," in which Hanson argues the Greek word *makarios* (often translated "blessed" in Matt 5:3–12) actu-

---

14. Herzog makes the following observation with regard to peasants in rural areas: "There are two thresholds at which peasants may lose their previous status, and it is at these moments that they will resist their decline most fiercely. As James C. Scott observes, 'downwardly mobile peasants may resist most bitterly at those thresholds where they risk losing much of their previous security.' The first threshold occurs when peasants lose their land. When threatened with the loss of their land and the security of their village, they will form movements and perhaps even rebel. The same is true when peasants reach the second, more desperate threshold, when the subsistence guarantees *within* dependency collapse," and the relative stability of tenancy gives way to the perilous life of a day laborer" (2005, 51–52). The question has less to do with whether or not Nazareth was experiencing such threats than how Jesus and his village authorities disagreed over the appropriate course of action for rising debt and the lost of land among the most vulnerable peasants.

ally conveys the cultural concept of "esteemed" or "honoured" (Hanson 1994). Neyrey contends that calling the destitute (*ptōchoi*) "honored" who suffer loss of honor as well as economic hardship makes the makarism an oxymoron: "How honourable are those who suffer loss of honour" (1995, 144). Following Hanson's findings, the four makarisms in Luke-Q can be read:

1. "How honored in God's eyes are the destitute because yours is the kingdom of God" (6:20).
2. "How honored in God's eyes are those who hunger now because you will be fed" (6:21a).
3. "How honored in God's eyes are those weeping now because you will laugh" (6:21b).
4. "How honored in Gods eyes you are when people hate you and exclude you and call you names and cast you out as evil on account of the son of man" (6:22).

Neyrey contends that these original four makarisms do not address the general peasant population in Galilee or the human condition universally, but rather they "describe the composite fate of a disciple who has been ostracized as a rebellious son by his family for loyalty to Jesus. This ostracism entails total loss of all economic support from the family (food, clothing, shelter), as well as total loss of honour and status in the eyes of the village (a good name, marriage prospects, etc.). Such persons would be 'shameful' in the eyes of the family and village, but Jesus proclaims them 'honourable' (*makarioi*)" (Neyrey 1995: 145).[15]

Having identified the cultural equation (loss of honor meant loss of status—economic and material support from families and villages), we can now also conceptualize the reversal of this phenomenon in Jesus's fictive kin groups. The new ascribed honor given to such destitute disciples by Jesus translated into a new religious, social, and economic status for them. Honor for the destitute in the Jesus movement because God accepted them meant that they enjoyed the benefits of their new fictive

15. Agreeing with Neyrey, I would also note that village authorities and fathers ostracized followers of Jesus for opting out of their villages' solution to the economic crisis and for electing to take Jesus up on an alternative model addressed below. In this manner they became "honorable." But it required rejecting traditional village power brokers as Jesus himself had.

kin groups, including daily food (Luke-Q 6:20–21; Matt-Q 5:6, 11–12). These honored poor experienced the kingdom of God materially. They became recipients of God's justice and compassion, which meant having something to eat, a place to eat it, and someone to eat with.

Mark's gospel still reflects this kingdom ideal. For example, when Peter reminds Jesus that "we have left everything to follow you," Jesus assures all his followers that greater blessings are in store for those who honor his kingdom call (10:29–30). But Jesus does not simply promise the restoration of former kyriarchal households. Consequently, no fathers are mentioned. The replacement blessings of the kingdom came "now in this time" (*kairos*) and were not postponed until the eschaton (10:30). Instead, the manifestation of God's kingdom brought something much better and yet still made up of earthly blessing in the present age. This idealized domestic economy that took shape in the earliest Jesus fictive kin groups would also influence Paul's, Mark's, and Luke's urban households (Mark 10:29–30; Luke 6:20–22; cf. 1 Cor 11:22b, 33).[16]

## The Movement's Patron-Client Domestic Economy

If not for the support that Jesus himself received from his own newly formed fictive kin groups, he too would have been listed among the destitute (*ptōchoi*) of Galilee and no longer simply part of the larger class of working peasants (*penēs*). Having left his father's village of Nazareth (*tē patrídi autou*, Mark 6:4), he ceased to participate in his family trade as a low-skilled artisan (*tektōn* Mark 6:3), and moved to Capernaum on the Sea of Galilee (Matt 4:13), where he began teaching, preaching, and healing (Mark 1:21, 25, 31; 2:1–4; Luke 4:23). We never again hear of Jesus's working with his father or brothers in his family trade, or becoming a day laborer or a fisherman in Capernaum; in this regard Jesus was unlike Paul of Tarsus, who apparently worked occasionally in his family trade (1 Cor 9:14–15).[17] Instead, Jesus traveled with the support of the women mentioned in Luke 8:2–3 and, if need be, he and his followers picked grain or figs when support groups or patrons were not available (Mark 7:2; 11:12ff.). Otherwise he frequented someone's house (*oikia*)

16. Refer to chapter 5 for a discussion on Paul's concept of fictive-kin groups.

17. See chapter 5.

and households (*oikoi*) hospitable to him and his traveling companions (Mark 3:32; Luke 9:4). Peasant households like Martha's "received him while he was traveling" (Luke 10:38). After Jesus was fed at the house of Peter, he subsequently moved on, traveling to other fishing villages in Galilee to preach and establish fictive kin groups (Mark 1:29, 38).

Q contains the provocative saying indicating that Jesus belonged to the begging poor (*ptōchos*). Having left home, Jesus reminds would-be followers that "foxes have holes and birds of the air have places to dwell, but the son of man has no place to rest his head" (Luke 9:58). But Jesus appears to have a place to rest his head in Capernaum. No doubt Simon's house became a temporary stopping-off place for Jesus and his itinerant followers in the region. However, Jesus would still have been without a permanent household or means to support himself. He also continued to bear the shame of abandoning his father and kinship network. In other words, he made himself poor. Neyrey utilizes Dennis Duling's social categories of "involuntary marginals" and "voluntary marginals" to characterize and distinguish those who followed Jesus as "voluntary marginals" (1995,154). Involuntary marginals "cannot participate in the normative social life of a group because of race, ethnicity, gender and the like; voluntary marginals, however, consciously and by choice live outside the normative social patterns" (Neyrey 1995, 154). Jesus can also be classified as a voluntary marginal, like his disciples. And like Jesus, all voluntary marginals in the Jesus movement found themselves in need of new fictive kin groups for support while their families now had to deal with their own downward mobility.

The function of hospitality and the creation of fictive kinship households provided the movement with living metaphors of Jesus's teaching about the kingdom of God, and became social institutions to establish this kingdom in villages. The message of the kingdom and loyalty to Jesus bound the followers together; this group held some features in common with the peasant households they left, yet showed some important differences. Malina and Neyrey note how the early Jesus fictive kin groups line up well with Mary Douglas's "strong group/weak grid" model to describe variables of control or non-control in a social body. A "strong group" derives from strong pressure for members to conform to the group's social norms, which makes for tight-knit communities where individuals always "think of themselves as group members first" (Malina and Neyrey 1988, 8). "Low grid" indicates that individuals in the group feel out of alignment with the "stated societal patterns of perception and experience" (ibid., 8). The new fictive kin group's most profound reform is suggested by the glaring absence of oppressive kyriarchal power relations that fed off agonistic competition between males for limited honor. The days of males' dominating all other males and essentially all peasant females subsided as the community shared a meal together in honor of "the heavenly father."[18] This provocative practice of open table fellowship also obliterated boundaries based on impurity, socioeconomic class distinctions, and ethnicity within the Jesus fictive kin groups (Mark 2:16; 7:24–30; Luke 7:36–50). John Elliott observes that Luke's presentation of his Jesus material still preserves the social and economic dynamics of the movement's households. According to Elliott, the "kingdom/household" in Luke demonstrates "acts of loving-kindness," "hospitality," "inclusiveness," "fellowship," and "status reversal," which made the household a "symbol for the kingdom of God" (1991, 227–28).[19]

Jesus's teaching and his "kingdom/households" even attracted some from the retainer class, who became patrons apparently without expecting anything in return (Luke 14:12–14). Rohrbaugh says, "Zacchaeus is willing to become the local patron Jesus needs" (2007, 84). The tax collector Zacchaeus received Jesus in his household (*oíkos*) "with joy" and vowed to give half his possessions to the poor (*ptōchoi*) and to redress extortion, not tax collection (Luke 19:6b, 8). In other words, patrons like Zacchaeus would suffer some depletion of their holdings but would not have necessarily become poor, let alone destitute. A patron like Zacchaeus could have recovered some of his or her redistributed wealth by continuing to function in his or her career or business—similar to Lydia in Acts and

18. I would maintain that the Jesus movement fictive kinship groups lacked traditional household kyriarchal structure. This had several social ramifications for all classes and women in particular (see chapter 3). But it did not eliminate struggles over power among particular fictive-kinship groups both during the time of Jesus and later, as evidenced by Paul's writings (see chapters 4 and 5 below).

19. Elliott's (1991) characterization the Lukan depiction of the Jesus-movement households as a "symbol for the kingdom of God" bears further exploration in light of recent conceptual metaphor theory. See Lakoff and Johnson (1981) and chapter 5. Conceptual metaphor theory would suggest that fictive-kinship households provided a transformational environment for such Jesus-group members to construct and experience a new social reality.

perhaps similar to Prisca and Aquila (1 Cor 16:40; see also 16:19b). One can assume that Zacchaeus continued to receive revenue as a reformed tax collector, which would have represented a stable source of support for Jesus and the local fictive kin group. Luke's Jesus raised no objection to the fact that Zacchaeus did not repudiate his profession; after all, his patronage to Jesus ultimately meant less for the Herodians and hence the emperor. Should this story turn out to have been part of Luke's creative rhetoric in order to get wealthier members to contribute to the poor in his second-generation Christian community, it still reflects the tradition's memory of Jesus's economic dependence on patrons with such resources to support him and his fictive kin groups. Luke's Zacchaeus story also stands out because it appears to represent a reversal of the political economies of the ancient world (Moxnes 1988, 161). Normally in ancient nonindustrial political-economic systems, rich patrons took resources from rural producers in villages and redistributed these goods to urban storehouses (Neyrey 1991, 156).

But a domestic economy emerged in the early Jesus fictive kin groups, where patrons redistributed their surplus goods among the groups' destitute—not reciprocally among the elite. In fact, the rich were expected to become patrons for the movement and its destitute members. The parable of the rich fool warns elite patrons about not "being rich to God" (Luke 12:21), and Luke's account of Ananias and Sapphira still sends chills down the spines of modern readers. This churlish tale suggests that even though patrons in Luke's urban community were not forced to sell property for the poor, the community expected them to do so voluntarily (Acts 5:1–10). In an ancient honor/shame culture, for those belonging to a close fictive kin group (as the text in Luke suggests), the social pressure on rich patrons to redistribute their possessions for the needs of the poor in their house churches had to be emphasized: "no one who had possessions said that any of it was their own, but all these things were shared in common" (Acts 4:32b).

Given this context, could it be that the destitute who received half of Zacchaeus's stuff were in fact those directly associated with Jesus's fictive kin groups, and not simply the destitute of Galilee in general? Those members of Jesus groups who became destitute voluntarily (resulting in alienation from their families and the loss of all support) needed support groups and/or patrons (Mark 1:16–20; 2:13–15; Luke-Q 9:57–58). Those kinship groups made up of those ostracized for loyalty to Jesus did not receive support. Such ostracized families may not have become destitute as a result of losing family members, but they would clearly have experienced some degree of downward mobility (Matt 12:36; Luke 12:52). Some of the destitute who received support were also like Jesus in that though they did not travel with him, they experienced alienation from families and village authorities (Matt 8:19–22; Luke-Q 9:57–62). We have no clear indication that the destitute in general received daily support from the Jesus movement. The needy who received alms were not necessarily outsiders (that is, the poor in general). It is more likely that they were the "needy" members of their new fictive kin group, as Acts 2:44–46 suggests. Peasants, having become destitute involuntarily by a variety of harsh circumstances exacerbated by Herodian-Roman taxation, would have been supported because they joined a Jesus kin group. These included the infirm, the impure, widowed and divorced women—all considered as having lost honor. I suggest that only these three groups (infirm folks, impure folks, and women widowed or divorced) found support as part of the Jesus-movement kin groups. They also found themselves liberated from anxiety about survival as members in their new fictive kin groups, through patron redistribution and the groups' reciprocity of goods (Luke-Q 12:22–34; cf. Matt 6:25–34). Again Jesus promised that "seeking the kingdom" ensured that all basic material needs "will be given to them" (Luke-Q 12:31). But nowhere is it clear that such promises were made to the destitute in general—although the destitute would have on occasion been given alms in acts of compassion (Luke 12:33). Thus, one needs to make a distinction even among the destitute poor (*ptōchos*). Destitute Galileans who were not members of a Jesus group meant those needing to find work or charity each day for survival. These involuntary destitute must be distinguished from the "honored poor" in the Jesus groups, who had lost or forsaken everything but shared the resources from their particular new fictive kin group.[20]

Social-scientific criticism also makes it difficult to imagine that the Jesus movement would have dispersed and shared its vital resources among the growing population of destitute peasants in Galilee when new

20. One must also differentiate between functionalist and conflict approaches among preindustrial, advanced agrarian peasant societies. I suggest a conflict model for the early Jesus movements. See Oakman (2007, 134–36).

fictive kin groups must have attracted their own significant number of destitute. Besides this, patron-client exchange in village economies took place mostly in the form of reciprocity between members who shared strong bonds of solidarity. Halvor Moxnes says that such groups based their exchange in part on defining "a member's privileges and duties, thus distinguishing between members and non-member" (1988, 36). Jesus divided the Galileans into two groups: those with him and those against him (Luke 11:32). Such division separating different groups was common in Jesus's day: "One of the basic and abiding social distinctions made among first-century Mediterraneans was that between in group and out group persons" (Malina and Rohrbaugh (1992, 354). This is not to maintain that Jesus or his movement lacked compassion for the plight of the destitute outside their own group. But social-scientific models point toward the formation of fictive kin groups that developed a domestic economy patterned after patron-client exchange and the patron's redistribution of resources among a group's own members as a means to survive Roman policies and the loss of family ties while implementing Jesus's kingdom-of-God agenda. This ancient Galilean movement did not resemble modern parachurch food pantries for the poor or shelters for the homeless, where such poor are almost exclusively marginalized members of society and not members of the churches who support such outreach ministries.

I suggest applying the following combination of two economic models to analyze the Jesus fictive kin groups in Galilee and how they provided for the needs of the honored poor among them: The first economic model is based on a model of "generalized reciprocity," where the solidarity of the group was very high, gifts were given without expecting something in return, and the exchange between parties was motivated by ideological, interpersonal relations that perpetuated the cohesion of the group (Sahlins 1966, 82; Malina 1986a, 101–2; Moxnes 1988, 36–42). The second economic model involves a variation of the typical patron-client redistribution, which both enhanced the elite group materially and strengthened its political structure. These two models help social scientists contrast peasant domestic economic systems based on types of reciprocity which distinguish "the household and the local village in first-century Palestine" from political economies where "typical large-scale societies with central storehouse economies" operated for the "interests of those in power" like ancient Rome (Elliott 1991, 232–33; Malina 1986a, 100–111). Elliott uses this distinction persuasively in order to highlight Luke's contrast between the generalized reciprocity of the "kingdom/household" and the "morally bankrupt" redistribution of the temple in Jerusalem (1991, 232–40).[21]

I have modified the second economic model to identify the phenomenon of different patrons' supporting Jesus and his local kin groups. Both Q's honored poor and Luke's accounts of wealthy people giving to the destitute indicate a "transformation of the very basis for patronage" (Moxnes 1991, 264). Moxnes points out that the patrons in Luke must not give expecting to create clients since the destitute could not repay. Such patrons gave without even expecting to receive honor for their sacrifices in the Jesus fictive kin groups: "This radical transformation of the concept of patronage" became a model for the domestic economy of the Jesus movement (Moxnes 1991, 266). Instead of taking resources from rural peasants for redistribution among the elites, patrons loyal to Jesus redistributed a generous potion of their wealth among the destitute in local Jesus fictive kin groups. This practice would in principle precipitate some downward mobility of the patrons themselves and would offset the flow of resources that normally went to the top in ancient agrarian political economies. This practice of generosity also indicates that patrons who honored Jesus and his movement dishonored those above them in the political-economic hierarchy of the ancient Mediterranean world. Such patrons would eventually draw attention to themselves and to Jesus. Jesus was not good business for small families or for the Herodians and Romans.

In the chapter before the Zacchaeus episode, Jesus tells a "rich ruler" to sell "all" of his possessions and give the proceeds to the "poor" (*ptōchoi*) and to come follow him (Matt 19:21b; Mark 10:21b; Luke 18:22b). In an honor/shame, patrilineal society people would surely have assumed that the proceeds from the rich man's possessions would go to his own family, with a special share to the eldest son. Jesus's instructions preclude such a cultural protocol and shock the listeners with a seditious request. The "poor" trumped the man's own family. That is, in ancient Mediterranean terms, the poor were being honored at the expense of the man's own biological family (Mark 10:19b). Again, these "poor" targeted to receive the

21. See Hanson and Oakman 2008, 48–50; 81; 113–16; 125–28.

proceeds of Jesus's new disciple's possessions were most likely the destitute already in the movement's new kin groups.

According to Luke, Levi (a potential patron) threw a banquet "in his house" for Jesus, which included Levi's fellow "tax collectors and sinners" (Luke 5:29). Mark's version of Levi's call says that Jesus's disciples also got an invitation to the banquet festivities (2:15). Unlike Zacchaeus, Levi travels with Jesus awhile and then decides to give this banquet to honor Jesus (Luke 5:28–29). Does this banquet bankrupt Levi or significantly diminish his economic resources? Levi appears to have been a small-time toll collector involved with the fishing industry at Capernaum (Stegemann and Stegemann 1999, 200). The banquet honors Jesus and serves to bind Jesus to Levi socially while further impugning Jesus's honor status (because he eats with those labeled sinners) (Neyrey 1996, 170; Talbott 2006, 30). But why did Jesus not demand that the resources and costs of such a banquet be used for the destitute? Jesus neither demands that Levi redistribute half his possessions nor requires him to sell all his things in order to give the proceeds to the destitute. The banquet with sinners functions theologically as a symbolic gesture of Jesus's understanding of the inclusive nature of God's kingdom, based on compassion and forgiveness. Luke's theology eclipses the more pragmatic economic needs of the movement and their destitute. But whether or not this was based on an actual account in the early Jesus Galilean movement or represents another literary device to draw attention to central theological ideals, social-scientific analysis again uncovers the economic ramifications of Levi's response to Jesus's call. It also sharpens the theological focus of this passage, which merged religious and economic factors for rhetorical purposes. Just asking what this story would have meant in the social and economic context of the ancient Mediterranean world brings up a range of possibilities not available to modern readers relying on theology or history alone. Speculating on the economic ramifications of such stories (given our general understanding of ancient political and domestic economies) enlivens our imagination and helps us to distinguish the various economic modalities that the early Jesus movement spawned.

## CONCLUSION

Social-scientific criticism exposes the causal relationship between social marginalization in the Galilean Jesus movement and downward mobility. Labeling led to losses. Deviants suffered alienation from families and villages, which in turn made disciples part of the honored poor (*ptōchos*). To choose loyalty to Jesus was essentially to make oneself a deviant for the kingdom of God. The concatenation between labeling, lost honor, banning, economic hardship, theological ideals, and the formation of new fictive kin groups should come as no surprise in the context of the ancient Mediterranean world, where religion and economics were embedded in political and kinship institutions. Therefore Jesus's kingdom-of-God agenda necessarily impacted the political and kinship structures at several Galilean villages and resulted in economic changes for individuals, families, and even some patrons in the Jesus movement. Membership brought the costly disadvantage of downward mobility but the advantage of compensation through community support for those doing God's will. But families who lost members to the Jesus movement faced the added prospect of accelerated downward mobility without a safety net to prevent becoming destitute.

Analyzing the Synoptics through social-scientific criticism also makes it problematic to imagine that Jesus was simply calling for poverty as a religious ideal for membership in the kingdom of God. He called households and villages to embrace ancient Israel's prophetic ideal of economic justice and distribution of goods. But Jesus's vision of such a kingdom of God came into conflict with kyriarchal authorities. This initial confrontation at Nazareth evoked envy over Jesus's attempts to dismantle kyriarchal and honor/shame kinship systems that manipulated religion for economic and political control. As the Synoptics tell it, the embarrassing event at Nazareth culminated in a labeling ritual of degradation and banning at the synagogue. And in an incredible act of rebelliousness, Jesus refuses to capitulate to village authorities but rather demanded that his followers "call no man father" (Matt 23:9). Jesus himself experienced the callous repercussions of defying the competitive and oppressive social systems in his own village. One wonders if Jesus's parable of the rebellious son in Luke's gospel could have been inspired by his own experience of rejection at home. The father in Jesus's story does not drag his rebellious child before village authorities for labeling and banning but instead restores his status as a son and distributes his finest possessions during a banquet—even in the midst of the obedient son's envy and name calling.

# 3

## Imagining the Matthean Eunuch Community

### KYRIARCHY ON THE CHOPPING BLOCK

The eunuch saying in Matthew's gospel is a gender metaphor that suggests women in Matthew's communit(ies) continued to experience the same equality in marriage and leadership roles as the women in Jesus's Galilean *basileia* movement.[1] The elevation of women's status created tension within the Jesus movements, discernable by reading the eunuch logion in its larger literary and social contexts. By examining the eunuch saying and Matthew's gospel in the context of the ancient Mediterranean world (where kyriarchal structures determined gender roles and eunuchs symbolized neither male nor female), I conclude that this Jesus saying challenged traditional male power rooted in kyriarchal marriage and households. This chapter consequently criticizes recent feminist historical-Jesus research that rejects the antikyriarchal and emancipatory nature of the *basileia* movement named after Jesus for women.

But is it possible to reread Matthew's eunuch saying as evidence that emancipatory struggles for equality in Jesus's Galilean movement were still operative in the Matthean house churches near the end of the first century in Syria?[2] I will argue so and maintain that the eunuch saying

---

1. *Basileia* ("kingdom") is used throughout this chapter to refer the Jesus movements as sociopolitical groups that used traditional Israelite religious ideology against the background of Roman imperial systems in their struggles for justice and egalitarian relationships.

2. Jesus movements were not the only emancipatory movements in the ancient

has special significance for imagining the status and role of women in the Matthean communit(ies).[3] Women in the Matthean communit(ies) were not marginalized like most women in the ancient Mediterranean world. The antikyriarchal structure of the Matthean communit(ies) led to new experiences of equality in their respective communit(ities) with some even functioning as leaders. This took place in spite of women's facing antipathy from traditional power brokers.[4] This tension surfaced rhetorically in Matt 19:3–12, a passage in which Jesus argues with some Pharisees and confronts his own disciples about marriage, divorce, and remarriage. The passage ends with the eunuch saying: "And he said to them, 'Not everyone receives this word even though it has been given to them. For some are eunuchs from birth; others have been made eunuchs by men; and some have made themselves eunuchs for the kingdom of heaven. Let anyone accept this that can'" (Matt 19:11–12).[5]

I maintain that Jesus's call for men to "make themselves eunuchs for the kingdom of heaven" challenged male power and helped to redefine social roles for women in the Jesus movement. The preservation of this difficult saying suggests that the Matthean communit(ies) wrestled with Jesus's ideal for male and female relationships in his *basileia* movement.

To imagine such a scenario, I rely on various feminist biblical scholars and especially the work of Elisabeth Schüssler Fiorenza, who characterizes her approach as rooted in historical and rhetorical biblical method

---

Mediterranean world; the rise of the Hasidim is an example of another such movement (*Jub.* 23:16–17; *1 En.* 100:2). Such struggles for equality are not necessarily the same as "egalitarianism," which, according to S. Scott Bartchy, belongs to the semantic field of politics, whereas "patriarchy" (the object of the emancipatory movements) belongs to the semantic field of kinship. Thus, Bartchy maintains that the "opposite of patriarchal domination is not egalitarian anarchy" but "non-patriarchy" (2003, 145).

3. I agree with Esther Fuchs, who has argued that the Bible is a "patriarchal text not in the sense that it describes an ancient patriarchal society but in the sense that *it prescribes an ideology of male domination*" (italics original). Fuchs states: "the Bible should not be interpreted as an authentic expression of women's voices." Rather, "the biblical text constructs women so as to validate male hegemony and superiority" (Fuchs 2003, 107). However, I think that the eunuch saying may illustrate a struggle against male hegemony and tyranny over women in Matthew's communit(ies).

4. Elaine M. Wainwright suggests that Matthew reveals different "voices" echoed in the Gospel, some of which may have come from an oral tradition of women. Conflict may have arisen within different Matthean households over the role and treatment of women (see Wainwright 1998, 38–42).

5. All biblical translations are my own.

as well as in feminist theory.[6] Schüssler Fiorenza's emphasis on a "soci-ological-theological model for the reconstruction of the early Christian movement" avoids weaknesses found in much current historical-Jesus research, to which I will return (Schüssler Fiorenza 1994, 92). I continue to embrace her neologism *kyriarchy* in this chapter to address the wider social context of the Matthean households and her characterization of the Jesus movement as an "emancipatory *basileia*-movement" against which the eunuch saying would have been understood.[7]

## KYRIARCHY IN THE ANCIENT MEDITERRANEAN WORLD

Deciphering the eunuch logion depends on insights about kyriarchy. Mediterranean societies were dominated by a kyriarchal sociopolitical system that gave control to the emperor/lord/master/father/husband over male or female subordinates and subjugated peoples (Schüssler Fiorenza 2001, 95). Kyriocentric symbols of male superiority and dominance per-meated cities and households.[8] Such kyriocentrism manufactured artifi-cial distinctions between male and female to legitimize and sustain male ascendancy. This sexual dimorphism established gender roles by which both men and women were judged. Gender status was blatantly correlated to biological differences in male and female anatomy, beginning with the genitalia. Interpreted sociopsychologically and underscored by kyriarchal religion, the male body became the symbol of culture's masculine ideals. Kyriocentric cultures grant power and privilege to those born with testi-

6. Schüssler Fiorenza (2001, 135). In addition to employing social-scientific disci-plines and historical-Jesus research, feminist theory also seeks to expose the rhetorical aspects of kyriocentric scholarship itself; see chapter 1, above.

7. Schüssler Fiorenza first used the term *kyriarchy* in *But She Said: Feminist Practices of Biblical Interpretation* (1992). She has defined *kyriarchal* as meaning "emperor, lord, slave-master, father, elite, male domination" (8); she states, "I have coined this analytic category to articulate the intersecting structures of domination: gender, race, class, and imperialism/colonialism." (117). Also see Schüssler Fiorenza 2005, 111–19. The char-acterization of the Jesus movement as an "emancipatory *basileia*-movement" draws at-tention to the role of conflict against kyriarchal structures in the ancient Mediterranean world, kyriarchal households, and Roman imperialism in particular, without implying they were anti-Jewish reform movements (see Schüssler Fiorenza 1994, xix; Schüssler Fiorenza 2001, 50, 113, 119).

8. Schüssler Fiorenza says that kyriocentrism "has the ideological function of natu-ralizing and legitimating not just gender but all forms of domination" (1994, xix).

cles. This distinction broke down, however, when men failed to fulfill their manly virtues or when women attained social status traditionally held by men (LiDonnici 1999, 85–86).[9] Masculinity in the ancient Mediterranean world was measured more by mastery over certain passions (*enkrateia*) and attainment of a higher societal status than by biological differences (Conway 2003, 164–68).[10] Women did attain power over some men and would ironically become more "masculine" than these males[11] based on the very kyriocentric symbolic gender constructions intended to subordinate females simply by their physiognomy.[12] The fluidity of the gender equation grows even more intriguing when one recognizes that a woman who acquired power and status apart from an ascribed elite status by birth had to do so without the benefit of testicles.[13]

Even in modern societies, few people think twice about the attention immediately given to a newborn's genitalia so that the infant's sex can be interpreted according to predetermined gender roles. The ancient Mediterranean world invested much more precision and control over ascribing gender roles and status. It began within the context of kyriarchal households, where the head of the household, usually a father, either performed or submitted the child to a human life-cycle ritual. These rituals determined kinship and encoded gender distinctions. Beginning at birth and throughout one's life, rituals attached meaning to biological

9. In the Roman imperial period, women gained both legal and economic opportunities and held public offices, and women from the upper classes took over for men during times of war and death. This threatened working-class and peasant men. See Schüssler Fiorenza 1994, 89–91.

10. See also Schüssler Fiorenza 1994, xix.

11. In ancient Greek mythology Artemis and Athena cross gender boundaries in their masculine activities of fighting and hunting as well as protecting the honor of violated women. Gwynn Kessler has recently offered examples from the Hebrew Bible and rabbinic literature illustrating that gender boundaries were breached in both directions (2005, 329–59).

12. For example, Hipparchia, wife of the Cynic Crates, had to defend herself for living a masculine lifestyle. Speaking in public, as she did, was considered very high on the scale of masculine traits in ancient Mediterranean honor-shame societies. Anderson and Moore suggest that Matthew's gospel obfuscates traditional masculine roles and opens the way for an alternative masculinity (2004).

13. Hesiod's monarchical myth about Uranus and Kronos illustrates the connection between power and testicles. Uranus began as the king of the gods until his son Kronos castrated him. The kyriarchal values of ancient Greek culture were so pervasive that Hesiod saw no need to explain Uranus's incapacity to rule following this shameful act.

relationships (Eisenbaum 2004.[14] The father in ancient Greek households performed the *amphidromia* rite, in which he carried his child around the hearth, as part of his decision to accept the child as a legitimate heir.[15] The Roman father (*paterfamilias*) inherited the responsibility for all religious rituals in his household; thus, he held a priestly status. Jewish fathers circumcised their infant sons under obligation of the law of Moses, following the example of father Abraham (Gen 21:4). Rituals such as marriage and banquets effectively continued the household's kyriarchal sociopolitical and economic structures founded on the symbolic significance of testicles.[16] Consequently, as Schüssler Fiorenza concludes, "household and marriage relationships generate the social-political inferiority and oppression of women" (1994, 86).

Ancient Mediterranean households reflected the city's kyriarchal religious patterns and social life on a microcosmic scale in the same way that the city mirrored the cosmos. Just as rulers found religion a reliable ally for administering the empire's political and economic agendas, fathers likewise had divine sanctions for sustaining their households. But Jesus in Matthew's gospel not only departs from these kyriarchal features of households but also challenges them with an alternative model. This departure did not involve the total emasculation of ancient Mediterranean culture. After all, the Matthean Jesus refers to God as "Father" (*patēr*; Matt 23:9), and Matthew calls Jesus "Lord" (*kyrios*; Matt 7:21–22) and "the Son of God" (*ho huios tou theou*; Matt 16:16).

This nuance serves as a reminder that Jesus and the movements he inspired in Galilee and Syria were part of two complex cultures: Jewish and Hellenistic. The crucial question in the historical reconstruction of

14. Eisenbaum maintains that "in both Greece and Rome, birth did not automatically bestow membership in the family or clan or citizenry; a child first needed to be ritually recognized by the father, who could also withhold such recognition" (2004, 681).

15. *Amphidromia* literally means "the running-around" ritual and was performed on the fifth or seventh day after birth for both sexes as a ritual of incorporation within the household. An olive branch placed on the door signaled the birth of a boy, and a swath of wool signaled a girl. This ritual had a counterpart in which the child was expelled from the household and exposed outside of the city's boundaries, as in the story of Oedipus (see Louise Bruit Zaidman and Pauline Schmitt Pantel 1992, 64).

16. Sawicki observes, "The Mishnah regards the householder as the central or basic kind of human being. Women, minors, and bond workers are defined by their lack of something that the householder has" (2000, 39).

Jesus is not whether syncretism between these cultures took place, but rather which model most shaped Jesus's life and teachings: a traditional Israelite culture or a Roman-Hellenistic one? Jonathan Reed expresses it this way: "In terms of culture, whether Galilee was Hellenized—that is to say Greek-speaking and conversant in the art, architecture, and thought of the broader Greco-Roman world—or essentially Semitic—that is to say Aramaic-speaking, aniconic, provincial in its architecture, and steeped in rabbinic teachings—makes a difference in the way scholars view the preservation of [Jesus's] sayings by his disciples and their interpretation" (2000, 8).

Archaeological data from Galilee prior to the second century CE continue to suggest that the population was mostly Jewish and that most villages remained distinctively Jewish. Even the urban center Sepphoris, once thought a bastion of Hellenism, now appears to have been a pre-dominantly Jewish city crafted in Hellenistic style (Reed 2000, 110–11; Chancey 2002). And although Roman imperialism was the chief means of Hellenization, "it was surprisingly accommodating to various indig-enous forms," according to Reed (110). Additionally, these Galileans ap-pear to have been staunchly independent, even showing signs of hostility toward Jerusalem's hegemonic efforts represented by "the scribes and Pharisees" (Matt 23:1–39).[17] Horsley and Draper find little room for a thoroughly Hellenized Galilee during the first century CE: "If anything, the increased economic pressures of Antipas's rule and his imposition of Roman-Hellenistic political culture would have driven the Galileans into deeper attachment to their traditional Israelite heritage" (1999, 59).

## KYRIARCHY AND THE JESUS TRADITION

Although the movements in Galilee and Syria remained Jewish,[18] they would have been distinctive from each other in various ways. These two

17. Reed writes, "Jesus and his first Galilean followers stood in the northern prophet-ic tradition calling for the revitalization of Israelite village communities and a return to covenantal principles as a means of redressing social, political, and economic injustices" (2000, 25). See also Richard A. Horsley 1995.

18. Schüssler Fiorenza had already labeled "the Jesus movement as a Jewish move-ment" prior to the growing consensus among those who have examined the archaeologi-cal evidence that Galileans were Jews. See Schüssler Fiorenza 1994, 107; and Reed 2000, 9).

socioreligious Jewish movements would have functioned differently: the former as a prophetic renewal movement within Israel and the latter as a missionary Jesus movement within a Greco-Roman city (Schüssler Fiorenza 1994, 100). They shared, however, an essential and overriding similarity. Both created tension and conflict with the dominant cultural ethos of the Greco-Roman world based on Jesus's vision of the *basileia* of God. According to Schüssler Fiorenza, the *basileia* movement in which Jesus participated was emancipatory and egalitarian, with women playing central roles in the struggle for justice (2000, 100–101).[19] The Jesus movements were not alone in this regard. Women functioned instrumentally in other ancient social movements from "Greek, Roman, Asian, and Jewish cultures" (Schüssler Fiorenza 2000, 41, 50–51). One should therefore understand Jesus and these intra-Jewish movements in their sociopolitical context as being neither unique nor anti-Jewish but rather antikyriarchal and anti-imperialistic.[20]

## Antikyriarchal Households

Each of these intra-Jewish movements interpreted Jesus's theological-social-political-economic vision for Israel and integrated it into its households.[21] Matthew's Gospel gives us one such memory and interpretation

19. Egalitarian must be used with caution based on the complex social structures in the Ancient Mediterranean World (see note 1 above). The inclusion of women and marginalized men at the communit(ies)' meals, and even allowing women to function as leaders in the Jesus movements, was made possible by requiring those empowered by culture with honor and power to relate to others based on God's justice and compassion—not oppressive power over others. Subsequently, members of the Matthean communit(ies) challenged kyriarchal marriage, divorce, and re-marriage that served to privilege men at the expense of women. Following Jesus, they re-defined marriage as a union between equals. But challenging and re-defining kyriarchal institutions based on dominating pyramids of power did not require the elimination of marriage, biological families, sexual differences, or possessions. Social and biological differences could no longer be the basis of establishing one's honor. This was accomplished by re-socializing how individuals in the communit(ies) exercised power in relationships than creating a polity that made every member equal in every aspect of the communit(ies)' life.

20. Schüssler Fiorenza's insistence on replacing the criterion of dissimilarity with the "criterion of possibility" in order to reconstruct Jesus within his Jewishness has been a salient strategy in modern historical-Jesus research (Talbott 2000, 136–37).

21. In the following chapters I will consider if Paul's communities were structured similarly to the early Jesus movements in Galilee, and whether or not Paul can be thought

of the Jesus tradition from the perspective of Matthew's alternative house-holds. Matthew has several sayings of Jesus that disrupt and displace kyriarchal households and marriage, the eunuch saying among others.[22] Deconstructing these sayings in order to capture the place and experi-ence of women requires a "historical imagination" enlivened by feminist theory (Schüssler Fiorenza 1994, xix). We can assume that women played decisive roles in Matthew's households in the first place because of simi-lar examples from the ancient Mediterranean world. Hellenistic religious cults, funeral societies, voluntary associations, and Jewish synagogues also used houses for assembling. The rigid separation between private and public space collapsed in these households, giving women new op-portunities and undermining kyriarchy (Levine 1999, 176, 180).[23]

The transition from a kyriarchal household to a Christian house church meant first eliminating the traditional role of fathers. Matthew's gospel represents this social maneuver with some eye-opening theo-logical rhetoric. Jesus has no biological father but only a surrogate who plays an insignificant role in the development of the Jesus story (Matt 1:18–25). Thus, symbolically, testicles have already been eliminated in the birth stories. At the same time, in Matthew's gospel, Jesus's mother and other women figure prominently (1:3a; 15:28; 27:55), and because of their greater justice or righteousness—not by virtue of their gender—they equal or exceed males in the gospel who show little faith (16:8, 23; 19:22–24; 23:1–36; 26:69–75; Levine 1988, 82). As discussed in the previous chapter, Jesus's community formation included a rather shocking tactic when he chose his first disciples: he called two brothers, James and John, the sons of Zebedee, who immediately left their father standing in the boat to follow Jesus (Matt 4:22). The new, alternative community was not established by the traditional concept of *patria potestas* (paternal power)

---

of as antikyriarchal.

22. Many of these antikyriarchal sayings may have originated in the Q communit(ies) from Galilee. For a thorough discussion of the origin of Q, see John S. Kloppenborg Verbin 2000, chap. 5. Christopher M. Tuckett writes, "The horizons of Q Christians seem thus to be firmly fixed within the bounds of Torah-observance" (1996, 425). Amy-Jill Levine says confidently that "women were among the group that preserved the Q tradi-tions" (1999, 151).

23. Elaine M. Wainwright, commenting on the leadership of women in Matthean communit(ies), says women "participated with men of their house-churches in the inter-pretation of the gospel story and its characterization of Jesus" (1998, 45).

or *paterfamilias* (father of the household) but on a new understanding of God as father: a model that competed with Roman theology in the imperial period, where the emperor was "often seen as a manifestation of God" and as *pater patriae,* father of the country (D'Angelo (1992, 624).

But if Jesus still called God Father, how could these households be considered antikyriarchal? This appellation can be elucidated if one considers Augustus's appropriation of the title "Father of the country" (*pater patriae*) that served to undermine Roman father's power over their households and especially over their wives. The Augustan marriage legislation in 18 BCE and 9 CE, drafted to strengthen the empire, subsequently gave certain rights—such as unsupervised control over their own financial affairs—to wives who bore three or four children.[24] Other forms of legislation changed family life in the early empire, further eroding the "absolute nature of patriarchal authority" (Kuefler 2001, 72). Ultimate paternal authority was reserved for the "Father" in Rome. The memory of Jesus's admonition in Matthew to "call no man on the earth your father, for you all have one heavenly Father" (23:9)[25] in a similar way undercut earthly fathers' power, by placing the entire community under the direct authority of God through Jesus ("All things were handed over to me by my Father" [Matt 11:27]). Two male figures still ruled over the Christian household with authority. But the "Father in heaven," who usurped the authority of *paterfamilias,* did not simply replace one form of male hegemony with another. According to Schüssler Fiorenza, "The 'father' God is invoked here—not to justify patriarchal structures and relationships in the community of disciples but precisely to reject all such claims, powers, and structures" (1994, 150).[26] Matthew's God mirrored neither the rule of fathers nor that of the emperor. The author of Matthew makes this clear through Jesus's ministry, one that hardly evoked ancient Mediterranean ideals of masculinity and power (see Anderson and Moore 2004, 68). As

24. Virtually all free Roman women were legally under one of three types of male power: *patria potestas* (paternal power), *manus* (subordination to the husband's legal power), or *tutela* (under a guardian). All slaves, male or female, were under the power of their master, male or female. A woman never had the legal status of *paterfamilias* (see Judith Evans Grubbs 2002, 20, 84).

25. Kathleen E. Corley thinks that this verse does not attack patriarchy but has to do with Jesus's theological concern for monotheism in light of the "extravagant burial practices for parents and the veneration of patriarchs and special prophets" (2002, 3, 76).

26. Bartchy has a similar interpretation and several good insights (1999, 71).

a servant representative of God's *basileia* (20:28), Jesus obscured gender distinctions by his identification with Sophia[27] and by using eunuchs (19:12) and children (19:14) as exemplary models for household members. The fatherhood of God in Matthew became ambivalent toward the prevailing Greco-Roman constructs of divinity, imperial rule, and Jesus's masculinity.

Matthew's households must have been considered dysfunctional according to kyriarchal standards, as Anthony Saldarini suggests: "Within this framework the author of Matthew consciously modifies the relationships among members of his households in light of Jesus's teachings" (2004, 158). Sayings left over from the Galilean movement, possibly the origin of the Q document, illustrate Matthew's communit(ies)' continued disregard for preserving kyriarchal households. In Matthew-Q 10:34–36, Jesus himself causes the acrimony between "a man and his father" and "a daughter and her mother" so that "one's enemies are in one's own household." Subsequently, fictive kinships in the Jesus movements are adjudicated by allegiance to God, not fathers: "Whoever does the will of my Father in Heaven is my brother and sister and mother" (12:50). Jesus's failure to mention fathers here not only indicates a structural change in households but also shows that "sisters" and "mothers" shared equally in honoring God with the "brothers." In comparison to this calling, Jesus did not allow sons to return home to bury their fathers, a heavily coded cultural dynamic that reinforced, replenished, and refurbished kyriarchy. Rather, sons were required to follow Jesus and "let the dead bury the dead" (8:21–22). The urgency of God's *basileia* surpassed even the most essential attachments to the kyriarchal household, which should be considered as good as dead anyway.

The elimination of the traditional father's role within antikyriarchal households invited the impeachment of kyriarchal marriage as well. In

27. Schüssler Fiorenza notes, "Only Matthew identifies Sophia with Jesus" (1994, 132). Celia Deutsch thinks that Matthew and Q's identification of Jesus with Wisdom serves to subordinate female to male and excludes egalitarian participation of women. According to Deutsch, one of the problems of Matthew's metaphorical use of Sophia has to do with the "dual gender" "Jesus-Sophia" that reveals the valorization of the male teaching/scribal class while subordinating females. But in these cases one could just as easily interpret the "dual gender" aspects of the metaphor as gender ambiguity, not male ascendancy (2001, 88–113). See also Schüssler Fiorenza 1994, 141–44; and Levine 1999, 161.

contrast to the Aristotelian tradition, Matthew says nothing about the wife's duties to her husband in the section of the gospel that deals with households: chapters 19 and 20.[28] Once again, the "sisters" and "mothers" receive a new calling: to "do the will of the Father," that transcends the old household codes.[29] Because women were equal disciples, wives' emancipation from subservient and oppressive roles would have been necessary to further validate the *basileia* of heaven.

The structural changes to households implicit in these texts convey an important aspect of social and political life in the ancient Mediterranean world. All social and political institutions were reinforced by serious theological considerations and legitimized by religious rituals (see Carter 2001, 20, 29–30; Horsley 2003, 29–31; and Price 2002, 16). For this reason, inquiries about the status of women in Matthew's communit(ies) must delve into both Jesus's teachings and his practice of inclusive table fellowship.[30] "Banquet ideology provided a model for creating community"; meals in Matthew were given theological significance and therefore helped shape the social role of women (Smith 2003, 279).[31]

## Antikyriarchal Meals

Meals communicated theological, social, political, and economic ideologies for ancient Mediterranean communities; they revealed a group's values and confirmed social boundaries that in turn defined and determined relationships among members of the group. Meals could maintain the status quo within different groups' social systems but also served to transform social status. Eating regularly with someone outside one's social boundary could break former class, status, and gender distinctions and enable one to cross over former social barriers. Dennis Smith characterizes five social dimensions of meals typical of the ancient Mediterranean world, which involve the following actions: (1) Meals establish social boundaries

28. On the egalitarian nature of this section of Matthew, see Carter 1994, 114.

29. Schüssler Fiorenza notes, "The household code would not have been formulated if other Christian institutional options had not already existed" (1995, 80).

30. Dennis E. Smith notes: "social reality and narrative world are significantly intertwined" (2003, 220).

31. Matthew's community, like the early "house-synagogues in Syria," would have held its meals in houses. See Duling (1995, 163).

for groups. (2) They form social bonds that did not exist previously between the participants (3) while also creating obligations between those
reclining. Smith's analysis also suggests that such meals simultaneously
reflected (4) social stratification and (5) equality (2003, 9–11).

Kathleen Corley has also addressed the social function of such meals
focusing on the subversive nature that ancient meals could play: "As a
social practice tremendously resistant to change, standardized meals
undoubtedly functioned to maintain and stabilize the class-based social
hierarchy of Greco-Roman society. Innovations in meal practice would
have undermined the basic social constructs and power relations in
Greco-Roman society. Innovations in the meal practice of women and
slaves, then, would undermine the gender-based hierarchy of Greco-
Roman society, as well as the gender-based division of that society into
"public" and 'private' categories" (1993, 22–23).

Matthew's communi(ties) also practiced baptism, which had become the decisive means of entering the community for Jewish women
and men as well as for Gentile women and men (Matt 28:19; cf. Gal 3:28).
According to Ekkehard Stegemann and Wolfgang Stegemann, "there is
no discernible gender-specific difference in the baptismal praxis of urban
Christ communities. On the contrary, it is of some significance that the
same ritual was practiced in the baptism of both sexes; that is to say, a
gender-independent 'ritual of initiation' could [promote] and must have
also fundamentally promoted the social integration of women into the
new community" (1999, 393). Meals and baptism in Jesus's name both
served as powerful vehicles for social transformation through which
women entered and overcame kyriarchal structures (see Bell 1992, 89).
Matthew's gospel suggests that women reclined at meals with Jesus publicly (9:9–13; 11:18–19; 14:13–21; 15:32–39; 21:31–32; Corley 1993, 22,
147, 153). These gospel scenes imply "an idealized characterization of
Jesus at table" (Smith 2003, 237).

In the ancient Mediterranean world, portrayals of women who ate
with men in public usually indicated that these women were included at
the meal for the purpose of sexual exploitation (Duling 1995, 163; Corley
1993, 22–23). The Epicureans and Cynics, for example, accused each
other of associating with "prostitutes" precisely because each group ate
its meals with women publicly (Stegemann and Stegemann 1999, 383).
Mixed-gender banqueting was not the only unconventional type of meal

that presented problems for ancient Mediterranean kyriarchal culture.[32] Men of low social class dining with higher-ranking males also breached social boundaries (Wainwright 1998, 47–48).[33] As indicated earlier in this chapter, the Mediterranean world generally valued class and status over gender in determining social roles (see Osiek and Balch 1997, 58). Women, especially those from a higher social class, would have been subject to accusations of promiscuity for attending a public banquet, but women of low status and class represented social irregularities that extended beyond the gender stigma. Stegemann and Stegemann observe the following important item with regard to meals: "For women of the lower stratum, participation in banquets was hardly a gender-specific taboo" (1999, 371). In other words, low class and status excluded both men and women from meals with the upper stratum in the ancient Mediterranean world.

## Why Were Women Included?

But why did the *basileia* movement named after Jesus include women from among the elevated social ranks with poor working women and men? If this mixing of different people at meals was analogous to some progressive religious and philosophical movements in the ancient Mediterranean world, could the inclusion of women have been a primary consideration for Jesus and for Matthew's communit(ies)? This question remains important for the historical investigation and reconstruction of Jesus and

32. Hal Taussig notes that "the general taboo against women and slaves reclining seems to have been quite regularly violated in a kind of social experimentation" (2009, 30). However, had it been a frequent practice in the ancient Mediterranean world it would have also continued to be viewed as nonconventional against the typical hierarchal and kyriarchal values and structures based on established social protocol for women and slaves. Based on Smith's extensive research of ancient Hellenistic type meals, banquets honored privileged persons in the patron-client network. But "clubs and associations were organized in such a way that individuals from a lower status in society could achieve higher status designated at the club banquets based on their rank within the club" (2003, 11). Caution must be exercised before assuming that inclusion of women and low-status men had become an acceptable trend across the first-century Mediterranean world and especially in rural Galilee.

33. See Hanson and Oakman's discussion on social stratification (2008, 39, 150, 158, 182–83, 186–87).

early Christianity. The answer also carries significance for those today who seek justice and equality for women within the Christian tradition.

Corley has addressed these questions and the role of women in the Jesus movement (2002; 1993, 444–59; 1996, 49–65). Her comprehensive work has contributed extensively to the discussion of Jesus's practice of dining as it relates to Christian origins and the development of other groups from the ancient Mediterranean world. Corley has also boldly challenged "Protestant historical models" and various feminist scholarly attempts to reconstruct Jesus and his movement as an apologetic for certain theological assumptions that she deems more mythical than historical.[34] While her criticisms have resulted in a more careful and nuanced examination of the available data, I would suggest that Corley's conclusions are no less susceptible to her own label of "foundational myth" than some of those she attacks. I base this critique on two pivotal methodological weaknesses central to Corley's assumptions and exemplified particularly in her text *Women and the Historical Jesus* (2002). But before I elaborate on these methodological weaknesses, I offer the following brief summary of Corley's conclusions about Jesus's inclusion of women.

Corley does not think that Jesus included women in meals as an essential strategy of his peasant ideology. She argues that Jesus's vision of the *basileia* of God had concerns for class but not gender issues: "The women seem to be around Jesus more as a matter of course than as a result of a gender-equal vision of the Kingdom of God" (2002, 114). In her analysis, the presence of women should be understood as part of a progressive social trend in the wider Greco-Roman world that began with economic changes. These alterations in the market economy of the Roman Empire precipitated social innovations that in turn led to certain freedoms and privileges for women—across the entire eastern Mediterranean world.[35] "The gender inclusivity of Jesus's movement, especially in its meals, has Greco-Roman rather than Hebraic roots, at least in the first century," she states (2002, 145). With regard "to the presence of women in his move-

---

34. Corley's criticisms have focused on Schüssler Fiorenza's work in particular (2002, 17–20; cf. Schüssler Fiorenza 2001, 128–37).

35. In *Private Women, Public Meals,* Corley stresses economic fluctuations for which she provides very little documentation, not even references to Augustan legislation regarding the financial affairs of women.

ment, Jesus appears more influenced by Greco-Roman culture than classic Hebraic culture" (2002, 146).

The first weakness of Corley's argument rests on her reconstruction of Jesus and the probable reasons for the inclusion of women in his movement. She bases this firmly on her insistence that Hellenistic culture not only "pervaded" Palestine but also shaped the "daily lives of Jews" (2002, 22). This pervasive Hellenistic paradigm also allows her to criticize those who make a sharp distinction between Hellenism and Judaism as either "Palestinian Judaism" or "Hellenistic Judaism." Corley rightly charges that such generalized distinctions can lead to anti-Jewish characterizations that make early Christianity appear unique and imply that Jesus superseded his kyriarchal Judaism.[36] However, questioning the degree to which Hellenism influenced Palestine need not constitute an apologetic for a theological agenda. Recent archaeological work and its assessments demand reconsideration of the overall impact that Hellenization had on Galilee in particular, as I have already mentioned earlier (see Horsley and Draper 1999, 9; Chancey 2004, 22–26).[37]

The problem does not have to do with "obscuring the diversity of Jewish culture" or with rejecting the notion that Hellenistic culture was part of the "cultural mix of Palestine" (2002, 22) or with denying the "presence of Hellenistic culture in Palestine" (Corley 2002, 23) or advocating either that villages like Nazareth were "cut off from Hellenistic contact" or that Galilee was in "complete isolation from Judea or rural areas from urban areas" (1993, 68). The crux of the matter revolves around archaeological evidence for Jews who fully participated in Greco-Roman culture in Galilee and for types of Jewish resistance to certain aspects of the Hellenization of Galilee. Recognizing that certain features of Hellenism could not be avoided (such as the use of Greek for legal documents or for Roman economic policies that emanated from Sepphoris and Tiberias), what evidence could be interpreted as attempts of some Jews to define themselves over and against others? Jewish diversity of the time involved

36. Schüssler Fiorenza's writing has done much to reveal and correct these problems in scholarship. Nevertheless, Corley accuses her of an "anti-Judaic model" (2002, 20).

37. Chancey's work is both thorough and compelling with regard to the question of the degree of Hellenization in Galilee before the second century CE. To be fair, it must be noted that Chancey's work (2004) appeared after Corley's *Women and the Historical Jesus: Feminist Myths of Christian Origins* (2002).

a spectrum of different groups that ranged from assimilating to resisting—all of which could be thought of as Hellenized to some degree. The Greek-speaking and Greek-writing Josephus represents one end of the spectrum, while the Aramaic-speaking and Aramaic-writing men and women at Qumran represent the other. Where on this scale would Jesus of Nazareth fit?

Corley looks for similarities with Greco-Roman culture in other forms of culture at the time and finds them even at Qumran (1993, 68).[38] She uses such examples to confirm her pervasive-Hellenistic model. But her justification for such a depiction of Palestine at the time of Jesus exposes some curious sources. For example, she refers to the thirty-two-year-old work of Martin Hengel, which adds nothing new to the current question of models of resistance in Palestine. She also claims that "many scholars in historical Jesus studies now recognize the extent to which Hellenistic culture pervaded first century Palestine" (1993, 68). Oddly, she mentions only a few scholars, including John Dominic Crossan, referring to page 18 of his book *The Historical Jesus* in a footnote (1993, 154 n. 134). This page in Crossan's text deals with the political relationship between the urban centers Sepphoris and Tiberias; here Crossan makes the innocuous comment that Nazareth "was not very far off" the major roads of commerce that went through Sepphoris (1991, 18).[39] The specific archaeological example that Corley offers in this part of her book comes, ironically, from the Roman cities of Ostia and Pompeii. She uses these artistic depictions of Roman women in the marketplace to suggest a Hellenistic style of public life for Jewish women in Palestine (2002, 23, fn. 137).

In 2001, one year before *Women and the Historical Jesus* was published, Crossan collaborated with the Galilean field archaeologist Jonathan L. Reed to publish *Excavating Jesus* (Crossan and Reed 2001). Crossan and Reed have interpreted the archaeological data to indicate that Jesus belonged to one type of Jewish resistance against the Roman-Herodian

---

38. Again, in reference to Hellenistic influences at Qumran one must ask, to what degree did Hellenism surface at Qumran? The problem resides with Corley's indiscriminate application of Hellenism in Palestine.

39. On the same page, Crossan has an interesting quotation by Sean Freyne, who speaks of the "'Galileans' detestation'" of the Jewish aristocracy in Sepphoris "'despite their sharing similar religious loyalties.'"

commercialization of Galilee (172). This conclusion does not impugn Corley's thesis, because it supports the presence of Roman Hellenization and her characterization of Jesus as one who had "a clear awareness of poverty and a critique of class inequity" (2002, 53). But the following observations by Crossan and Reed refute Corley's premise that Greco-Roman styles of dining fully account for Jesus's gender inclusivity and even ritual cleansing (*miqwaoth*)[40] among Jews in Palestine:

> It is not incidental that [certain] implements of purity uncovered by archaeologists challenge two main cultural encroachments from the Hellenistic and Roman worlds, modes of bathing and modes of dining. Bathing in *miqwaoth* contrasted with elite Roman-style bathing practices and offered an alternative that reinforced Jewish distinctiveness and strengthened resistance to foreign domination. Similarly stone vessels offered an indigenous and inexpensive alternative to expensive imported glasses, metals, or ceramics . . . In this case, Jewish self-definition was the profoundest act of non-violent colonial resistance . . . It was still possible to observe Jewish purity laws and still collaborate fully with Rome. But if they did not observe those customs at all, would it have been possible to resist in any way, violently or non-violently (2002, 172)?

Stressing the Greco-Roman recumbent posture of Jewish women eating with men at meals does not preclude the strong possibility that "implements of purity uncovered by archeologists" may have symbolized the meals themselves and represented covert attempts to stave off the tide of the foreign culture (Corley 2002, 26, 49).[41]

The claim that Jesus was primarily influenced by progressive Greco-Roman dining habits to explain his inclusion of women at meals remains tenuous in Corley's work in light of the growing body of archaeological evidence. As it stands, Corley's reconstruction of Jesus appears to be (to

40. Corley writes that *miqwaoth* "were probably not baths used for ritual purification, but are rather modifications of Roman style cold stepped pools (*frigidaria*)." The debate over whether *miqwaoth* were used as ritual baths for purification or for cooling off is far from settled. But I think Crossan and Reed come much closer to understanding their function in the Galilee. I would also suggest that the *miqwaoth* functioned as religious rituals of social resistance within the conflict happening in ancient Palestine.

41. Corley questions whether Jesus actually had disputes with the Pharisees over purity matters in the meal. The people of Qumran and the *haberim* (the self-designation of dining associates among the Pharisees) were exceptions with regard to their continued concern for purity, according to Corley.

use her terms) as much the result of "myth" making as are the reconstructions by those scholars whom she criticizes for constructing an "egalitarian" Jesus. Her presuppositions about a generic Jesus within Greco-Roman culture also fall prey to an anti-Jewish notion: that Jews could not have been innovative without Hellenism (2002, 53).

The second weakness in Corley's argument centers on how Jesus may be thought of as egalitarian. Corley thinks that "although his teaching demonstrates a clear awareness of poverty and a critique of class inequity in ancient Palestine, it does not show an equivalent critique of patriarchy, nor a similar interest in gender concerns. Thus, although there is reason to describe aspects of his message concerning the Kingdom of God as 'egalitarian,' this egalitarianism does not extend to the concerns of women, nor was it aimed at a clear social program geared towards major social change for women" (2002, 53). Corley has painstakingly sought to dismantle the claim of Schüssler Fiorenza and others that Jesus's egalitarian ideal included women and was rooted in his teachings about the *basileia* of heaven.[42] Corley's methodological penchant for a Greco-Romanized Palestine "makes it more plausible that the inclusion of women at Jesus's meals reflects progressive (although controversial) cultural practices found throughout Greco-Roman society and in Hellenistic Judaism, rather than a peasant egalitarian ideology or Sophia-inspired prophetic vision" (2002, 60).

Lurking here are some menacing methodological weaknesses found in modern historical-Jesus research when scholars either rely on outdated social-scientific models or use current ones uncritically. Cross-cultural models from the 1960s and 1970s tend to obfuscate "unique and distinctive" aspects of particular groups, thereby losing sight of their "creative agency" (Sawicki 2000, 6–7).[43] Social models that relegate religion to the maintenance and manipulation of social structure make it almost impossible to recognize subversive and distinctive aspects of religion.[44] Using

42. See Schüssler Fiorenza 2001, 16–21, 53, 60, 144–46; Corley 1990, 291–325. The exchange between Schüssler Fiorenza and Corley in these texts is provocative and illuminating. Also see Schüssler Fiorenza 2001, 129–37.

43. For helpful critiques on this subject, see Sawicki 2000; and Mary Ann Tolbert 2001, 255–71.

44. For example, the major works of Emile Durkheim, Claude Lévi-Strauss, Clifford Geertz, and later from others in the 1970s, including Gerhard E. Lenski's macrosociological model of the first-century's "advanced agrarian" society, do not take into full ac-

such functionalist models of religion exclusively for Jesus research im-poses general categories onto particular data without asking whether the religion of Jesus may have functioned differently.[45] Religion, like gender, belongs to a complex historical process that constantly interacts with oth-er features of culture and society. Additionally, some reduce religion to a mere "epiphenomenon."[46] In this case, researchers assume that religion is a superficial and isolated phenomenon undergirded by more objective and powerful political and economic social forces. Following this model predisposes one to trivialize Jesus's and his movement's transcendent concerns. But faithfulness to the God of Jesus seems to have eclipsed the dominant culture's kyriarchal political and economic requisites, creat-ing an alternative social system in which sons leave fathers and the rich sell their possessions and give to the poor for the *basileia* of God (Matt 19:21).

These methodological flaws explain how Corley can imagine Jesus's "progressive" inclusion of women as a product of Greco-Roman social forces rather than his theological vision of equality in the *basileia* of God.[47] One wonders how any social aspect of the ancient Mediterranean can be understood apart from a serious analysis of the religious dimensions, both social and theological (not to mention political and economic). Even Solon's economic and political reforms of Athens in 594 BCE were connected to new ethical and theological features associated with Zeus and Dikē. It is for the reason that Jesus made a political-theological vi-sion central to his inclusion of women at meals that he can be considered rather typical of the ancient Mediterranean world. It may sound rather absurd to some, but in the case of Jesus and the early Jesus movement,

---

count these aspects of religion.

45. This tendency resonates in the work of Burton L. Mack (see 2001, 84–85).

46. The sociologists Rodney Stark and Roger Finke criticize enlightenment models in the study of religion up to the present for failing to accept the decades of social-scientific data that refute many assumptions about religion. According to this "old paradigm," religion is an "epiphenomenon" based on something false, while the underlying reality concerning "religion" rests on political and economic social dynamics (see Stark and Finke 2000, 27–79).

47. Corley does recognize a distinctive Jewish feature in Q that represents Jesus's con-cern for idolatrous pagan burial customs based on his Hebraic monotheistic theology. But she minimizes these exceptions in order to portray a more Greco-Roman–influenced Jesus (2002, 79, 146).

theology shaped economic considerations. Schüssler Fiorenza soundly advises that "biblical scholarship must investigate not just the philological, historical, archaeological, or literary features of biblical texts but also their theological rhetoric" (2001, 135).

The inclusion of women because of economic opportunities also runs counter to Matthew's depiction of Jesus and the Matthean communit(ies). In Matthew the poor are honored (Matt-Q 5:3), have good news proclaimed to them (Matt-Q 11:5), are to be recipients of rich disciples' generosity (Matt-Q 19:21), and are invited to banquets (Matt-Q 22:9). According to Matthew's Jesus, economic advantages could jeopardize one's devotion to the *basileia* of heaven as a distraction (Matt-Q 6:19; Matt 16:26; 19:21–24). Ideally, loyalty to God takes priority over economic gain for all who would follow Jesus (Matt-Q 6:24–33). Corley suggests that wealthier women would have been attracted to Jesus for one reason, while poor, enslaved, and working women would have joined for other reasons. However, why would class-conscious wealthier women participate in meals that would have undermined their status when the poor were also included? Something must have transcended mere status considerations in order to get people of higher rank to break with conventional social and gender hierarchy.

## Matthew 19:3–12

With the previous discussions in mind, I shall now address the following three questions: (1) What was the relationship of the eunuch saying (Matt 19:11–12) to the preceding passage on divorce and remarriage (19:3–10) as well as to other divorce sayings in the Synoptic Gospels (Hanson and Oakman 2008, 40–43)?[48] (2) How would males in Matthew's communit(ies) have understood becoming eunuchs for the *basileia*? And (3) what does this eunuch logion suggest about women in the Matthean communi(ties); how would women have understood it in the wider context of their experience as members of the *basileia* of heaven?

---

48. The Synoptic Gospels have three other passages on Jesus's divorce sayings (Matt 5:31–32; Mark 10:2–12; and Luke 16:18). Matthew 19:3–10 appears to be an adaptation of Mark's saying with the addition of the clause "except for *porneia* [sexual intercourse outside of marriage]" in 19:9, also found in 5:32.

First, like Mark 10:2–10, which Matthew used, Matthew's passage on divorce and remarriage exhibits androcentric attitudes about marriage (see Schüssler Fiorenza 1994, 143; and Carter 1994, 59). Yet both Mark and Matthew turned the tables on kyriarchal marriage, divorce, and remarriage. Matthew's eunuch saying served not only to intensify Jesus's antikyriarchal comments but also to suggest equality between all members of the household(s), despite the fact that Jesus preserved marriage. This was possible because Jesus restructured marriage by undermining traditional gender roles. The ideal marriage and relationship between genders was not new for Jesus but reformulated from the ancient Genesis creation myths (Gen 1:27; 2:24). In Matthew, becoming a eunuch (19:12), a child (19:13–14), or a servant (20:27) made one an ideal member of the *basileia* of heaven and also put one at odds with kyriarchal households and social structures. This alternative model opposes "the authorities of the Gentiles who lord over them" and their "great ones who exercise power over them" (20:25).

Matthew makes the Pharisees and Jesus's male disciples the foils for his antikyriarchal comments. The Pharisees' androcentric question about the rights of a man to divorce " his wife for any reason" (19:3) gives Jesus an opportunity to treat divorce as a mere symptom of the more serious problem of a "hardened heart" that distorts God's ideal union. He focused instead on creation and the first marriage.

The Pharisees' initial question to Jesus assumes the man's authority under the law to initiate a divorce; they just wanted Jesus's interpretation (19:3).[49] But Jesus broadens the discussion to what the Creator did in the beginning, by quoting Gen 1:27: "he made them male and female" (Matt 19:4). Jesus follows immediately in Matthew's text with another quotation from Gen 2:24, referring to the first marriage (Matt 19:5) with a midrash (Matt 19:6): "'For this reason a man shall leave his father and mother and be joined to his wife and the two shall become one flesh.' So they are no longer two but one flesh. Therefore, what God has brought together let no one separate" (Matt 19:5–6). The Matthean Pharisees ask why, then, Moses gave them the right to divorce (Matt 19:7). I read Jesus's riposte

49. Mark's passage reflects the right of Roman wives to divorce husbands (Mark 10:12). Jewish women also divorced husbands in the Hellenistic period, and divorce by wives is attested as early as the Elephantine community, that is, around the fifth century BCE.

as, "Because of the hardness of your hearts" (19:8), you oppose what the "Creator" intended "from the beginning" (19:9) for humans as "man and woman" (19:4) and "husband and wife" (19:5).

Jesus answers the question about an appropriate cause for divorce only after he has reintroduced females into the Creator's purpose and has reminded the Pharisees that the first marriage resulted in a "one-flesh," permanent relationship (Matt 19:9). His answer also suggests that men were equally culpable for adultery. Infidelity might lead to divorce, but remarriage perpetuated inequality in a kyriarchal system, thereby further thwarting the ideal marriage. Having removed the advantage for men in divorce and remarriage, Jesus so utterly confounds his own male disciples by these antikyriarchal comments that they wonder what the sense of marriage is in the first place if men lose their privileges! The text literally says, "If this is the way of a man with a woman, it is no advantage to marry" (19:10). Jesus responds to his male disciples' dismay with the eunuch saying (19:11–12).

The eunuch saying did not justify celibacy or the renunciation of marriage for males.[50] This would have implied either that Jesus agreed with the disciples' churlish reaction that marriage ought to be abandoned because it eviscerates male privilege, or that Jesus allowed an elite class of celibate men to attain special status in the communit(ies)! I suggest instead that it affirms the disciples' startling realization that the ideal alternative marriage, like their alternative household(s), required males to symbolically sever their testicles as the symbolic bases of kyriarchy.[51] All Jesus's male disciples were expected to voluntarily operate under a new

50. Both blatant and subtle forms of androcentrism continue to obscure the eunuch saying in the history of interpretation from as early as the second century. Commentators continue to gloss over both the impact this saying would have had on the relationship between men and women in the early Jesus movement as well as what its preservation in the Gospel reveals about Matthew's communit(ies). See Albright and Mann 1979, 225–28; Meier 1991, 332–45; and Allison 1998, 175. The NIV perpetuates this assumption by translating the last part of 19:12 ("others have renounced marriage because of the kingdom of heaven"). Translating *eunouchisan heautous* ("make themselves eunuchs") as "have renounced marriage" goes well beyond merely euphemizing. This translation depletes the text of its poignant physical, social, and theological impact.

51. Malina says that "male honor is symbolized by the testicles, which stand for manliness, courage, authority over family, willingness to defend one's reputation, and refusal to submit to humiliation" in the ancient Mediterranean world (2001, 4).

definition of being male. This was the first step in reclaiming what the Creator had in mind for humanity "from the beginning" (19:4, 9).

Jesus's comments should not be construed as anti-Jewish for disagreeing with the Pharisees, in light of the later Mishnaic disputes between Shammai and Hillel over the appropriate cause for divorcing one's wife. Furthermore, Jesus was not the only Jew of the time who used Genesis to advocate an ideological notion of contemporary marriage. In the Hellenistic period some Jewish groups, especially from Palestine, used the Genesis myth of the first marriage between Adam and Eve as their idealistic marital model. The marriage of Tobias and Sarah (Tob 8:5–8; third or second century BCE); Ben Sira's allusion to Gen 2:18 (Sir 36:24; 132 BCE); and the Qumran's use of the phrase "one flesh" (4QMMT), quoting Gen 2:24 and early Christian communities (Eph 5:31), are examples similar to Jesus's use.[52] Unlike Philo,[53] but similar to later Talmudic midrashim on Gen 1:27,[54] the Matthean Jesus did not obscure the text's allusion to equality.

One must also ask, how would males in the Jesus movements have understood "making oneself a eunuch for the sake of the kingdom of heaven"? The reference to eunuchs, familiar yet curious persons, would have evoked a variety of connotations in the ancient Mediterranean world. The law of Moses excluded eunuchs from the covenant with Israel (Lev 21:20; 22:24–25; Deut 23:1), but Isa 56:3–5 praises faithful eunuchs. The *galli*, who most likely originated in Asia Minor, castrated themselves in the cult of Attis as a devotional gesture to the goddess Cybele.[55] Although Cybele became popular among the Roman upper classes by the second century

52. This trend continued in latter Palestinian rabbinic marriage ideology (see Satlow 2001, 57–67). Both Jesus and the Damascus Document (CD 4.20—5.2) cite Gen 1:27. However, Qumran commentators used Gen 1:27 as a prohibition against polygamy, whereas Jesus was making a statement against divorce. Josephus does not mention Adam and Eve when dealing with creation (*Ant.* 1.32–36), and Philo fails to link the primordial marriage to contemporary marriage.

53. Philo (*Creation* 134) separates the first creation, in Gen 1:27, as an "incorporeal, neither male nor female," able to reflect the image of God, from the second, in Gen 2:7, which is a corporeal "man or woman," where woman was created from man and was given a secondary and subordinate status.

54. Rabbis contended that Adam included both male and female (*b. Ketubbot* 8a): "The Talmud asserts that male and female were created in God's image. Nahmanides thought that 'both partake of the divine spirit'" (quoted in Judith Romney Wegner 1991, 47).

55. See Garth Thomas 1984, 1500–35; see also Vermasern 1977.

CE, castration was against the law in the Roman empire and was considered "weird" and "obscene" (Juvenal *Satires* 6.511–41). So eunuchs were hardly the quintessential model of celibacy in the ancient Mediterranean world. Matthew Kuefler notes that "sex between women and eunuchs was always possible," and "sex was as likely a motive for the castration of a slave as resale" (2001, 98–99). The Roman poet Claudian (in *Eutropium*) left a clear testimony, articulated in a witty double entendre, concerning eunuchs as sex partners for other males. Before the second century CE, eunuchs did not evoke the simple image of sexual asceticism claimed by so many modern commentators. Saldarini notes, "Consistent with the Jewish tradition, Matthew nowhere praises celibacy in itself. Unlike other writers in the Greco-Roman tradition, the evangelist does not encourage control of sexual passions for the sake of individual self-mastery" (1999, 22). The Stoic Epictetus wrote, "Even those who castrate themselves are not able to cut themselves off from the desires of men" (Epictetus *Discourses* 2.20.19). According to Eusebius's *Ecclesiastical History*, Origen actually took the eunuch passage literally, perhaps thinking he was on the "cutting edge" of theology. Although Origen criticized castration in his own writings, the rumor of his self-mutilation inspired several later Christians to practice sexual asceticism by castrating themselves in devotion to Christ.

Clearly the eunuch saying targeted male power based on gender distinctions that legitimized kyriarchy at the expense of women's equality and hence opposed Jesus's vision of the *basileia* of heaven. The eunuch saying essentially called men to refuse to play this Mediterranean machismo game, which was rooted in a culture characterized by an honor-shame protocol. Eunuchs symbolized the opposite in such a society; that is, impotence, effeminacy, impurity, and shame.[56] The essential stigma surrounding eunuchs in the ancient Mediterranean world was due to their gender ambiguity. They were highly ambiguous members of society, even though some held high-ranking positions: "In terms of gender scripts, the eunuch leads a boundary-blurring, altogether subversive ex-

56. Moxnes deals extensively with eunuchs and the implications of Jesus's eunuch logion (2003) Of particular interest to my treatment of this passage are Moxnes's observations that households were "masculine places," and that for Jesus to have required young men to leave home would have meant obscuring an important part of their identity as men (73).

istence" (Anderson and Moore 2001, 90). "Eunuchs for the sake of the *basileia* of heaven" meant becoming neither male nor female according to social scripts; that is, it meant stepping outside the structure of ancient Mediterranean kyriarchy. This paved the way for men and women to relate to one another as it was "from the beginning."

Last, it should be noted how Warren Carter can find examples of egalitarian discipleship, antikyriarchal structures, and equality between husbands and wives in Matthew's gospel (2000, 384; 2001, 35–37), and how Saldarini can speak of men in Matthew's household(s) taking on "roles of service usually relegated to women" without discussing the impact the eunuch saying might have had on women (2004, 166). Carter understands the eunuchs as some males who renounce remarriage (1994, 71), and Salderini thinks they are celibate, divorced men, or men seeking to remain unmarried for the work of God's *basileia* (2004, 164). What about Matthean women who were divorced? Would the same special exemplary status be granted to women if they practiced celibacy? Would Jesus create a special class of spiritually elite males elevated by *enkrateia*? Ironically, neither Carter nor Salderini seems to be able to imagine how a gender-blurring metaphor like the eunuch saying could have anything to do with gender relationships.

## CONCLUSION

I am convinced that the eunuch metaphor reflects the *basileia* movements' inclusion and equal treatment of women as a theological ideal rooted in the vision of God's *basileia,* an ideal in which male-female relationships were patterned after Gen 1:27. This model most likely created tension not only against the background of the kyriarchal ancient Mediterranean world but also within the Jesus movements in Galilee and the Matthean household(s) in Antioch. The harsh reaction of Jesus's male disciples to the loss of their advantage in divorce may reflect some males' inner conflict over women's roles. The eunuch logion may have been a cynical response to such in-house social tension rather than a general critique of kyriarchy. (The move from text to social reality remains a precarious journey.) But to enjoy inclusion and equality, women would have had to experience a breakdown of the era's sexual dimorphism that strictly defined gender roles. "Castrating" kyriarchy was necessary to open the way for women in the Matthean house churches so that all could be judged on the basis of how they functioned as faithful disciples—not by virtue of their biological differences.

Who would have preserved such an embarrassing and offensive saying? One can imagine that at least some women would have enthusiastically, remembering that Jesus used it to voice resistance against any who would deny to women what the Creator had willed—even against his own male disciples. But neither surgery nor sexual asceticism could overcome such systemic forces. Jesus's challenge for men to renounce power "for the sake of the *basileia* of heaven" required males to take on a new identity in a community in which traditional kyriarchal roles were redefined by eunuchs, children, and servants. The poignant eunuch saying must have inspired women and some men to resist kyriarchy and to embrace the vision of the *basileia* of God despite forces within their own communit(ies) to conform to traditional gender-based roles.

Rhetorical analysis of the Matthean eunuch metaphor in the context of the divorce and remarriage passage reveals the communit(ies') struggles and discourse on power relations—with the status of women precipitating the conflict. Rhetorical criticism also enlivens what Schüssler Fiorenza calls the "historical imagination" that allows one to hear the voices of those women and subaltern males who were resisting the reinscription of kyriarchal power and domination. Jesus's challenge to kyriarchy and the vision of the *basileia* of God lived on within the Matthean communit(ies) and other later Jesus-movement groups throughout the ancient Mediterranean world. We now turn to the question of power relations in Paul's communities.

# 4

## The Bifurcated Paul: Kyriarchy and Kyridoularchy

Paul of Tarsus, one of history's most influential authors, has also become one of the most controversial figures among those who interpret his ancient letters. Scholars characterize Paul from one end of the speculative curve to the other: from an authoritative apostle of domination (Castelli) to an antidomination teacher (Ehrensperger), from an anti-Jewish prophet of Christianity (Sanders) to an Israelite prophet addressing Israelites in the Hellenized world (Malina and Pilch), and from a typical ancient Mediterranean kyriarchal male (Marshal) to an anti-imperial prophet (Horsley) who established nonpatriarchal, radically inclusive communities (Bartchy). It may seem futile in light of such disparate and diverse interpretations of Paul to attempt yet another reading without appearing to be either pretentious or pedantically redundant. In this chapter I critique several current approaches to Paul's use of power, taking note of both their strengths and weaknesses. I go on to suggest that Paul responded in a typical kyriarchal fashion to conflict in his Christ communities even while calling for a nonkyriarchal model I have termed *kyridoularchy*, which will be explained below.[1] Kyriarchy and kyridoularchy conflict with each

1. Here I distinguish nonkyriarchy from antikyriarchy when referring to Paul's Christ-communities which were neither typically kyriarchal nor antikyriarchal—in the same way that Jesus structured his communities in the Galilee. Essentially, Paul's kyridoularchy required power to be used to empower or honor those with less status in his communities. In this case, power remained a strategy towards community solidarity and cohesion aligned with Paul's ideology. However, Jesus's eunuch model required those with power to relinquish status, privilege, and class in order to challenge hierarchal pyramids of power situated in the very structures of ancient Mediterranean kyriarchy.

other and represent the inconsistencies and ambivalent aspects of Paul's writings that deal with power relations: especially in 1 Corinthians.

Helpful insights from archaeology,[2] cultural anthropology, rhetorical criticism, social-scientific criticism, and feminist studies make navigating through the dark passages of ancient history less precarious—but nonetheless adventuresome. Several treatments of Paul's writings also rely on insightful feminist biblical postcolonial criticism (Marchal 2008; Schüssler Fiorenza 2007; Kwok 2005). All these scholarly approaches have no doubt advanced the quest for Paul. But it appears clear that certain aspects of Paul's writings will remain an enigma as long as people read his letters. Both normative, theological readings that take Paul's writings as timeless, authoritative Scripture, and descriptive, critical approaches that analysis Paul's letters as artifacts from first-century Mediterranean culture must accept this dilemma.

This does not mean that the case for deciphering Paul's ancient and elusive writings should be left merely for TV evangelists' anachronistic and sexist exegesis; neither should Paul's writings be used to buttress further neocolonial exploitation at the hands of subtle or overt forms of Christian domination theology. Too much is riding on interpreting this important figure's documents for scholars and devout Christians. Paul's writings continue to influence the values and attitudes of nearly two billion people who identify with the Christian tradition. Additionally crucial is the realization that many peoples outside the Christian tradition remain subject to dehumanizing perceptions drawn from Pauline texts, not only by Fundamentalists but by pious believers' misinformed, anachronistic readings. Such views of Pauline texts unwittingly interwoven with other biblical texts have long since been assimilated into our culture's value system. Regrettably, not everyone recognizes the detrimental attitudes toward women, Jews, non-Christians, gays, and non-Europeans engendered by those who claim to speak for Paul—who claimed to speak for God. Some who do recognize the connection between Pauline interpretations and our culture's colonial, misogynistic, and intolerant practices are attempting to draw attention to such abuses by situating Paul's texts in their original cultural and historical milieus.

2. For example, significant work has been done to uncover several Roman colonial cities where Paul established Christ communities, improving our knowledge of these "contact zones."

Thanks to the scholarly perspectives on Paul's writings mentioned above, we now have valuable approaches that allow for nuanced readings and varieties of interpretations to stir one's historical imagination. Many of these new approaches to Paul also criticize the anti-intellectual, anti-woman, antigay, or anti-Jewish subtexts of other works (Marchal 2008; Schüssler Fiorenza 2007). Although these works may vary widely, recent scholarship on Paul has delimited the parameters from which to analyze our sources. The following is not meant to be a pretentious criticism of other attempts to understand Paul's writings. It rather participates in the exciting scholarly enterprise that recognizes the difficult questions surrounding Pauline scholarship and his enduring historical, social, political, and theological significance. Nonspecialists are encouraged to participate as well by first becoming familiar with the major issues surrounding contemporary Pauline scholarship. The next two chapters provide one step in that direction by a serious attempt to come to terms with a contextual approach to Paul's use of power under the rubric of various critical models, not as a defense for Paul's authoritative position in modern Christianity.[3] In other words, the normative ramifications for traditional Christian doctrines and faith are left to readers. Such personal and devotional considerations remain secondary to the descriptive and critical nature of my treatment of Paul's writings. I realize that the two cannot be completely isolated from one another, nor should they be, considering the above-mentioned abuses of Pauline texts by both those merely uninformed and those seeking to legitimize their own power.

I rely on social-scientific criticism, feminist analysis, and rhetorical criticism to analyze Paul's rhetoric and metaphors. Insights from these disciplines help us recognize the complexity of Paul writings are also products of his culture in dialogue with his various Christ communities. Paul attempted to re-socialize diverse Christ communities through his "political-theology,"[4] personal rhetoric, and religious rituals. Such re-socialization was pervasive and encompassing in all aspects of these

3. Joseph Marchal's comments are especially helpful in this regard (2008, 111–23); see also Polaski 1999, 124–36.

4. I have borrowed this compound term from Neil Elliott, who uses it to describe Paul's argument in Romans. Elliott borrowed it from Jacob Taubes, who said: "The Epistle to the Romans is a political-theology, a *political* declaration of war on the Caesar" (2004, 13).

communities—even requiring new adaptations for their economic life (1 Cor 4; 2 Cor 8–9). This hermeneutical tactic underscores the significance of Paul's theology for his communities by drawing attention to the synergistic relationship between political-economic forces and the role of religion in the ancient Mediterranean world—as in the chapters dealing with Jesus. Careful attention will be given to this hybrid socioreligious phenomenon with specific examples from Paul's writings.

I also think it is essential to determine (as far as possible) when and for what reasons Paul either followed or deviated from the social and cultural patterns of the ancient Mediterranean world. Can Paul be thought of as a social innovator or radical? Or did he always speak and function as a typical ancient kyriarchal male living in the Mediterranean world? If Paul was at times innovative but in other circumstances typical for his day, how can we account for his vacillation by means of the above-mentioned critical tools of analysis? I find Paul's use of power both typical and innovative for his culture. But this vacillation must be examined in the cultural web of interrelated artifacts, such as Paul's own religious experience (altered state of consciousness), his political-theology, the type of communities he founded, their rituals, and his rhetorical use of metaphors. Identifying various social features among Paul's communities presents valuable information when reconstructing the complex nature of his letters.

As stated earlier, Paul, like Jesus, should be viewed as a product of his social and cultural environment. Paul remained part of his ancient Israelite tradition while also operating in an urban, Hellenistic, and Roman imperial environment. Any innovation, therefore, must be measured against standardized expectations and values for males and females, the person's social status, and one's particular group association living in the wider ancient Mediterranean world. Such instances need also be evaluated as responses to specific sociopolitical and economic dynamics found in Paul's communities—taking care not to separate these social factors from religion. Clearly Paul responded to various issues facing his communities, based on a political-theology that both targeted Roman imperial ideology and addressed specific struggles over power within his Christ communities. Although these dual contexts obviously differ in scope and historical particulars, both involved politics and power that Paul viewed as impediments to his gospel. Therefore, with kyriarchal language prevalent in his culture, Paul directed his rhetoric against any perceived rival. For example,

Paul said that the God of Israel had established his promised messianic order when he made the crucified Jesus "Lord" by raising him from the dead (1 Cor 2:8; 15:3–4; Phil 2:6–11). This illustrates part of Paul's anti-imperial rhetoric, a seditious political claim that maintained Jesus Christ was Lord—not Caesar. Paul infused his gospel message with such Roman kyriarchal ideology while embedding it in his revised interpretation of ancient Israel's tradition (1 Cor 2:8; 15:27–28; Rom 15:7–13; Isa 11:10).[5] "Paul's portrayal of the crucified Jesus' vindication through resurrection was rooted in Judean apocalypticism. So also is the focus of his gospel on a figure executed by the imperial rulers" (Horsley 2000, 93). One might say that Paul, like modern apocalyptic preachers, read current events through the lens of his ancient prophetic texts. Those Christ-community members whom Paul perceived as challenging his authority and disrupting the communities' calling were also subject to the same authoritative rhetoric Paul used to exalt the crucified Lord over imperial Rome!

Such politically inspired theology laid the foundation for many of Paul's social innovations within his Christ communities. His self-disclosed religious experience or altered state of consciousness formed the basis of his claim to ultimate authority over his communities (Gal 1:12; 2 Cor 12:1–5). According to Paul, this "revelation" from Christ reoriented both his participation within Judaism and his relationship with "Gentiles";[6] he exhorted both Jews and Gentiles to relate together in an alternative social order as fictive kin—a highly innovative social maneuver for the first century (Gal 1:11–16; Bartchy 2003). Paul maintained that God had fulfilled his promises to Israel's ancestors as evidenced by the inclusion of the *ethnē*, "nations" (Rom 15:7–13). And according to Paul, this redemptive act did not replace Israel with a new religion we now anachronistically refer to as Christianity. Paul used the Greek word *ekklēsia* for these fictive kinship groups. The usual English translation of *ekklēsia* as "church" unfortunately conjures up many anachronistic concepts for modern in-

5. Neill Elliott says, "His [Paul's] scenario of the nations turning in faithful obedience to Israel's Messiah was a peculiarly Israelite vision, informed by Israel's scriptures. Those scriptures explicitly identified the Messiah as the one "who rises to rule the nations" (2008, 46).

6. See discussion on the use of this term in Malina and Pilch 2006, 364–66.

dividuals, which obscure the original political overtones associated with *ekklēsia* in ancient Mediterranean culture.[7]

Paul's early experiences living and sharing meals with culturally and ethnically diverse Christ communities also contributed to his theological vision and shaped the social structure of the communities he later established. Just as his revised theology of Israel brought Paul into an uncommon association with Gentiles, it likewise led him to follow other unconventional social practices, such as including all women at the communities' meals and placing some women in prominent roles (Rom 16:3–4, 6–7, 15; 1 Cor 11:5, 11–12; 12:7; Gal 3:28; Phil 4:3). One of Paul's most controversial responses to God's apocalyptic new order (and surely one that he must have first witnessed and experienced among Christ communities shortly after his altered state of consciousness) was his new awareness of having to deal with typical ancient Mediterranean kyriarchy. I will argue that while kyriarchy continued in Paul's language and the structure of his communities, he also modified it to accommodate his political-theology and vision for how he felt members of Christ communities should relate to one another in the new, apocalyptic age. Paul himself emerged as a "co-worker" (*synergos*) with other local *ekklēsia* leaders—several of them women—as they resocialized members based on an early christological model of power relations found in Phil 2:6–11. Before Paul, someone had composed this hymn that proclaimed the servant-lordship of Christ over every authority (Phil 2:5–11). Paul was not the sole voice exalting Christ's lordship, as the ancient hymn reveals. Paul also declared the "crucified" Christ as "the lord of glory," which would have functioned to rival the emperor and his imperial institution. This anti-imperial rhetoric also mimicked the kyriarchal terms used in the hymn (1 Cor 2:8; see below). While Christ inaugurated or reinstated the lordship of Israel's God as the true ruler of earth's peoples, the *ekklēsia* bore witness to the servant-lordship of Christ in their midst through ultimate allegiance or faith in Christ and obedience to Paul (Rom 1:4–5; 1 Cor 3:11, 16–17; 4:14–17; 2 Cor 10:6; Elliott 2008, 45).

Paul articulated this new order of God's rule with the rhetoric of his christological perspective—a political-theology constructed from a kyriarchal backdrop with kyriarchal language. Paul operated in a kyri-

---

7. See Koester 2007, 211–13.

archal environment under Roman imperial ideology, and within ancient Mediterranean households modeled after kyriarchy. Neil Elliott maintains that Paul "seems incapable of imagining the end of Roman kyriarchy without describing the ascendancy of a new and better kyriarchy, that of the Messiah, the *kyrios*, who will subdue and rule, *archein*, over the nations with justice" (2008, 52). As mentioned above, I would also stipulate that although Paul relied on kyriarchal rhetoric, he also redefined and transformed it according to Christ's self-humiliation and subordination to God—even becoming a "slave" on behalf of others (see the next chapter). Paul operated under a divine kyriarchy similarly to ancient Greco-Roman rulers (1 Cor 15:27–28; Phil 2:7; Price 1997, 47–71). But Paul's Christ, the crucified, servant-lord, called into question all human relationships based on hierarchy, including traditional patron-client relationships.

Traditional kyriarchy attempted to eliminate vulnerability and victimization for those in positions of power by establishing social boundaries through honor-shame competition, through the religion of the status quo, through the economic control of clients by patrons, through the institutions of slavery and marriage, through labeling, through Hellenistic meals, and through violence. Christ's lordship not only challenged these kyriarchal strongholds but required those with honor and status to use their power for the benefit of the weaker members of their households (Rom 15:1; Phlm 16). Paul exercised his power based on two models: ancient Mediterranean kyriarchy and Christ as crucified servant-lord (1 Cor 1:23; Phil 2:7). He expected Christ communities to imitate the latter, his christological version of kyriarchy.

In order to express Paul's christological version of kyriarchy, I will use a neologism (*kyridoularchy*) based on the three Greek words: *kyrios* ("Lord"), *doulos/ē* (masculine and feminine for "servant" or "slave"), and *archē* ("ruler"). We recall that kyriarchy refers to the convergence of gender, sexuality, race, ethnicity, imperialism, and status that shaped social structures and institutions in the ancient Mediterranean world to dominate others (Schüssler Fiorenza 2001, 118–19). Kyridoularchy characterized both males and females who enjoyed an elevated status by virtue of kyriarchal institutions but who exercised their power on behalf of others in their fictive kinship groups with subordinate social positions and statuses. Kyridoularchy resulted in honor for lower-status kinship members, who would not have normally received honor based on ancient

Mediterranean standards. This also meant that the poor received food and other resources through participating in the communities' shared meal. Kyridoularchy honored and therefore empowered vulnerable and marginalized members (Rom 12:10; 1 Cor 11:33; 12:24). Kyridoularchy did not necessarily require one to forfeit his or her status or economic means simply to identify with lower-status members. The object was not repudiating one's power but ascribing honor to others. This will be discussed further in the next chapter.

Naturally in his environment, Paul's lordship of Christ contains both religious and political significance typical of the ancient Mediterranean world, where the emperor's lordship reigned over earth's peoples with divine sanction, as a "son of God" (Neil Elliott 2008, 44, 198). Paul could rely on similar divine legitimization for resocializing his communities with an appeal to Christ as "son of God" yet "servant" for others: kyridoularchy (Rom 8:3; 15:8; Gal 5:13; Phil 2:7). But again, Paul's christological version of kyriarchy inscribes Christ in the place of the emperor as Lord, and alters typical kyriarchal-based power relationships in the Christ communities. Subsequently, kyridoularchy does not mirror the kyriarchy of the imperial household, with its hierarchy of elite Roman classes; neither does it echo the traditional patriarchal households that stretched across the ancient Mediterranean basin and beyond. Those who found themselves with culturally ascribed honor and therefore in social positions to exercise or translate honor into power over others for their own benefit or for the advantage of their patrons are now expected to use all forms of kyriarchy to empower and benefit those of lower status! Poor members of the *ekklēsia* are to experience equal access to food and drink at the communities' meals as an expression of mutual honor (1 Cor 11:17–22). The predominately "Gentile" communities in Corinth were required to respond to the needs of "poor saints" in Jerusalem out of their own economic resources (2 Corinthians 8–9). Members with greater "knowledge" are asked to "take care" that their "authority" (*exousia*) not be used to injure "the weak ones," who are now their "brothers and sisters" (1 Cor 8:7, 9, 12). Paul acknowledges that some members (including himself) continue to have authority, power, economic means, and honor, but his understanding of how these status markers are to be used in the *ekklēsia* was determined by members' identity as fictive kin, a new family in Christ. Notice, for example, Paul's provocatively reconfigured kyriarchal language to those in positions of power with regard to those with socially inferior status in the Christ community at Rome.

> We, the powerful ones (*hoi dunatoi*) ought to bear the weaknesses of those without power (*tôn adunatôn*) and not please ourselves. Let each please the neighbor for the neighbor's benefit—for [the neighbor's] edification. For Christ did not please himself. But as it is written: 'The shameful things of the ones reproaching you fell on me.'" (Rom 15:1–3).[8]

I realize that characterizing Paul's use of power even based on a model of self-humiliation and service still raises the question of asymmetrical relationships between Paul and members of his communities. It can also function to legitimize an authoritative hierarchy ruling over others in the Christ communities. This did take place later, evidenced in Deutero-Pauline texts as Horsley (2000, 93) observes in connection with Paul's anti-imperial rhetoric:

> Paul's redeployment of key terms from Roman imperial ideology, however, meant that he "reinscribed" imperial images and relations within his arguments aimed at reinforcing the discipline of an anti-imperial movement. In offering his assembly an alternative to Caesar, Paul in effect presented Jesus Christ as the true emperor, the true Lord and Savor who was in the process of subjugating all things to himself! Such imperial language could have been difficult for the emergent polity of the Christian movement to appeal to and build on Paul's imperial counterimperial language. Already in the deutero-Pauline letters the implications of such language for relations within the movement and its adjustment to the dominant social order are abundantly evident. In its imagery of Christ as the true emperor, the Christian church was already well prepared for its own establishment under Constantine.

8. See Martin for a discussion on this passage (1990, 141–45).

## SOME RECENT EXAMPLES OF SCHOLARSHIP
## ON PAUL'S USE OF POWER

### Foucauldian Analysis and Pauline Studies

The following brief summaries and critiques of recent scholars that ad-dress Paul's use of power provide a framework to further analyze this topic. Such a discussion has become essential for serious students of Paul because of the excellent contributions several scholars have made to this central issue, and because of the implications for understanding Paul as an advocate for either traditional kyriarchal power over others or self-effacing service to empower others. Many of these studies use Michel Foucault's analysis of power.

Since virtually everything Paul wrote involved some aspect of power relations in the Ancient Mediterranean world, the modern task of inter-preting his writings remains incomplete without a careful analysis of the political dimensions of power. Interpretations based on the theological assumption that Paul's letters are an authoritative part of the Christian canon continue to convert this canonical authority into power over others for a variety of purposes assumed to be for the good of those seeking to follow Christ. This approach has historically failed to question Paul's use of power in terms of kyriarchy and in fact tends to valorize Paul as a time-less and absolute authority, which often perpetuates the abuse of power. Elizabeth Castelli critiques Pauline scholarship for either "skirt[ing] the question of power or reinscrib[ing] it unproblematically" (1991, 23). Paul's rhetoric of obedience, subordination, humility, and imitation have all been decontextualized, leaving only spiritualized, devotional material for modern believers. Others reduce Paul's rhetoric to theological keys for understanding Paul's apostolic role in the church (see Castelli 1991, 25).

This is certainly not the approach of scholars questioning Paul's rhe-torical use of power—especially not of those who use feminist hermeneu-tics, social-scientific criticism, postcolonial biblical criticism, rhetorical criticism, and Michel Foucault. I shall briefly refer to a handful of such scholars as examples of more recent approaches to Pauline texts that tackle the issue of power as central and essential for any analysis of Paul. Such works deserve credit for making it more difficult to "skirt" the question about power for all those delving into Paul's writings. This has become even more important, because the social sciences—now central to biblical studies—have demonstrated that the basic tenet of all social relations implies the dynamic use or exercise of power. In addition to the social sciences, several modern cultural theorists have also drawn attention to the significance of critically analyzing power relations. No one in recent Western intellectual life has made this clearer than Michel Foucault. So naturally, several biblical scholars have familiarized themselves with Foucault's major works and employed his poststructuralist critique to varying degrees. Foucault stipulates that "to live in society is, in any event, to live in such a way that some can act on the actions of others. A society without power relations can only be an abstraction" (1994, 343). Power only exists "as it is exercised by some on others, only when it is put into action" (1994, 340). This aspect of Foucault's concept of power appears irrefutable and quite helpful. Yet the highly selective use and interpretation of Foucault's works for the First and Second Testaments raises its own questions. These questions arise because of Foucault's own inconsistencies but more important because of the structural differences between the ancient Mediterranean world and the postmodern world of Foucault and his dialogue partners.[9] Nonetheless, Foucauldian critiques and guides for Pauline studies have served to complement rhetorical criticism, feminist hermeneutics, and postcolonialism.[10]

I think it also important for biblical experts to supplement their use of Foucault with social-scientific criticism and cultural anthropological models based on the ancient Mediterranean world. These supplements would address the lack of methodological structure in Foucauldian analysis and at the same time connect it to the ancient world.[11] For example, the ancient Mediterranean concepts of honor and shame illustrate the relation between power and honor as well as the dynamics of how power was

9. Ehrensperger criticizes Foucault's attempt to avoid making universal and theoretical comments on human culture, the subject, and power while essentially constructing new theories on all with an ubiquitous application (2007, 11ff.). However, it should be noticed that Foucault insisted on finding specific examples within culture and limiting them to a particular occasion with regard to the use of power. See Foucault (1994) *Power*.

10. Joseph Marshal does an excellent job of this (2008, 63, 65–67, 75).

11. After all, Foucault himself rejected having his work function as some rigid methodological paradigm (1977).

"exercised" when "put into action by some on others."[12] Honor and shame took place in the public domain where one party initiated a challenge to another's honor or family honor. This public response or riposte to such a challenge represents (in Foucauldian terms) an "act on the actions of others." By way of contrast, the honor-shame model could supplement Foucauldian concepts with a more appropriate social-scientific model for the ancient world. Foucault says that power can be exercised by subordinates in their struggles against dominant individuals or institutions. Although this was not generally the case for public challenges in the ancient Mediterranean world, Zeba Crook has just recently argued convincingly that some men and women with lower status actually challenged higher-status men successfully![13] The former notion that those with lower status could not challenge others perceived to have more honor in the eyes of the community must be revisited. Jewett's assertion that "this occurs only between persons of the same class, because superiority over those of lower status was assumed and did not have to be proved" represents the position originally formulated by Malina (Jewett 2003, 552; Crook 2009, 592–604). Asymmetrical challenges by those from the lower status also came in the form of an indirect or coded rhetorical response that the political scientist James C. Scott has termed a "hidden transcript" (1990; see below).[14] The point is simply this: existing biblical research on honor-shame addresses the exercise of power in the specific context of ancient Mediterranean agonistic society and provides extensive concrete examples. Scott's model of resistance against dominant powers through "hidden transcripts" also helps to link Foucault's notions about power to specific Pauline texts and contexts. This type of social-scientific analysis of power provides a methodological frame of reference to supplement Foucault's basic concepts while confirming one of his observations—that "power relations are very complex" (1980, 208). Such heuristic examples applied to the ancient Mediterranean world confirm this.

12. Bartchy (2003, 137) makes a connection between honor and power in the ancient Mediterranean world.

13. See Zeba Crook's article, which challenges former assumptions about honor and shame operating only among males with equal status and class (2009, 591–611). See chapter 1 (above) and particularly notes 17 and 18.

14. See chapter 1 above.

Therefore, selective and limited uses of Foucauldian concepts of power for Pauline scholars should not necessarily mean that one recuse him- or herself from using Foucault in some capacity. But the use of Foucault remains problematic without some methodological mooring to tie it to the ancient biblical world. One could, for example, use Foucault's "forms of resistance against different forms of power" to analyze Jesus and Paul, but it would first require placing Jesus and Paul in the category of resistance against dominant powers. This of course is not only an easy thing to accommodate but necessary (1994, 329). Foucault provides examples of modern resistance "struggles" that challenge "the power of men over women, of parents over children, of psychiatry over the mentally ill, of medicine over the population, of administration over the ways people live" (1994, 329). Foucault chose categories that ostensibly differentiate between the dominant and subordinate pair. Foucault went on to identify what he called the "three types of struggles: against forms of domination (ethnic, social, and religious); against forms of exploitation that separate individuals from what they produce; or against that which ties the individual to himself and submits him to others in this way (struggles against subjection [*assujettissement*], against forms of subjectivity and submission)" (1994, 331). I offer the following brief comparisons using Foucault's three types applied to both Jesus and Paul to illustrate this point.

Foucault's first type follows Jesus's struggles with Roman imperialism in Galilee as well as with the elitist temple-state in Jerusalem. The second type can apply to resistance to Herodian tax collection by Jesus and the peasant population of lower Galilee. And Foucault's third type could be represented by Jesus's rejection of kyriarchy, honor-shame, and labeling as forces of alienation. I can also apply the same three types of resistance to Paul, but with less exactitude. For example, Paul's political-theology opposed Roman imperial ideology and challenged the emperor's claim to have divine sanction to rule the nations (Foucault's first type). The second type seems applicable to Paul's concept of ancient Israel's justice for workers but is less clear than Foucault's first type above. It could be argued that Paul believed that workers were due their wages (1 Cor 3:8b). "Even solders get paid; farmers and herders consume what they produce" (1 Cor 3:7, 10b). Based on this, Paul argues that he and Barnabas have a right to "food and drink" from the community of faith they had produced— especially in light of the fact that the Corinthian *ekklēsia* gave material support to others (1 Cor 3:4, 11–12). Foucault's third type is also some-what problematic for Paul but could be massaged a bit to fit Paul's resis-tance to any form of abusive power in relationships. But this presumes that Paul challenged traditional kyriarchy, sexism, and ethnocentrism, or any use of power that alienated people from themselves and others. But again, one must first determine if Paul's rhetorical use of power served kyriarchal or nonkyriarchal ends. This would be further complicated, be-cause Foucault's notion of power was limited to power-over others. So my somewhat-selective and limited example based on Foucault could serve to analyze certain aspects of power relations for Jesus and Paul. But it should also remind us that we still face the arduous task of interpreting both Paul and Foucault along predetermined lines, not to mention the fact that Foucault never meant his analysis of power to function as a method.[15] Foucault himself admitted to a selective use of others' works that suited his interest even if he was "unfaithful" to the author (1980, 53–54).[16]

The full spectrum of benefits and problematic issues for biblical scholars employing Foucauldian models cannot be fully explored here.[17] The present investigation seeks to clarify and find an interpretive path to understand Paul's rhetoric and use of power. Since some Pauline schol-ars continue to use Foucault's work, I have suggested a couple benefits and caveats for doing so. The rather selective use of Foucault by certain scholars is of less concern than examining interpretive machinations that predetermine Paul's use of power patterned after kyriarchy.

### Recent Treatments of Paul's Use of Power

Elizabeth Castelli's important book, *Imitating Paul: A Discourse of Power*, relies on aspects of Foucault's notion of power and rhetorical criticism surrounding the Greek term *mimesis*, "imitation" (1991). Castelli makes

15. This is true of postmodern theories in general; see Ingraffia 1995.

16. This surfaced in one of Foucault's interviews, which included a specific reference to his use of Nietzsche; see Rabinow 1980, 37–54.

17. See Ingraffia 1995 for an extensive summary and critique. I reject Ingraffia's use of "true Christianity" as one of postmodern theorists' intended victims—even if some postmodern critics express open hostility toward Christianity. His use of "ontotheology" to characterize postmodern theory's approach to biblical theology is not appropriate for social-scientific criticism.

mimesis the central rubric for deciphering Paul's writings. She begins
with the thesis: "The notion of mimesis functions in Paul's letters as a
strategy of power. That is, it articulates and rationalizes as true and
natural a particular set of power relations within the social formation of
early Christianity" (15). She selects Foucault's conceptual categories of
"regimes of truth" and "technologies of power" for her "interpretive lens"
(15). Castelli claims to be able to use this "lens" to bring Paul's discourse
on power into focus by analyzing the relationship between his texts and
rhetoric "on the one hand, and social formations on the other" (15).
Castelli sums up the concept of mimesis in Greco-Roman culture that
"Paul inherited" as follows:

1. Mimesis is always articulated as a hierarchal relationship, where-
   by the "copy" is but a derivation of the "model" and cannot aspire
   to the privileged status of the "model."

2. Mimesis presupposes a valorization of sameness over against
   difference. Certain conceptual equations accompany this move:
   unity and harmony are associated with sameness while difference
   is attributed characteristics of diffusion, disorder, and discord.

3. The notion of the authority of the model plays a fundamental
   role in mimetic relationship (16).[18]

Castelli's combination of Paul's audiences' social context and her tri-
partite characterization of ancient mimesis predispose Castelli to view
Paul within a "hierarchal economy of sameness" in which Paul enjoys a
"privileged status" as the "model" for his communities' "monolithic social
formation" and is enabled to "reinscribe" his elevated status (17, 54, 96).
"'Become imitators of me' is a call to sameness which erases difference and,
at the same time, reinforces the authoritative status of the model" (103).
According to Castelli, Paul underscores his requirement of "sameness"
for subordinates with the possibility of one's jeopardizing one's salvation
for noncompliance (16–17). While acknowledging Foucault's concept
of power as "affecting both the dominator and the dominated," Castelli
restricts her analysis of Paul's sparse use of mimesis under Foucault's

18. I find it odd that here Castelli embraces these three generalized notions of the
rhetorical use of mimesis from Greco-Roman examples to characterize Paul's power,
because later she says that she does not base her interpretation of Paul's letters "particularly" on the "Greco-Roman schools of rhetoric" (54).

"system of differentiations enabling the hierarchal relationship between dominant and subordinate to be continually enacted" (43, 122).[19]

How representative is Castelli's characterization of Paul? Her interpretation exemplifies the marriage of a rather limited and highly selective use of Foucault with a conspicuously narrow and highly rigid use of mimesis that gives birth to her hermeneutical conclusion regarding Paul's use of power. That Castelli establishes Paul's use of mimesis from a hierarchal, top-down role in his communities (which served to eradicate differences and enshrine Paul's authoritative status) without giving serious consideration to Paul's modified kyriarchal rhetoric and metaphors cast suspicion on her overall thesis.[20] Why, for example, does her work not include some treatment of the extensive Girardian literature on mimetic theory? This would have been useful by way of comparison. Hamerton-Kelly, using a Girardian interpretation of Paul, claims "Girard's universal 'scapegoat' mechanism can be applied to Paul's writings as evidence of Paul 'counteract[ing] mimetic rivalry'" (1985, 70).

> This suggests that Paul understands the situation in the same way as the Girardian hermeneutic does! It is mimetic rivalry that has caused the members of the [Corinthian] church to puff themselves up with reference to one anther; mimesis is endemic to human community, so since the apostle knows this, he urges the right kind of mimesis; not the kind that covers up the mechanism of the victim and enables them spuriously to claim that they are wise and strong and held in honor (4:10), but the kind which enables them to see that their community was brought into being by a victim imitating a victim, a scapegoat imitating a scapegoat . . . (70).

Hamerton-Kelly's reading presents some in the Corinthian communities as causing problems through mimetic rivalry. Paul addresses this crisis by modeling "interdependence," "vulnerability," and "weakness"—not coercive rhetoric for his own power play (76). According to Hamerton-Kelly,

19. Paul uses the term *mimesis* in three letters: 1 Cor 4:16; 11:1; Phil 3:17; and 1 Thess 1:6–7; 2:14.

20. Castelli ties Paul's use of paternal imagery and roles in the ancient Mediterranean world to "mimesis-language," which again is assumed unproblematically, to suggest an "ontological superiority." S. Scott Bartchy challenges the assumption that Paul simply advocated paternal power in his Christ communities and claims that Castelli "misses entirely Paul's undermining of precisely those justifications for the patriarchal system" (2003, 143).

Paul's strategy of mimesis empowers those in the communities "who are willing to imitate, not one another in rivalry, but the crucified Christ in humility" (77).

Castelli's work has provided an invaluable challenge to uncritical and narrow approaches to power relations in Paul's writings and remains essential for current debates on Paul. The questions she raises about "sameness" and rhetoric of hierarchal domination have not been fully or adequately answered by more traditional interpretations of Paul—but need to be. Her Foucauldian selections and the rhetorical use of ancient mimesis, however, are subject to accusations of generalization and omission.[21]

Cynthia Briggs Kittredge (1998) and Sandra Hack Polaski (1999) have also addressed the issue of power in Paul's rhetoric. While Kittredge does not use Foucault, Polaski adapts and builds her thesis on Foucauldian concepts and several references to Castelli. Both authors provide helpful explanations of rhetorical criticism, and they employ it methodologically in conjunction with historical reconstruction.[22] Their historical reconstruction attempts to "distinguish Paul's voice" (Kittredge 1998, 11) from his audiences' voices as evidence of the "competing claims" (1998, 7, 36) and power relations "the text may mask" (Polaski 1999, 21).

"In order to recover the voices submerged in the text, one must move from rhetorical analysis to reconstruction of the historical situation. The distinction between the inscribed rhetorical situation and the possible historical situation is critical: the inscribed rhetorical situation is inscribed in the text itself; the historical situation must be reconstructed from other sources as well" (Kittredge 1998, 9). "Within that rhetoric of Paul's letters, there is evidence of points of conflict. Those points of conflict constitute the exigencies of the rhetorical situation" (7). This is an invaluable point.

Kittredge and Polaski also place Paul in a dominant, kyriarchal role as he wrestles for power against his Christ communities' alternative vision. Kittredge extends this rhetorical and historical reconstruction to imagine the early Christ communities' struggles for equality against

21. I am thinking of Eherensperger's work in particular, introduced below (2007).

22. Briggs Kittredge relies especially on Schüssler Fiorenza's works on rhetorical criticism and on historical reconstruction. (See Schüssler Fiorenza 1987, 386–403; and 1994, 443–69).

"the forces of the dominant patriarchal ethos of the Greco-Roman world (1998, 6).[23] Paul's letters reflect this struggle inasmuch as "one can see that the competing visions of the community are articulated with different cultural languages and social metaphors" particularly evident in the "language of obedience and metaphors drawn from the patriarchal family" (6). Kittredge's feminist perspective rejects the "inevitability of the symbolic universe of kyriarchy" represented by Paul's "voice" (36). Paul constructs a "symbolic universe where sons obey father and congregation obeys God"—a universe that simultaneously functions to legitimize and preserve Paul's authority (Kittredge 1998, 7, 36, 178; Kittredge 2000, 106–8). Both Kittredge and Polaski examine several Pauline texts and metaphors; Kittredge pays special attention to Philippians, and Polaski concentrates on Philemon. Each author also incorporates and critiques rival interpretations of Paul's use of power, so providing helpful background to the complex nature of interpretations of Paul. Polaski even references Hamerton-Kelly's Girardian interpretation of mimesis but rejects it because it fails to address the question of where Paul gets his authority to wield power (1999, 120).[24]

Polaski, in spite of her statements about the complexity of power relationships in Foucault and about "his recognition that power is granted, as it were, from the bottom up," nonetheless like Castelli and Kittredge characterizes Paul in a typical kyriarchal fashion (1999, 87). Even Paul's "egalitarian tone" and "metaphors" in Philemon "serve to establish the base of power claims Paul will make later" (60). According to Polaski, Paul's use of "grace" "both establishes a place for everyone and strives to keep everyone firmly in place, attributing to Paul a place in the top, with the authority both to describe the structure and to assign others their places in it" (118). Polaski and Kittredge make Paul's kyriarchal discourse stand out like Jesus's words in a red-letter edition of the Gospels. This makes their efforts a must for all Pauline scholars. "Points of conflict" in Paul's rhetoric do evidence other voices struggling against kyriarchal domination. But Kittredge and Polaski also too easily dismiss the same conflict in Paul's own voice and his own ambivalence toward kyriarchy.

23. She again relies heavily on the works of Schüssler Fiorenza, (1983; 1992).

24. This response seems somewhat quixotic given Girard's well-known scapegoat mechanism. The issue of Paul's authority is taken for granted, and it is superfluous for Paul to function as a scapegoat to disarm the communities' struggles for power.

Joseph A. Marchal has recently published an important book that also deals with Paul's use of power. In *The Politics of Heaven: Women, Gender, and Empire in the Study of Paul*, Marchal identifies his approach as a "feminist, postcolonial analysis" (11) and part of a "paradigm shift" for Pauline studies (37). Following Schüssler Fiorenza's now-familiar rhetorical criticism and historical reconstruction—Marchal sets out to show how "Paul's letters and most (elite imperial pale malestream) scholarship on Paul are the results of imperially gendered rhetorical activities" (11).[25] Marchal has drawn attention to "gender, sexuality, ethnicity, and empire" through his feminist, postcolonial analysis in order to "revitalize biblical scholarship['s] task for the twenty-first century" (111). He chides "malestream biblical scholarship" for failing to notice the contributions of feminist scholarship on Pauline literature and to recognize how crucial gender analysis can be for understanding the imperial system of Paul's time (19).[26] Marchal relies less on Castelli and Foucault, opting rather for a "people's history," that is, "history from below" to supplement his feminist, postcolonial analysis—a type of "transdiciplinary" strategy (36). A "people's history" approach suggests that the non-elites also shape history and should be considered as significant for studies in Paul (24–36).[27]

Marchal's book provides an excellent overview of feminists and postcolonial scholarship as applied to Paul's letters and to the use of the rhetoric of imitation in Philippians. Like Castelli, Kittredge, and Polaski, Marchal sees something essentially hierarchal in Paul's use of mimesis (63). But Marchal goes further.

> The letter [Philippians] is Paul's opportunity to characterize the community as in need of his authority and the progress it can bring to them. This attitude is justified in light of the violently dualistic way he conceives of difference in the letter. Enemies are condemned and those who "belong" are required to be obedient. Paul casts the community in the dependent, subordinate role of

25. Marchal tends to place less stress on historical reconstruction, aligning himself with Musa W. Dube's rhetorical approach, (Marchal 2008, 128 fn 70).

26. Marchal refers specifically to Kittredge's contributions of strategies for "reading against the text." He also criticizes Castelli and Polaski for not using postcolonial feminist works, (2008, 135 n37). Polaski also is rebuked for underemphasizing the role of Roman imperialism in Paul's writings (2008, 19–20).

27. Marchal mentions the failure of Marxist forms of history to recognize the importance of women in the labor force—as in phrases such as "the working man."

a hierarchal system, a system explained and maintained by reference to particularly gendered power dynamics endorsed by the
divine. Even if one can argue that Paul makes these claims over
against the empire of his time . . . it is not significantly different
from the imperialism of his time. In Philippians, Paul argues and
thinks imperialistically, possibly so that he might "both subvert
and reinscribe the imperial system." These patterns indicate that,
even if this is an effort to subvert the Roman Empire, this letter can
be easily re-assimilated or co-opted to an imperialist or colonialist
agenda. (54)

Marchal continues, "This analysis suggests that Paul reinscribes and
mimics the imperialism of his time in the letter to the Philippians" (55).
"Thus, Paul is not just repeating imperial images in his letters; he is also
mimicking imperial-style power arrangements in an effort to consolidate
his own authority" (57).

Marchal, having exposed Paul's letters and Pauline interpretation as
a "cultured complicity in kyriarchy," feels responsible to "decenter Paul
in the study of his letters" (116). Those who continue to work within the
"traditional bounds of this field (Pauline letters)" should avoid "focusing
on the perspective of Paul per se" (121). I agree; no one should defend
Marchal's Paul.

Marchal adds a final creative strategy to decenter Paul and resist
"oppressive practices of biblical argumentation in contemporary re-
uses" (121). He borrows Gayatri Chakravorty Spivak's term *catachresis*.
In Spivak's work this term characterizes the "improper use" of a word
"re-appropriated to describe anti-colonial practices that reuse colonizing
techniques or institutions against the purposes of colonization" (121). But
could this not have been a similar strategy found in Paul's use of kyriarchal language for his Christ communities' anti-imperial practices, as in
the call to imitate him as he imitated Christ: the anti-imperial, crucified
one? Marchal speaks of a "resistant form of mimicry or mockery" by the
colonized and "denotes a productive ambivalence where transgressive resistance becomes possible" (70–71). Which was Paul more interested in:
inscribing his own authority over small Christ communities that he eventually left in the hands of their own spirit-filled leaders, or empowering
these communities as political groups for Christ's apocalyptic, anti-imperial rule over the nations? The latter would include evidence of "ambiva-

lence" and "mockery" toward the imperialism of Paul's day. This seems possible in light of the absurd metaphorical references to Jesus Christ. For example, Jesus as the "son of God"—of the God of the Judeans at that (Rom 8:3). Jesus as the one executed by Rome but exalted by God as Lord over even imperial magistrates (1 Cor 1:23; 15:27; Phil 2:8–11). Jesus as a servant-lord—the archetype for kyridoularchy (Phil 2:7). One also must take stock of the puzzling counterkyriarchal social structure of the Christ communities' inclusion of women as leaders, of the poor, of slaves, and of non-Israelites as equal partners in a politically charged fictive kinship movement that appears to have actually challenged and altered typical kyriarchal power relations (Rom 14:1; 15:1–3; Gal 3:28; Phil 2:3–4). Paul's kyriarchal rhetoric of imitation must be read in the context of his counterkyriarchal metaphors, of his language of service and mutual care, and of rituals—without predisposing Paul as mere proponent of self-serving kyriarchy. Significant departures from traditional kyriarchy would have created an ostensible environment of confusion, tension, and conflict in Christ communities. Paul's response to his communities' evolving struggle for survival hardly resembles the Pastoral Letters or *1 Clement*, let alone the ecclesiastical kyriarchy institutionalized by Constantine and its later hegemonic juggernauts.

Kathy Ehrensperger's most recent book presents a formidable challenge to the above-mentioned scholars' theories on Paul's kyriarchal use of mimesis and his language of obedience.[28] In *Paul and the Dynamics of Power: Communication and Interaction in the Early Christ-Movements*, one finds a thorough and compelling analysis of Paul's use of power. Ehrensperger's extensive—though selective—use of Foucault's perception of power relations differs from the Foucauldian treatments of Castelli, Kittredge, and Marchal by way of application. Ehrensperger determines that "Foucault's approach is significant to this study since he is one of the theorists who raised fundamental criticisms against an understanding of power which presupposes as the paradigmatic model, the relation of a powerful agent who imposes his will on a powerless subordinate. His emphasis on the all-pervasiveness of power and the differentiated per-

---

28. Ehrensperger does not refer to Marchal's (2008) book, *The Politics of Heaven*; evidently it was not available for her book (2007). However, her critiques apply to the Marchal's general thesis.

ception of asymmetry and hierarchy in social relations deserves further consideration on our reading of the Pauline discourse" (2007, 21).

Ehrensperger, however, notes that a Foucauldian approach to power undermines "positive and empowering impacts on social relations" (2007, 21). In turn, she focuses her investigation of power on recent theorists who suggest beneficial outcomes from certain types of power relations. One such scholar is Hannah Arendt, who, according to Ehrensperger, argues that power is not always asymmetrical, exclusively dominating, and controlling but can emerge in "communicative action for the enhancement of all involved in the process" (14).[29] Ehrensperger turns next to the feminist scholar Amy Allen, whose work combines aspects of Foucault and Arendt to distinguish three forms of power: "power-over, power-to, and power-with" (26). Ehrensperger also utilizes Thomas Wartenberg's social-field theory in which he claims that "power-over" need "not necessarily lead to domination or oppression" (27). Naturally, Ehrensperger is drawn to Wartenberg's concept of "transformative power" that aims to "render itself obsolete by means of empowering the subordinate"—a mixing of "power-over and power-to" (27–28). Using Socrates's relationship with his Athenian students to illustrate "transformative power," Wartenberg notes how the students' empowerment moved them from subordinates to equals with their teacher. Ehrensperger draws attention to the fact that "the relationship changes from one of power-over and power-to to a relationship of power-to and power-with," and hence "not all power-over relations are perceived to be necessarily exercised to the disadvantage of the weaker agent" (29, 31). Ehrensperger surmises from this conflation that "asymmetry and hierarchy as inherent aspects of power relations" are not "problematic as long as the goal of the exercise of transformative power renders itself obsolete" (33). When applied to Paul, Ehrensperger says, "Thus the power-over operative between Paul and the communities is aimed at rendering itself obsolete, in that their asymmetrical relationship will be transformed and Paul should eventually become one among many siblings. This perception of Paul's differentiated use of power resonates with transformative and communicative aspects of power highlighted by Arendt, Wartenberg and Allen" (62).[30]

29. See chapter 1, above.

30. She comments on the limitations of modern theories of power to analyze Paul's warning that "all of these concepts have been developed from within contemporary

Since the pivotal motifs surrounding Paul's rhetorical use of power hinge on questions concerning his "authority" as a self-declared "apostle" (Gal 1:11–12) and his subsequent use of "mimesis" (1 Cor 4:16; 11:1; Phil 3:17; 1 Thess 1:6–7; 2:14) in the context of his language of "obedience," "submission," and "slavery"—(Rom 1:5; 5:18–19; 6:12–19; 13:1–7; 16:2; 1 Cor 7:23; 9:19; 12:13; 14:32–34; 2 Cor 10:5ff.; Gal 4:1, 7; Phil 2:6–12; Philemon)—Ehrensperger offers a comprehensive response. For example, she says that Paul's claim of authority and leadership must be understood in the specific context of the *ekklēsiai*'s plurality of "apostles" and "co-workers in Christ" (14, 37–61). Ehrensperger suggests that the communities' shared "purpose" or "calling" to live out the gospel in "grace" (*charis*) mitigated both mimesis and submissive obedience that served kyriarchal domination for Paul.[31] Challenges to Paul's authority or the communities' unity amounts to derailing their shared "calling in Christ (Rom 1:1; 8:28; 1 Cor 1:26; 7:15, 17–24; Phil 3:14). Ehrensperger therefore understands "obedience as faith and as submission to God['s]" calling not Paul's rhetorical attempt to reinscribe his own authority and power-over Christ communities (156). However, Polaski and others before her have made much of Paul's concept of "grace" in direct relation to Paul's authority to rule over others, not only his communities but the Christ communities in Rome, Christ communities he did not establish (1999, chap. 4).[32] The following statement by Paul to the communities in Rome is a case in point: "But I dared to write to you in part as a reminder for you because of the grace given to me by God that I might be a servant of Christ Jesus to the nations" (15:15–16a).[33] Again, Ehrensperger renders Paul's discourse on "grace" very differently. She actually sees it as part of Paul's "subversive

---

western societies as conceptual tools for analyses of contemporary twentieth- to twenty-first-century societies. This puts a question mark against their usefulness for an analysis of a discourse of power not of a contemporary society but of letters which reflect only in fragmentary form social institutions of small groups in the first century CE in the Roman Empire" (2007, 34).

31. While "authorial intent" plays little to no role in postmodernism (Foucault 1994, 298; Polaski, 1999, 19–20), Ehrensperger's concepts of not only Paul's purpose but also the prophets of Israel, Israel, Christ, and Israel's God represent a departure from Foucauldian thought (2007, 90–91).

32. Ernst Käsemann, (1980, 335).

33. My translation.

discourse" and connected to his calling or purpose on behalf of "the nations" (2007, 73).

Ehrensperger's innovative book on Paul's use of power acknowledges that while "Paul did claim authority for himself in relation to his communities he founded, he did so in a differentiated way which cannot be subsumed under an exercise of power-over in the vein of a command-obedience structure" (2007, 155). Even the hierarchy between Paul and his communities changed to equal status when each community could function according to the pattern modeled after their servant-lord (Phil 2:5–12). Ehrensperger suggests that 1 Thessalonians indicates that the community's imitation had taken over for Paul "in exemplifying the life of Christ to others," thus making Paul's power-over them obsolete (1 Thess 1:6–7; 2:14; 2007, 154–55). She maintains that throughout Paul's letters one finds examples of Paul's use of "transformative power" for the communities' alternative life—a life that subverted Roman imperial values and the use of power (2007, 79, 91).

Ehrensperger's critique of those who limit Paul's use of power in terms of domination and control through his rhetoric of imitation, obedience, and grace expands our options for analyzing power according to its variable forms and dynamic social possibilities. But Ehrensperger's positive spin on Paul's temporary use of power to empower his communities does not explain how power relations functioned among those empowered. Did such empowerment eventually result in egalitarian communities or less obtrusive forms of hierarchy? Did everyone attain equal status, distribute goods equally, and have an equal voice? Were differences tolerated, especially if they conflicted with Paul's vision of the gospel? The question about the roles and status of women and slaves still seems problematic in light of Ehrensperger's analysis (1 Corinthians 7, 11, 14). Paul's praise for the Thessalonians as an exemplary model for other communities because they imitated him, Silvanus, Timothy, and Christ could just as easily be understood as Paul's successfully inscribing his authority over them (1 Thess 1:6–7)! What happened when empowered others resisted Paul's authority, as in the Corinthian letters? Did Paul return to a "power-over" rhetoric? It seems that Ehrensperger ultimately fails to address Paul's ambivalent rhetoric, which vacillates between kyriarchy and kyridoularchy.

All of the above works I have touched on make constructive contributions to the discourse on Paul and power. I remain aware of the "theoretical discourses" that valorize Paul's politics of "othering" or "vilifying" his own communities' dissenting voices (Schüssler Fiorenza 2000, 45). This means that I also have to recognize the fact that it was still Paul who determined the scope and content of his communities' mission and life together by virtue of his use of power. "Faith," "grace," "submission," "obedience," "mutual love," "service," and "imitation" were all constructed by Paul's rhetoric in response to his communities' specific issues and conflicts over authority. His voice was inscribed over the "other voices" in his writings as Paul established the communities' standards.

But what are we to make of the fact that Paul's voice was not always that of a typical kyriarchal male in the ancient Mediterranean world, chiding his communities as disobedient children in order to maintain his privileged status?[34] Based on my selected theoretical and methodological approaches to Paul's writings, it is problematic to label Paul simply as an advocate of "hegemonic kyriarchal structures of superordination and subordination" in all cases (Schüssler Fiorenza 2000, 40–57). Rather, I find Paul—like Seneca (*De Constantia* 13.2, 5) and Epictetus (*Discourses* 2.9.15)—could also be critical of kyriarchal socialization. The very kyriarchy that had conditioned Paul and other male members of his communities to accept and defend fell under the scrutiny of Christ's kyridoularchy (1 Cor 9:19; Gal 2:20; Phil 2:1–11; also see Bartchy 2003, 136).[35] Paul's attempt to resocialize his communities appears to have been misunderstood by some (1 Cor 3:1–4), rejected by others (Gal 1:6), but embraced by those who patterned their relationships after this new evolutionary and traumatic process of transformation from kyriarchy to kyridoularchy (Rom 16:3–16; 1 Thess 2:14). This dynamic process required the reconfiguration of kyriarchal power for the empowerment of others, or to restate this with Ehrensperger's borrowed terms: power-over others to power-to and power-with each other. This means that kyriarchy remained central during struggles for power in Paul's communities, even if Paul negotiated

34. This also puts my interpretation of Paul at odds with some social-scientific depictions of Paul as "typical" for his time—for example: "Even when Paul did not make explicit use of familial concepts, he acted out typical role expectations associated with that of a *paterfamilias* and at the same time also conferred the role of 'children' upon the Corinthians" (Joubert 1995, 217–18). Cf. Ehrensperger 2007, 41, 118 n5, 128–36; Bartchy 2003).

35. See Glad for an extended discussion of Paul critique of ancient Mediterranean honor and shame (2003, 7–41).

to modify power relations in the direction of kyridoularchy characterized by their new Lord in a new, apocalyptic age. Kyriarchy and kyridoularchy coexisted in a contentious dynamic that never completely eviscerated the other.

## *Ambivalent Paradigms as Methodological Yin and Yang*

Similar to the above-mentioned controversies over interpreting Paul's use of rhetoric, a rather heated but fruitful dialogue continues between feminist, postcolonial approaches to Paul and traditional historical-critical methods. For example, Robert Jewett maintains "the historical-critical method is more promising than a postmodernism that imputes hegemonic motives to dissenting participants and asserts theories and conclusions that must finally be accepted on authority" (2000, 60). Schüssler Fiorenza quips: "Feminists and postcolonial scholars in turn have pointed to the ideological deformations of Pauline texts that are often reinscribed by malestream Pauline scholarship" (2000, 44; Kwok 2009, 196).[36] Horsley comes close to combining the two approaches, according to Schüssler Fiorenza (2000, 50). As elaborated in chapter 1, I have suggested the integration of feminist, postcolonial studies with rhetorical, historical-critical, and social-scientific criticism. Such a collaborative approach serves to sensitize each interpretive paradigm to the implications of Paul's writings in their complex contexts. Viewing Paul's Christ communities' gendered sociopolitical life against Roman imperialistic ideologies that his communities sought to oppose and overcome continues to be advantageous for investigating Paul's use of power. Ideological antagonism between scholars does not have to prevent the insights that both can afford one another. Such differences provoke necessary critical analysis and critiques between the two. Notice this brief yet direct response to Schüssler Fiorenza's critique of biblical scholarship by Robert Jewett.

> A related issue is the evidentiary force of voices within the early church that have been inferred from Pauline letters. The reconstruction of such voices is one of the most subtle and controversial achievements of the historical-critical method. Schüssler Fiorenza

36. Also see Marchal 2008, 15–38, for an excellent characterization of the hermeneutical issues between the two camps. Also cf. Horsley 2003, 152–73; Horsley 2002, 72–102).

argues that such voices should always take precedence over Paul's own views, because, on the basis of her interpretation of the letters, Paul is an advocate of kyriarchy. "Whenever Paul's rhetoric vilifies and belittles [the community]," she writes, "one must resist his rhetoric rather than valorize it." I believe there is substantial evidence to confirm her insistence that the early church was at times engaged in "a radical egalitarian politics of *Ekklēsia*." Elliott's reflections on the functions of persuasion within imperialistic contexts provide a framework for understanding what was at stake for the early church. I would like to suggest, however, that Paul's conversation partners were frequently on the imperialistic side of the ledger. (2000, 60)

Part of this disagreement over who actually represents the voice for "egalitarian" relationships in Paul's communities—Paul or other voices he was trying to silence—rests on Schüssler Fiorenza's suspicion that the historical-critical method does not actually represent the historical reality of Paul's conflict with certain members of his communities.[37] She begins by delineating between the "inscribed rhetorical situation" and the "possible historical situation." Rhetorical analysis reveals that Paul constructed the rhetorical situation in conjunction with his attempt to persuade his audience and his audience's reactions. Schüssler Fiorenza next imagines a historical scenario reconstructed from her rhetorical analysis combined with her reliance on extrinsic sources to better understand the audience's historical and social setting (1987, 386–403; 1994, 443–69). This has been an invaluable contribution to biblical scholarship in general and to feminist hermeneutics in particular, as seen above. Jewett's comments regarding Schüssler Fiorenza's assumptions about "other voices" can serve to temper the conclusions based on this supposition so that each (whether biblical scholarship or feminist criticism) refines the other instead of nullifying the other. I would further stipulate that all investigations of Paul's use of power utilize both approaches under the general purview of social-scientific criticism as I above combined social-science criticism, rhetorical criticism, and Foucauldian understandings of power. I shall return to this point below.

37. Once more I draw attention to Bartchy's distinction between "patriarchy" and "egalitarianism." "In response to this diversity, Paul's apparent goal was not the creation of an egalitarian community in the political sense, but a *well-functioning family* in the kinship sense" (2003, 146; italics original).

First, I would like to address a basic methodological issue that impacts studies on Paul that deal with power in particular. One continues to find a propensity to view religion in a rather dismissive (read: negative) or uniform (read: oversimplified) manner. Social-scientific critics' admonition not to separate religion from politics in the ancient Mediterranean world has advanced biblical scholarship beyond merely theologically based interpretations and continues to net important insights, including theological ones. At times, religion is still viewed as a static phenomenon that always functions to maintain social order: as an "epiphenomenon" that masks the essential underlying political and economic "realities."[38] This outdated Western-Enlightenment concept of religion has been eclipsed by those thinkers who include religion as an integral part of the social-political network of power relations.

Bruce Lincoln's works continue to challenge hegemonic concepts of religion that obscure its role in politics and economics. Lincoln illustrates how the popularized definition of religion by Clifford Geertz meshed well with Protestantism's concept of the individual's inner moods and perceptions—religion as a personal belief. Various influential Enlightenment figures had either relegated religion to a uniform social function that legitimized domination by elites, or viewed religion as a manifestation of ancient prescientific psychology that repressed modern individuals (2006, 1–2). This concept of religion characterizes most Marxist and many postmodern approaches to religion. Anthony Giddens's "structuration theory" also falls into this categorical use of religion. Under a section titled "The Naturalization of the Present: Reification," Giddens writes, "The interests of the dominant groups are bound up with the preservation of the *status quo*" (1979, 195). This is part of an extended discussion in Giddens about how "ideology" functions in society. Religion comes under this ideological framework and his Freudian take on religion (126). The use of Giddens's works seems more appropriate to post-Pauline, mid-second-century Christianity and beyond. But Lincoln presents a variety of models to account for the operations of religion in society that guard against reductionistic and inappropriate generalizations for Pauline scholars. Lincoln's three types of religions "are a step beyond the formulations of the 'romantic' and 'materialist' theoreticians . . . wherein religion

38. See chapter 3, above.

was seen as a monolithic entity invariably championing the interests of stability, social integration, and the status quo" (Giddens 1979, 91).

Lincoln calls his first model "the religion of the status quo."[39] His primary example for this type is based on the Chinese literati class and their use of Confucianism during the Han dynasty (206 BCE—220 CE). Lincoln notes that filial obligation and the cult of ancestors provided the model for all social relationships (80). He compares this with the Church of England under James I and Charles I, noting that "here, as in China, we see a religious ideology that serves the interests of the dominant social fraction, and a religious institution supported by that dominant fraction" (81). Certainly this can be applied to the Roman imperial cult but not to Paul, although it does match well with later Christian hegemonic traditions and with institutions that have and continue to speak for Paul.

As a second model of religion, Lincoln identifies a "religion of resistance" that emerges from the ranks of the lower socioeconomic strata and protests against the religion of the status quo (82–84). This group, says Lincoln, "has the least interest in preserving social stability and [their] sufferings are too great for the solace extended by the religion of the status quo" (82). Religions of resistance are evidence that the dominant religion of the status quo has not been able to persuade or permeate all segments of society. These are "insular communities," according to Lincoln, most interested in surviving hegemony and not accepting any part of the religion of the status quo (83). Religions of resistance "espouse a set of values that differs in some measure from that of the religion of the status quo," which makes them also "encourage practices of deviance" (83–84).

Lincoln's observation about leaders in religions of resistance is also helpful with regard to Paul's claim to divine authority. Lincoln notes that while the members of religions of resistance tend to come from the lower strata, "their leadership as a rule does not" (84). These "marginalized intelligentsia" often gain needed material support from their communities. Lincoln adds another important characteristic of the leaders of religions of resistance. His comparative analysis with leaders from religions of the status quo distinguishes leaders from religions of resistance in that the latter "regularly have recourse to an altogether different and superior

---

39. Lincoln constructed another type he called "religions of counterrevolution." These rise from the ashes of defeated religions of the status quo (ironically) as resistors of the victorious religion of resistance (2006, 91).

source of legitimacy: claiming that their authority rests on revelations or visions, direct experience of transcendent reality" (85).[40] Paul and his Christ communities compare well with Lincoln's "religions of resistance," especially as communities that "define[d] themselves in opposition to the religion of the status quo, defending against the ideological domination of the latter (85).[41]

Examples in Lincoln's third model of religion, "religions of revolution," "define themselves in opposition to the dominant social fraction itself, not its religious arm alone, promoting direct action against the dominant fraction's material control of society" (85).[42] Lincoln warns against thinking of this last type according to "secular theory" rather than it being another "religious theory of legitimacy" like his three other types. "Religions of revolution" characterize themselves as the "true religion." And their religious ideology animates their political and economic action against the dominant social fraction (87). But this type does not best suit Paul and his communities, because of Lincoln's description of "direct action against the dominant fraction's material control of society." Paul's sociopolitical challenges to Roman imperialism were indirect rhetorical attacks on Roman imperial ideology that were masked in what Scott refers to as "hidden transcripts" (1990, 4–5).

## THE BIFURCATED PAUL

Even this brief and selected overview of current research on Paul's use of power shows the need for further discussion on this important topic. Two predominant and ambivalent paradigms have surfaced: one follows feminist, postcolonial hermeneutics; and the other rests on various applications of the historical-critical method. Several scholars from each camp

40. This "different and superior source of legitimacy" refers to traditional titles, training, ordination, and the like (84). He uses Weber's "charismatic" type for his leaders of religions of resistance (84–85). Communal meals and ritual healing promote solidarity for this type.

41. Lincoln recognizes that "no movement or ideology is frozen into a single sociopolitical stance . . . they are part of a dynamic process, shifting their orientation as the result of external events and their confrontation with other movements and ideologies rooted in difference segments of society, representing different interests" (91).

42. Lincoln gives several examples, including the Nizari (Assassin) revolt against Sunni orthodoxy and the Seljuq Empire (88).

also include rhetorical analysis as a substantial part of their interpretive grids as well as modern theorists on power—especially the works of Michel Foucault and the political scientist James C. Scott. As mentioned above, although the two general approaches depart from each other over the characterization of Paul's use power, each stands to benefit from the other. Feminist scholars using rhetorical analysis and postcolonial theory have sensitized the entire scope of Pauline studies to critically reexamine Paul in light of ancient Mediterranean rhetoric in order to detect those "voices" inscribed in Paul's letters to specific communities. Thanks to these scholars, those "other, gendered voices" are being heard, and Paul's voice should never be heard again as a monologue on power relations. The controversial question about whether Paul's voice or other voices within his communities advocated a challenge to traditional kyriarchy should continue to evoke more innovative research on power relations in the early Christ communities.

The pioneering works of Schüssler Fiorenza and Horsley have been paradigmatic in this current venture in Pauline studies. Horsley's numerous works addressing Paul's anti-imperial rhetoric have helped to narrow the gap between the two general approaches to Paul by incorporating postcolonial studies and using Schüssler Fiorenza and other feminists as dialogue partners (Horsley 1997, 224–52; 2000, 40–50, 85; 2008a, 20–34). But as we have already seen, Horsley's Paul remains conspicuously different from Schüssler Fiorenza's reconstructed Paul. The feminist, postcolonial reconstruction of Paul and his audience differs from historical-critical approaches for two very important and interrelated reasons. This bifurcation of Paul reveals something of methodological interest. First, historical-critical scholars have gleaned political insights from Scott's works, which have both confirmed and expanded scholars' insistence that "political resistance" played an essential part of the early Jesus movements and Paul's Christ communities (Neil Elliott 2008, 2008; Horsley 2003; 2005; 2008a). In Horsley's words, "The key to understanding the dynamics of power relations is the recognition that political resistance by the subjected is rooted in the off-stage hidden transcript" (2008, 184). Put briefly, this approach to Paul's use of power understands his rhetoric as informed and conditioned by the sociopolitical dynamics of participating in a resistance movement against a dominant political force.

This social-scientific perspective subordinates Paul's machinations
for personal status under the larger canopy of the dyadic values and
political operations of subjected peoples in ancient Mediterranean culture.[43] For example, Horsley views Paul as directing a broad anti-imperial
rhetoric against Rome and its culture (2000, 101). Paul established "alternative ekklēsiai" similar to Lincoln's "religions of resistance." According
to Horsley, these alternative *ekklēsiai* were to live in opposition to "the
dominant imperial order" as a necessary part of Paul's apocalyptic vision
of God's kingdom for the nations (2000, 97, 101). For Paul, God's rule
had already begun in "the body of Christ" where the risen Christ was
mystically present through the "Spirit," the initiation ritual of "baptism
into Christ," and the Lord's Supper (Rom 6:4; 1 Cor 3:16; 6:19–20; 12:13;
Gal 4:6). Scott's concept of resistance by means of the rhetoric of "hidden
transcript" suggests that Paul's rhetoric of imitation and obedience should
first be understood within this macrocontext as these alternative Christ
communities functioned as *ekklēsiai*. This does not negate the communities' inner political struggles nor should it silence the other voices—
especially those of women. It rather prioritizes the larger phenomenon
of the communities' shared political resistance as subjected peoples as
they struggled among themselves for a variety of reasons. This approach
suggests that Paul's "hidden transcript" was initially and primarily framed
in the context of political resistance against dominant, elite institutions by
his subjected communities. Struggles between certain members within
these communities and against Paul developed after the formation of
these communities of resistance against their macro-sociopolitical matrix.
Paul's rhetorical response to these later micro-sociopolitical situations
must not be separated from the larger rhetorical and historical contexts.
This contextualization mitigates the charge of Paul's intended or unin-
tended inscription of his own authority, suggesting that the communities'
self-identity, ideology, and sociopolitical structure also constructed Paul.

In this regard I want to draw attention to two more aspects of Scott's
analysis of resistance movements. First, Scott recognizes the key role that
an individual can play: "The inclination to dismiss 'individual' acts of
resistance as insignificant and reserve the term 'resistance' for collective
or organized action is as misguided as the emphasis on 'principled' ac-

43. I would suggest that this is one reason Foucault's analysis of modern, individualistic cultures should be used judiciously. See also Ehrensperger 2007, 3.

tion" (1985, 297). No doubt Paul played a central role in the communities' resistance to imperial ideology and order—and used his power and authority to resocialize these groups to that end. Paul provided the ideological framework for these communities with his overarching political-theology of Christ's lordship for the nations (Rom 1:5). Combined with this anti-imperial rhetoric and subordinated to it was Paul's rhetoric of imitation and obedience crafted with metaphors about Christ's sacrifice and servant status that accomplished God's will. This rhetoric served as a reminder to his communities that God was also "the one working in you, in order to accomplish his will and good pleasure" (Phil 2:13).[44] This line of persuasion directs attention to the collective role of the communities in accomplishing what Paul perceived as God's will and work—not simply Paul's kyriarchal status. This secondary and subordinate use of rhetoric actually "decenters" Paul by calling for the communities' ultimate loyalty to God—not himself or others (1 Cor 3:4–11; 9:12, 15, 19, 23).

I find that Paul's role also resonates with another of Scott's concepts of "hidden transcript." On the one hand, Paul played a major role in his communities' structure and life. But on the other hand, Paul would have had to use his rhetorical skills to actually win and maintain support of his restructured kyridoularchal kingdom agenda. According to Scott:

> Charisma, as it is normally understood, has a suspect air of manipulation about it. In ordinary usage, it suggests that someone possesses a personal quality or aura that touches a secret nerve that makes others surrender their will and follow. The term *personal magnetism* is frequently used, as if charismatic figures had a force that aligned followers like so many iron fillings caught in their field of force. I would not deny that instances of charisma along these lines exist, but the complete surrender of personal will to a figure of power is, I believe, a comparatively rare and marginal phenomenon. (1990, 221)

One can easily imagine with feminist scholars that Paul's dominant role in his subjected communities of resistance would have been challenged. But who challenged Paul and for what reasons? This is taken up in detail in the next chapter. Suffice it for now to say that, based on the social-scientific analysis above, Paul would have perceived any such challenge to his personal honor and authority as an impediment to his communi-

---

44. My translation.

ties' divine calling and purpose as well. In this sociopolitical context of resistant-group religions (it is a purpose-driven Paul) that conditions his ambivalent uses of power bifurcated into kyriarchy and kyridoularchy.

## CONCLUSION

Paul played a central role in helping to empower community members to fulfill their mutual loyalty to Christ and honor the true God in opposition to the empire. But this took power, and it manifested in the form of Paul's kyriarchal rhetoric in his kyriarchal environment. Community formation was accomplished by Paul's rhetorical force of persuasion rather than by his "magnetic" charisma. When Paul perceived that his communities were threatened by paralyzing discord, and when his authority was challenged, he turned to kyriarchy and his rhetorical skill to reinforce his message by reinscribing his authority.[45] The question of whether Paul manipulated people for his own benefit or not—intentionally or not—has little to do with the realization driven home by Catelli and others: Paul controlled and dominated others. It is more significant to determine if Paul's exercise of power to dominate was meant to be permanent or temporary. It appears that Paul would have always stepped back into any situation that deviated from kyridoularchy with kyriarchal authority. Although this power-over others stands out as counterintuitive to his modified kyriarchal message in the larger context of his anti-imperial ideology, it does represent the conflicted, ambivalent, and paradoxical nature of Paul's writings with regard to power relations.[46]

Kyriarchal rhetoric in Paul's world led to kyriarchy. But Paul also tried to persuade his communities to modify kyriarchal power relations with one another as a means to affirm the crucified Lord's reign over all the nations, relations modeled after Christ's kyridoularchy (Gal 5:13). Ironically again for modern readers, Paul responded to alternative vi-

45. He would have had to convince them that his hegemony was for their common good (Scott 1990, 4).

46. Note Schüssler Fiorenza's important observation based on Michael K. Halliday's work: "Anti-language is used by outsiders for constructing a reality that is an alternative reality to that of the dominant society. Even though anti-language uses words of the dominant group in a different way, so that they can only be understood by "insiders," anti-language still re-inscribes language patterns of the dominant speech community" (2007, 5).

sions for his Christ communities' kyridoularchy with kyriarchal authority (1 Cor 4:21; 2 Cor 11:15) while in all circumstances claiming to model kyridoularchy (2 Cor 11:23)! God may have been replacing the old oppressive order with a new one modeled after his own son's kyridoularchy, but in Paul's view it took power for this transition to take place. Paul and his Christ communities were participating in this transition by modifying kyriarchy while anticipating a consummation yet to come (1 Thess 4:10b–18). Paul's apocalyptic vision of God's reign through Christ and his *ekklēsiai* may have meant that all forms of imperial kyriarchy were to be rendered obsolete. But kyriarchy still threatened the kingdom of God from both without and within, and it appears that some in Paul's communities thought he represented one such threat!

I have characterized Paul's use of power above with the neologism—kyridoularchy. It now remains incumbent on me in the following chapter to substantiate this interpretive claim according to my primary methodological rubric by examining some key passages in Paul's first letter to the Corinthians.

# 5

## Kyriarchy and Kyridoularchy:
## The Bifurcated Paul in His Own Words

I have coined the term *kyridoularchy* in order to characterize one of Paul's power strategies as a modified or reconfigured form of ancient Mediterranean kyriarchy. This did not mean an end to typical kyriarchy in Paul. Paul also continued to conscript kyriarchal language against Roman kyriarchy and members in his own communities, when he perceived that some among them had challenged his authority and undermined his gospel. This bifurcated approach to power in Paul suggests that both traditional kyriarchy and Paul's modified form of kyridoularchy coexisted in a paradoxical and ambivalent relation. Paul's vacillating approaches to power relations have caused much confusion and controversy among all those who continue to read Paul's writings.

Part of understanding Paul's vacillation between kyriarchy and kyridoularchy begins with the recognition that kyriarchal language and concepts shaped all discourse on power relations in the ancient Mediterranean world. As a language user, Paul was no exception as he targeted different polemical situations in his Christ communities and resisted the political-theology of imperial Rome. Paul's rhetoric about God as "Father" and Christ as "Lord" (1 Cor 1:3) or "son of God" (Rom 1:4); about himself as an "admonishing" (1 Cor 4:14), threatening (4:21) "father" (4:15); about "power" in the "kingdom of God" (1 Cor 4:20); about "rule," "authority," "subjection" (1 Cor 15:23–28) illustrate the inscription of ancient kyriarchal metaphors. Even his message about the crucified and risen Christ as "Lord" (1 Cor 2:8; Phil 2:7) reveals Paul's christological kyriarchy inscribed as a "hidden transcript" that both repudiated and undermined

Roman imperial ideology and Caesar's claim as "Lord." Therefore, Paul's political-theology must be read as embedded in the complex matrix of ancient Roman imperial theology, ancient Mediterranean values and urban social structures, and the specific historical circumstances of Paul's Christ communities as types of religious resistance movements that were experiencing their own internal struggles over power. Such contextualization leads to a more nuanced comprehension of Paul's complex and ambivalent rhetoric.

Coming to terms with Paul's bifurcated approach to power also requires that we see him as a product of converging cultural streams. For example, one finds Hellenistic-style rhetoric (Forbes 2003, 134–73),[1] and familiarity with some Stoic, Cynic, and Epicurean concepts in Paul's writings (Deming 2004, 80–83, 87–89). These substantial Hellenistic influences made up only part of Paul's cultural hybrid that shaped his writings. We must also take into account Paul's self-disclosed affiliation with the traditions of ancient Israel and his association with Judean-style apocalyptic Christ communities (Wright 2005, 21, 40, 91; 2009, 67–68; Hays 2005, 1–5, 119–20, 143; Horsley 2000, 93–100). In other words, Paul's ambivalent use of power stems from the complexity of his background and circumstances. Paul is both a product of and a respondent to these cultural, sociopolitical, economic, and theological factors. On the one hand, one should expect Paul to have been a rather typical kyriarchal male, considering that all power relations in the ancient Mediterranean world were defined, regulated, and maintained by kyriarchy. But on the other hand, Paul's variegated use of kyriarchal language must be contextualized and problematized against his participation with typical religious resistance movements in imperial and colonized locations that articulated their resistance through apocalyptic images and metaphors taken from ancient Israel.

I have selected certain passages that reveal Paul's rhetorical shifts between kyriarchy and kyridoularchy. The object is not only to hear Paul's voice but the other voices he addressed and suppressed. In the process of this rhetorical criticism, I also intend to nuance Paul's different uses of power by examining how some of his favorite metaphors functioned to shape his communities' power relations. This will include consideration

1. According to Forbes, Paul's use of ancient Greco-Roman rhetoric does not evidence a thorough acquaintance with or reliance upon it (2003, 150–51).

of the communities' rituals—baptism and the Lord's Supper—since rhetoric cannot be isolated from a ritual context in the ancient Mediterranean world (Taussig 181–84).

I examine 1 Corinthians since this document has many examples of Paul's attempts to persuade the communities regarding a variety of issues.[2] These correspondences reflect both kyriarchy and kyridoularchy. First Corinthians requires special attention for the obvious reason that Paul spent a good deal of time with these communities in this Roman colonial city.[3]

## 1 CORINTHIANS 7

One can easily find examples of Paul's ambivalent and paradoxical language in 1 Corinthians covering a wide range of topics—and always having some connection to power relations. Paul's advice on celibacy and marriage in 1 Corinthians 7 is one such case. First Corinthians 7 has also evoked a great deal of disagreement and confusion.[4] Will Deming discuses this controversial chapter with great acumen and clarity, especially by debunking the charge that Paul advocated sexual asceticism (2004, 216–19).[5] With regard to Paul's vacillating discourse on marriage and celibacy Deming observes that "the diversity of issues Paul addresses in 1 Corinthians 7 has also put limitations on his discussion in another way. Inasmuch as he argues here in favor of marriage, here against it, here in favor of celibacy, here against it, he has restricted the range of what he can

2. White estimates that there may have been as many as six house churches in Corinth during Paul's time there (2003, 467).

3. Corinth was actually a Roman city, rebuilt by Rome in 44 BCE after having been destroyed by Rome in 146 BCE. At the time Paul wrote to the Corinthian communities in Greek, the official language was Latin; see Joubert 1995, 214; and Murphy-O'Connor 1992, 1135–39.

4. Deming has refuted the long-held argument that Paul was to be considered an ascetic advocating celibacy over marriage as an inferior state before God (see 2005, chap 4).

5. Cf. Vincent L. Wimbush. Deming's Stoic and Cynic comparative analysis refutes Wimbush's older, generalized Hellenized ascetic model. In a somewhat ironic twist, Wimbush begins by insisting on keeping "praxis" and "motive" together in their specific Hellenistic-Roman context but retreats to generalized models—like Bellah's "transcendental religions" and the old evolutionistic notion of "primitive religion" (1–10).

say. He does not want to set the value of marriage too high and thereby discourage all forms of celibacy, nor does he wish to praise celibacy in a way that undermines the institution of marriage" (2004, 211). Deming first contextualizes this passage to shed light on Paul's wavering and seemingly inconsistent statements about celibacy and marriage by noting the popularized Stoic and Cynic arguments on these subjects. Deming shows how Paul used Stoic idioms concerning marriage against the Cynic predilection for celibacy to frame his advice on a variety of specific questions and issues that the Corinthians inquired about. Deming asserts that Paul's statements in 1 Corinthians are not the "deliberations of a systematic theologian formulating a general definition of Christian marriage" (213). His exemplary analysis also reveals how Paul subordinated his diverse comments about marriage and celibacy to the overarching concern about the Corinthians' "calling" (7:17–24; see below) and about "keeping God's commandments" (7:15, 35) (214).

Deming's treatment of this passage illustrates one more case where Paul's response to complex layers of issues could be paradoxical and ambivalent. Given the fact that marriage and celibacy had traditionally been perceived as in direct conflict by rivaling Stoics and Cynics, Paul embraced both as possibilities in different situations as long as God was honored and as long as the Corinthians considered not only one another but even "nonbelievers" (vv. 3–5; 13–14). Paul's advice depended on the particular questions or statements involving issues about marriage and celibacy in Corinth.[6] Part of his response was influenced by a reference to some temporary situation involving the Christ communities (v. 26) and by his apocalyptic statement about the "passing away of this world in its present form" (v. 31b). Whatever the particular crisis in Corinth involved, Paul juxtaposed it to his apocalyptic proclamation, and so indicated that ordinary life had been disrupted (vv. 29–31). The reality of such disruption appears to be part of Paul's justification for some of his rather unconventional remarks about not only marriage and celibacy but relationships between men and women—which we shall consider shortly. Clearly, all this had ramifications for power relations among the Corinthians.

None of Paul's rhetoric addressing any of these issues relied on mimetic "sameness" even though each topic was laden with implica-

---

6. Wire suggests that Paul is responding to "statements" by some Corinthians, not necessarily answering their questions (1990, 80).

tions for kyriarchal power relations in the Corinthian communities. In fact, Paul's responses and comments reflect not only the diversity in the Corinthian communities but also their (including women's) liberty to make decisions. Apparently Paul had not demanded much in the way of prescriptive laws to shore up kyriarchal marriage and sexuality during his long association with the Corinthian communities. These issues surfaced only after Paul had departed Corinth, and he had either been asked or had received word about their statements, concerns, and specific situations confronting the communities ("Now concerning . . . ": 7:1, 25; 8:1; 12:1; 16:1, 12). The Corinthians may have asked Paul for some revelation from Christ on these matters inasmuch as Paul made it clear when he was only offering his own opinion (7:6, 12, 25). It is also likely that some among the Corinthians may have addressed these issues based on their own revelations and access to divine wisdom (Wire 1990, 81–87; Horsley 2008b, 153–55). Certainly Paul expressed his views of what was best in each circumstance but without demanding childlike obedience as he had elsewhere (cf. 4:14–16).[7] The Corinthian request for advice would have seemed to be a perfect opportunity for Paul to exert his kyriarchal authority at every point, but he refrained. Except for prohibiting both the woman and the man from separating from each other by the authority of "the Lord" (7:10–11), and his "command" for each to live as "the Lord" and "God" had determined according to one's "calling" (7:17), Paul's language seems rather docile and actually compliant concerning matters that impacted the very structure of the communities' social life. His nonkyriarchal rhetoric stands out:

- "I say this according to a concession not a command; I wish that all could be like me" (7:6–7a; note, Paul does not say, "imitate me");[8]
- "I think it is good for you" (7:26);
- "I am saying this to you for your benefit, not in order to restrain you" (7:35);
- "In my opinion, she is happier if she remains [unmarried]; and I think I also have the spirit of God" (7:40).

7. I will return to these verses below.
8. Cf. 1 Cor 4:16

Wire observes, "there is no question that Paul is rhetorically accentuating the equal and reciprocal nature of sexual responsibilities" (Wire, 1990, 80), and "he repeats the rhetoric of equality four times in four sentences" (1990, 85), while at times he "disclaims any authority for his words beyond his own trustworthiness due to the Lord's mercy" (1990, 87).[9]

Paul's mercurial comments on gender relations in 1 Corinthians 7 in the context of ancient Mediterranean culture are just as striking as is his lack of kyriarchal rhetoric and call for rote obedience in this passage. His nonkyriarchal rhetoric and failure to demand obedience here are accentuated by the fact that any consideration of Paul's use of power must also include an analysis of its implications for gender relationships by gender analysis.[10] But again, scholars disagree whether it was in fact Paul or "other voices" who encouraged and defended ameliorated roles for women in marriage and their communities at large (see John H. Elliott 1995, 111; and Wire 1990, 36–37, respectively).[11] Deming's seminal treatment of this chapter in light of Stoic, Cynic, and Hellenistic Jewish views on marriage should also be taken into consideration when examining Paul's comments.[12] Wire's groundbreaking feminist analysis and rhetorical criti-

9. I find some of Wire's comments on this section of 1 Corinthians perplexing in as much as she attempts to mitigate or invalidate what she has already observed by way of Paul's "rhetoric of equality." She thinks that "his careful rhetoric may reflect wariness in approaching strong and fixed positions at odds with his own" (1990, 80). Paul's rhetoric of equality and reciprocal responsibilities between men and women "appeals more to" and "demands more from women" (1990, 81–82). In fact, "the women are a problem to Paul" (1990, 85). These comments are provocative and obviously very important in relation to Paul's use of power. However, Wire's explanations amount to more speculation rather than her otherwise skillful rhetorical analysis. The fact that some women were a problem to Paul is not in question—the issue has to do with the reason(s). The text in chapter 7 does not indicate that all women in general constituted a problem or challenge for Paul (1990, 32–34; 206–7). See also Wire 1990, 226.

10. See Marchal 2008, 19 and Kittredge 2000, 103–4, 108.

11. According to Wire, these voices represent the "women prophets" who believed their baptism placed them in an unmediated relationship with Christ (167–69). Paul, she argues, responded with a hierarchal model justified by Christ's own subordination to God (1 Cor 15:28), which begins with women at the bottom, then men, then Christ, and finally God at the top. This model, in turn, afforded Paul a rhetorical device to subordinate the Corinthians to himself (36–37).

12. Cases supporting gnostic influences behind 1 Corinthians 7 have not proven to be adequate at this point due in large part to the difficulty of defining a discernable form of "gnosticism" for first-century Corinth (see Deming 1995, 30–44. Peter Brown addresses the diversity of the gnosticisms in the second century and beyond (65–139) Karen King's

cism of 1 Corinthians likewise must be factored into this hermeneutical scheme to do justice to this ancient text. I suggest that 1 Corinthians 7 lacks kyriarchal force because the *ekklēsiai* in Corinth had already began to move away from traditional kyriarchal marriages and gender relations. Paul's tempered comments indicate that the communities' modifications of power relations were still in process toward kyridoularchy. Nothing in chapter 7 suggests that some were attempting to return to kyriarchy-based relations. As we shall see below, the same cannot be said about other polemical situations at Corinth, especially not about the communal meal or Lord's Supper.

In addition to these general observations on 1 Corinthians 7 above, I now turn to specific parts of Paul's text for analysis with regard to gender and power. Note that Paul begins chapter 7 (vv. 1–2) as an extension of his concerns and warnings about sexual immorality (1 Cor 5:1, 11; 6:13, 18). He adds a statement about the possibility of married persons being tempted if they cease to meet each other's conjugal responsibilities (7:5) and adds a similar caveat for the unmarried and widows, who might lack control (*egkrateuontai*, 7:9). Nothing requires one to conclude that Paul's concern about immorality or about lack of control stems primarily from the women simply because of their gender, although assumptions about women's inferiority were commonly held in the androcentric and misogynistic ancient Mediterranean world. According to Paul, a believing wife could actually sanctify her unbelieving husband—perhaps in order that some in the community would not see him and their children as a threat to the communities' spiritual status (7:14).[13] Paul gives no indication that husbands or male members of the communities in Corinth need to protect the honor of "their women" in sexual matters. Instead, Paul goes so far as to speak of the woman having "authority" over her husband's body (7:4b). It appears that traditional male honor was of less concern to Paul than was Paul's concern that women in the communities be considered

---

(2003) crucial work brings the difficulties that have plagued the history of interpretation on *gnosticism* into relation with the complexities of attempts to define *gnosticism* according to the gnostics' own writings; see also Horsley 2008, 65–88. Deming, who also rejects suggestions that Paul's comments on marriage and celibacy can be understood based on Philo's "dualistic spirituality," and parallels with Jewish wisdom literature (33).

13. Such purity concerns may have arisen over unbelieving spouses and their children participating in the Lord's Supper in Corinth.

equal and responsible partners in protecting honor for all. Paul's stance marked quite an innovation for such a kyriarchal culture.

Why did Paul not simply tell the women to submit to their husbands' authority and the unmarried to their fathers in these contentious matters? First, according to the kyriarchal standards of ancient Mediterranean households, these women would have been required to submit to their husbands and fathers (14:35). But 1 Corinthians 7 suggests the communities' households had already begun to supersede individual households. In the first place, these issues had already become public; that is, they had already surfaced in the communities' household gatherings (7:1). Paul did not try to repress this public controversy by placing it back on the authoritative shoulders of fathers and husbands to deal with in their private households. Bartchy draws attention to this social anomaly: "Here Paul urges followers of Christ who are married to understand that the husband belongs to the wife in exactly the same way that the wife belongs to the husband, with the consequence that decisions regarding their sexual life together are to be made by mutual agreement rather than by patriarchal fiat" (2003, 140).

Second, Paul makes it clear that any question or problem regarding celibacy or sexual immorality impacts both husband and wife equally! Regardless who initiated or was suggesting celibacy among married couples at Corinth (Wire's "women prophets" or Horsley's "spiritual elite"),[14] Paul's concern and advice applied to both men and women equality. Certainly this mutuality with regard to sex between the man and woman in marriage reflects the social elevation of women and wives at Corinth and in other Christ communities. Bartchy makes another noteworthy suggestion based on his reading of 1 Corinthians 7. He says, "All the advice Paul gave regarding marriage assumes that his readers would respond with decisions made without respect to their blood family's interests and wishes" (2003, 140). Even the nonbelieving wife's decision to remain with a "brother" was considered binding on this husband; he was not to leave her (7:12). In Paul's opinion, the unmarried woman and virgin were better able to "please the Lord" than a married man (7:33b–34). Women's having the capacity to please and honor God apart from marriage may seem a rather mute point for modern readers. Examples of women's practicing

---

14. See Horsley 2008b, 153–55; and his comments on "spiritual marriage" between the individual and Christ, 2008b, 60–64.

sexual asceticism in the ancient Mediterranean are rare, but this did occur.[15] But such cases for Christians expressing devotion to Christ through
sexual asceticism only began to appear as paradigmatic for both men and
women in the middle of the second century. The stigma against sexual relations was not simply about sexual relations for either men or women in
1 Corinthians 7. Rather the stigma against sexual relations derived from
calling sex a distraction from serving the Lord (7:19b, 24, 32–34, 35b, 40).
Deming's distinction between celibacy and sexual asceticism is central to
recognizing the significance of Paul's suggestion here that women had an
equal opportunity and responsibility with men to serve the Lord outside
of kyriarchal marriage and bring honor to their communities. A widow
may decide on her own to remarry as long as the new partner is "in the
Lord" (7:39). This is yet another incident where Paul subordinated marriage to one's devotion to Christ—not sexual asceticism or kyriarchy.

This also accounts for Paul's endorsing the communities' diversity
regarding marriage, remarriage, and celibacy. He remains firm on the
"Lord's" prohibition against divorce: "a woman must not be separated
from the husband" (7:10).[16] Yet even here one finds a rather sinuous
departure from his "command" based on the "Lord's" strict prohibition
against divorce in the following verse: "but if she is separated, let her
remain unmarried or be reconciled to [her] husband, and the husband
[should] not divorce his wife" (7:11). Bartchy's adroit comment about the
woman's power to make choices after being separated from her husband
captures the import of Paul's addendum to the Lord's command in v. 10:

> When Paul then addresses the case of a woman in 1 Corinthians
> who left her husband, he neither chides her for having rejected
> the authority of her husband nor advises her to return to the au-
> thority of her father (7:11), both of whom were surely shamed by
> her actions. Not even Paul's awareness of a command from Jesus
> opposing divorce leads him to suggest in her case that family piety
> was more important than her freedom in Christ. The condition he
> mentions is that she should be reconciled to her husband, *if she*

15. Noteworthy are Philo's descriptions of the Therapeutae (*Contempl. Life* 12, 13,
18, 34–37).

16. I think that the aorist passive infinitive (*choristhēnai*) lessens the force of most
translations, ; most translations indicate Paul addressed his command only to wives. He
may be referring to any situation that led to separation initiated by either wife or husband. Note that Paul at the end of v. 11 tells husbands not to "leave" (*aphienai*) wives.

> *should choose* again to live a married life. With such advice, Paul
> risked provoking the resentment and retaliation of non-Christian
> husbands and fathers. (140; italics added)

Having identified Paul's nonkyriarchal approach to the volatile gender issues raised in 1 Corinthians 7, how can one account for this? Was it
part of a ploy to restrict and silence the women that had created problems
for Paul, coupled with his "wariness from approaching strong and fixed
positions at odds with his own" (Wire 1990, 80–85)? Paul's language in
this chapter stands in contrast with his kyriarchal rhetoric and tone elsewhere, especially compared with 1 Cor 3:23 and 4:14–21. Could he have
grown wary and decided to try a more tactful approach to reinscribe his
waning authority? Determining whether or not Paul's bifurcated use of
power stems from some psychological state due to stress and fatigue may
be important, but the truth remains elusive. Answers to such questions
would shed light on whether Paul's ambivalent and paradoxical use of
power was intended to reinscribe kyriarchy or to redefine power relations:
to inscribe kyridoularchy. But to assert an answer to this question implies
knowledge of Paul's emotional state to account for his nondomineering
and nonauthoritative tone in 1 Corinthians 7.

I have suggested above that Paul subordinates his diverse comments
on marriage and gender relations in chapter 7 to his concept of God's "calling" (*klēsis*).[17] But translating this word has itself obscured Paul's use of it
in 7:17–24. Mistranslating *klēsis* as "occupation," "condition," and "situation" has resulted in many thinking that Paul meant to prevent people in
his Christ communities from changing "their social and legal status, giving such social conservatism a divine sanction" (Bartchy lecture 2009).[18]

17. Paul's use of this word in 1 Corinthians 7 has been much disputed by translators and scholars since Martin Luther translated the Greek *klēsis* as *Beruf*, German for
"occupation/status"—instead of *Ruf* ("call, summons") in 7:20: "Ein jeglicher bleibe in
dem Beruf darin er berufen ist." Bartchy, in a yet-to-be-published paper, has convincingly argued against translating *klēsis* as "condition," "state," "station," "situation," or
"position"—terms used by most modern English translations. Bartchy insists that many
scholars continue to mistranslate *klēsis*, which continued to both obscure Paul's use of
the term and perpetuate justifying the status quo for subalterns as it once was used to
subordinate slaves. Bartchy bases this important corrective on the use of *klēsis* in Paul's
writings and the ancient Mediterranean world up to the fourth century, with an example
from the Roman writer Labanius.

18. Taken from a document given to students by S. Scott Bartchy during a lecture at
California State University, Northridge, in May 2009.

Paul did not exhort slaves to "remain in slavery, even if presented with the possibility of freedom" (Bartchy lecture, 2009; 7:21).[19] Anachronistic treatments of the complex phenomenon of ancient Mediterranean slavery also add to the confusion about Paul's use of "calling." Slaves "were constantly becoming free; while still slaves, many of them had money, power, and influence that belied their legal status" (Martin 1990, 42). In this context, it makes little sense for Paul to expect slaves to try to remain in this transitory social condition that they would have had little or no control over! To consider Paul pro-slavery also vitiates Paul's concept of "God's call." Why would God have called some to bondage under others rather than to full service to himself (7:23)? Furthermore, God's "call" was expressed symbolically at one's public baptism, which indicated that "in Christ" everyone enjoyed equal status in the communities, including slaves (1 Cor 12:13; Gal 3:28).

Others in Corinth apparently assumed that one's social status (especially one's marital status) was necessarily linked to or contingent on one's status in the Christ communities (7:24). Some may have inferred from this that one could improve his or her status in the communities by either practicing sexual asceticism or repudiating marriage, circumcision, uncircumcision, and slavery—after initiation by baptism "in Christ" (7:17–24). Part of this thinking may have been directly associated with the ecstatic experiences of some women at Corinth during worship (MacDonald 2004, 155–61) or, again, at baptism (Wire 1990, 69). Some men would have also been included among these spiritually elite women, based on their own ecstatic religious experiences (Horsley 2008, 154–55). Both women and men would have interpreted these altered states of consciousness in a variety of possible modes already available to them based on similar phenomena in their ancient Mediterranean culture (Malina and Pilch 2006, 331–34).[20] Such experiences would have also elevated their status in the communities (Wire 1990, 69; Horsley 2008, 154–55). Women prophets imbued with special "knowledge" and "wisdom" may have also claimed to have "transcended sexual differentiation" and demonstrated their new status "by becoming men; they removed their veils—

19. It was unlikely that a slave could refuse a change in his or her social status since it would have been under the control of the master.

20. All religious experiences are historically and culturally conditioned. See Hollenback 1996, 8–12.

symbols of the inferiority and subordination that characterized their day-to-day living" (MacDonald 2004, 157). All or any part of this would have meant challenges to the communities' unified social structure and to Paul's concept of the communities' calling: "for we all have been baptized by one spirit into one body, whether Jew or Gentile, slave or free, and we all have been given one spirit to drink (12:13).[21]

By embedding his concept of God's "calling" in his kyriarchal po-litical-theology, Paul was able to move the Corinthians further toward kyridoularchy. Paul refers to "power" throughout 1 Corinthians, using the Greek term *dynamis* more than in any other of his letters. Note, for ex-ample, Paul's kyriarchal terms and political language for God and Christ associated with his rhetoric of God's calling. Paul begins the letter with the claim that God had "called" him by his will to be an apostle of Christ Jesus (1:1a). He follows in the very next verse with highly politicized lan-guage, addressing his hearers as "the *ekklēsia* of God in Corinth, set apart in Christ Jesus, called saints, with all of those who call on the name of the Lord Jesus Christ in every place, their Lord and our Lord: Grace and peace from God our Father and the Lord Jesus Christ God is faithful, through him you were called into participation with his son, Jesus Christ our Lord" (1:9). As part of Paul's closing kyriarchal rhetoric, he speaks of "the end," "when [Christ] delivers over the kingdom of God the Father, af-ter having destroyed all dominion, authority and power; for he must reign until he places his enemies under his feet" (15:24–25)."When [Christ] submits all things to [God], the Son himself will be subjected to the one having subjected all things to him in order that God might be all in all" (15:28). Paul twice threatens to come to Corinth in a demonstration of power against those who have used arrogant speech against him and are not imitating him (1 Cor 4:16, 18–21; 2 Cor 13:1–4). This rhetorical *topos* follows the communities' "crucified Lord" (1 Cor 2:8), who will destroy the very powers that killed him (15:24) "who was crucified in weakness but lives in the power of God. And we are weak in him, but we shall live in

---

21. Paul may have eliminated the phrase "neither male and female" (found in the baptismal formula in Gal 3:28) from his text to the Corinthians because some women were using it to erase sex differences not social divisions (MacDonald 1987, 129–36). Replacing it with "having been given one spirit to drink" still expressed the social unity of their calling.

him by God's power against you" (2 Cor 13:4).[22] In this way, Paul relies on kyriarchal metaphors when his kyridoularchal vision for the Christ communities (the kyridoularchal edifice he engineered and helped to build [1 Cor 3:9–10]) had been recently compromised.

Interspersed with Paul's kyriarchal rhetoric one still finds his modified approach to kyriarchal power (kyridoularchy). For example, Paul juxtaposes his "weakness" (1 Cor 2:3), Christ's "weakness" (2 Cor 13:4), and God's "weakness" (1 Cor 1:25) with those claiming to be wise in Corinth (1 Cor 1:17, 19–31; 2:1–13; 3:19; 2 Cor 1:12). He also makes a distinction between injurious "knowledge" and community-empowering "love" for those with a "weak conscience" (1 Cor 8:1b, 12), appealing to those with a strong conscience to "take care least somehow your authority [in this matter] does not become a stumbling block to the weak" (8:9; see also 13:1–7). Paul refers to himself as free and yet a slave to all (1 Cor 9:17).

Paul's rhetoric in 1 Corinthians 7 comes across tolerant and non-kyriarchal to the point of affirming equality between men and women in the very institution that subordinated and abused women: kyriarchal marriage. Paul's ameliorating approach to power relations also involves three additional things: First, Paul subordinates everyone to God's call to serve Christ and one another. Second, Paul addresses everyone in the communities concerning a range of questions and issues that concerned most—not just a few who had challenged Paul's authority or what he had previously taught. Third, the communities' equality reflected in gender relationships stems from Paul's earlier resocialization of his Christ communities toward kyridoularchy before they are disrupted in Paul's absence by new questions and struggles for power within the communities. In fact, Paul throughout both 1 and 2 Corinthians seems to assume kyridoularchy as the communities' basis for power relations. However, neither chapter 7 nor the entire correspondence with the Corinthians can be isolated from the general kyriarchal rhetoric mentioned above. This also accounts for Paul's ambivalent, paradoxical, and bifurcated use of power.

---

22. I have rendered the Greek preposition *eis* as "against." This meaning is part of the lexical possibilities and this translation makes most sense from the confrontational context.

## 1 Corinthians 9:19–23: Paul as "Servant to All"

Perhaps no better example of ambivalence in Paul's writings can be found than between his kyriarchal role as "called apostle by the will of God" (1 Cor 1:1a) and his claim to be "servant to all," a model of kyridoularchy (1 Cor 9:19b). Paul's servant role may be what he was referring to when he asks the Corinthians to "imitate him" (4:16). The only indication here of what Paul may have meant by this is disclosed in Timothy's task to remind the Corinthians of Paul's "ways in Christ Jesus" that he taught in "every *ekklēsia*" (4:17b). We once again find Paul's kyridoularchy fully embedded in typical kyriarchal rhetoric. Paul's appeal for mimesis came directly after he called himself the Corinthians' "father in Christ Jesus through the gospel" (4:15b). This is similar to Paul's use of mimesis later in the letter: "Become imitators of me as I am of Christ"—followed by kyriarchal hierarchy (11:1ff.). How does this kyriarchal context relate to Paul's claim to be a "servant to all?" Is Paul's kyridoularchy a pretense for an elevated reinscription of kyriarchal hierarchy in his communities?

Paul writes,

> While being free from everyone, I have enslaved myself to every-one in order to gain many. To the Judeans I became as a Judean, in order to gain Judeans. To the ones under the law [I became] as one under the law, though not being under the law. To the ones without the law [I became] as without the law—not being with-out God's law but under [the law] of Christ—in order to gain the ones without the law. I became weak to the weak, in order to gain the weak. I have become all things [to everyone] in order that by any means I might save some. I do everything on account of the gospel, in order that I might become a co-participant in it. (1 Cor 9:19–23)

Referring to the persecution suffered by the *ekklēsia* in Thessalonica, Paul says, "You became imitators of us and the Lord" (1 Thess 1:6). Paul also writes to the communities (*ekklēsia*) in Galatia saying, "You have been called to freedom, brothers and sisters; only do not [use] this freedom for an opportunity in the flesh, but through love serve one another" (5:13). "Carry each other's burdens and thereby fulfill the law of Christ" (Gal 6:2). To "the beloved and called saints in Rome," Paul says he and others with power had an obligation to help the weak, and to look not to their own interests but to the interests of their neighbors, "because Christ did not please himself" but suffered for those who were shamed by others (Rom 15:1–3). Taken together, these comments from 1 Thessalonians, Galatians, Romans, and 1 Corinthians indicate that Paul did expect "every *ekklēsia*" to imitate a model of kyridoularchy based on his ways in Christ (1 Cor 4:17). By this expectation, Paul simultaneously shores up his own authority over them.

Paul claims that his communities should imitate his servant model because it is part of "God's call" and their devotion as "Christ's servants" (1 Cor 7:17b, 22b). On a larger scale, Christ himself became a servant in order for God to eventually subdue imperial powers (1 Cor 15:24–28; Phil 2:7, 11) and bring "all nations" into faithful obedience to the one, true God (Rom 1:5). Obedience to Paul through such imitation honors God (Phil 2:12; 3:17). Paul praises those who do it (1 Thess 1:6; 2:14) and chides those who resist as unfaithful (1 Cor 4:19–21; 2 Cor 13:1–3; Gal 1:6; 3:1; 4:12–20; 5:7–8). Kyriarchal manipulation aside, how would Paul's communities have understood this in their culture? No doubt they expected any male figure of authority to use such rhetoric. But what models were available for them to associate Paul's machinations towards kyridoularchy?

### Ancient Models of Kyridoularchy

People in the ancient Mediterranean world were accustomed to many forms of devotion and submission to patrons like fathers, rulers, and gods (White 2003, 458–60; Price 1998, 3, 182–88).[23] We also have examples of such patrons either calling themselves servants/slaves or being referred to as servants/slaves.[24] Several ancient authors speculated and wrote about leaders, philosophers, and kings as servants to the gods (Martin 1990, 86).[25] Homer likened Odysseus to a god and portrayed him as suffering tragic hardships ("ill fated above all men"), which captured the attention of both Stoics and Cynics alike. Stoics and Cynics used Odysseus as a

23. Koester gives examples of slave girls' being given to temples in Macedonia (Beroia) as an expression of devotion to the mother goddess (2007, 177–79).

24. The Greek word *doulos/doulē* can mean "male/female servant or slave."

25. The Cynics in particular spoke of the "ideal king" as the "slave king" who even "suffered for the good of others" (see Martin 1990, 86–87).

model for self-sufficiency (*autarkeia*) and wisdom (*sophia*). The scene in Homer's *Odyssey* where Odysseus is tied to the mast of his ship was even compared to Jesus's crucifixion by some later Christians (MacDonald 2000, 16–17).[26] Certain traditions in ancient Israel called Moses and their greatest king, David, servants of God (Exod 14:31; 1 Kgs 11:34; Jer 33:26); but I would argue that these are in fact status claims: Moses and David had *direct* lord/servant relationships with Yahweh, with no intervening lords (Hanson 1988). Second Isaiah speaks of a paradigmatic "suffering servant" whose afflictions serve the benefit of others (Isa 53:3–6, 11). The fact that such models of idealized servant leaders existed is not nearly as revealing as how they functioned socially.

Dale Martin has analyzed and articulated how certain Greco-Roman authors' rhetoric idealized different leadership roles. The social impact of such leaders on both high- and low-status classes has clear implications for better understanding Paul's metaphorical use of the concept of slavery and the word "servant/slave" as he applied the concept to Christ, himself, and Christ communities (Rom 13:4; 1 Cor 7:23; 9:19; Gal 1:10; 5:13; Phil 2:7; Phlm 1, 16). Martin's insightful observations on the metaphorical use of slavery in the ancient Mediterranean world also reveal part of Paul's paradoxical use of power and its consequences for his communities' social status—kyridoularchy. Martin names and elaborates two major models of leadership. The first he calls "the enslaved leader," or "the populist model, by which the leader attempted to identify himself with the common people and therefore lowered himself socially to their level" (87). Martin calls his next model "the benevolent patriarchal model." He observes that "the leader ruled benevolently but from a secure, firm position of social superiority" (87). The idealized leaders following the first model enslaved themselves to their followers. They would have been considered a leader of the people (*dēmotikos*). Such leaders took up the cause for the common people "against the interests of the upper class" (87).

The Cynics, according to Martin, venerated the slave leaders for their "individual-ethical" freedom. And in spite of their external, self-imposed circumstances and low status, Cynic philosophers labeled slave leaders as truly wise (88). On the other hand, Martin's "benevolent patriarch" operated as a stabilizing factor for patron-client hierarchal relations between

---

26. The *Acts of Andrew* characterized Andrew as a "Christianized Odysseus" (MacDonald 2000, 17).

social inferiors and their upper-class patrons. Upper-class, idealized patrons ruled their households as "kindly fathers," encouraging inferiors to
remain in their social positions as faithful and obedient children, which
position was said to be for their own good, even having the potential to
improve their circumstances (89). Martin points out that Aristotle rea-
soned in his *Nicomachean Ethics* that the type of political government did
not matter as much as the type of ruler(s). But it was very crucial that the
person or persons in power "rule in the interest of the entire population"
(89). Aristotle also thought of the ideal government as paternal—the king
was to be like a father to his family (8.10.1).

Martin concludes that the two models of ancient Greco-Roman leadership served as rhetorical devices for the elite to contemplate the ideal
type of leader. Whereas the "benevolent patriarchal" leader functioned to
"maintain and reinforce prevailing structures of authority," the "enslaved
leader" or populist leader "disrupted the structure of society either by attempting to move up from the lower class in a position of leadership or
by moving down from a high-status position and betraying his own class's
interest in identifying with the lower class (114–15). Martin also notes
that such an enslaved leader could actually "gain power" by appearing
to relinquish it and "move down the social scale" (115). Several upper-
class authors condemned the populist model because it was thought to be
shamefully catering to the lower classes (115).

Martin rejects the "benevolent patriarchal" model of leadership for
Paul, because Paul identified with the "weak" (as in one's social status)
and even did manual labor because he refused financial support, to show
solidarity with the lower classes (120, 121, 128). Martin criticizes Gerd
Theissen's "benevolent patriarchal" model because the leader does not
sacrifice status or money for the common good; after all, leadership was
about preserving the status and security of the upper classes: "Paul refuses to lead from the secure position of social superiority" (125). Martin
instead places Paul under his rubric of populist-enslaved leader and
stipulates that "self-lowering functions to express concerns about status
reversal or status confusion. The leader challenges the assumptions about
the givenness of prevailing status indicators and may well be castigated for
causing status chaos by not remaining in his traditional social position.
The self-lowering leader says that normal status indicators are indifferent
if not downright harmful, and that the salvation of the community may

necessitate the self-lowering of the leader. The leader takes on a humble role in order to save or elevate those whom he leads" (124–25).

Following this example would have undermined the social hierarchy and status in Corinth. But does Martin's "enslaved leader" model of "self-lowering" that required members of higher status to render service to those of lower status amount to kyridoularchy? Yes, inasmuch as the enslaved leader used his or her power and elevated status to serve others in lower or more vulnerable social positions who were especially subject to kyriarchal abuse and domination. Theissen identifies at least nine persons of high status in the Corinthian communities. These could have functioned as "enslaved leaders." But the majority of the members were most likely poor and of low status (Theissen 1992, 94–95). Paul's kyridoularchy did not simply apply to persons with high social status. Even persons of low class and status were expected to use whatever power they may have had over other, more lowly members of their households for their good and to render service for the community's common good by virtue of empowered community status through the gift of the spirit (1 Cor 1:26–29; 12:7). Most of the husbands/fathers in Corinth would have fallen into this category and would have been expected to check their kyriarchal power and authority over wives, children, and in some cases slaves.

Three prominent women, Chloe, Phoebe, and Prisca (with her husband Aquila) led house churches in Corinth (1 Cor 1:11; 16:19; Rom 16:1–2). Here, such women would have also been able to exercise kyriarchal power over their households, but would also have been expected to practice kyridoularchy. In the case of wealthy, patron heads of households, part of Paul's kyridoularchy would have meant the house churches' considerable financial support in the form of hosting the communities' gathered meals and worship with special attention to the poor (1 Cor 1:11; 11:22). We have already mentioned above that some women elevated their status in the communities by means of their religious experiences and public performances during worship (1 Cor 11:5). These woman prophets may have used public worship as an opportunity to raise their personal status, and would also have been pressured by Paul to practice kyridoularchy (1 Cor 11:5; 12:7). So Martin's models reflect rather androcentric and predominately elitist depictions of power, centered on the male upper classes.[27] This leaves one in the lurch with regard to power relations across the entire spectrum of different social classes in Paul's communities; few were in positions of high social status, but most exercised power in relations with a variety of social equals, subordinates, and superiors. Martin's models are especially problematic because they lack attention to gender relations—again, essential for any consideration about power relations.

Additionally, Paul vacillated between kyriarchy and kyridoularchy. Martin's enslaved model implies that such a leader (and Paul in particular) continued to function at a "self-lowered status" in order to identify with the "weak." Martin contends that Paul's "slavery to all" belonged to the "common rhetoric that portrayed leaders as gaining power by giving up their normal high status and enslaving themselves to the masses" (132–33). He cites Paul's refusal to accept financial support from the Corinthians as such an example (120). But Paul maintains that he continued to have the right to their financial support (1 Cor 9:12). Paul does not refuse their support in order to identify with the poor but rather to contest the accusation that he used his status and authority for monetary profit only (9:11–12b, 17–18). Had he truly lowered his status and permanently joined the ranks of the poor and low-status members, how could he—as an enslaved leader now on their level—have claimed any such right? His argument may have been more compelling to the weak if he had claimed that he had not given up his higher status, which still entitled him to support. But to claim to merit monetary support because of his apostolic status to instruct the communities and preach the gospel actually distinguishes Paul from the low class and illustrates that he has not relinquished his kyriarchal authority and privilege!

Again, Martin's model fails to account for the fact that Paul's kyriarchal rhetoric obviously applied to members of low status (1 Cor 7:16–17). Paul does not simply identify with the plight of everyone with low status in the communities, against the interests of the high status. Again, Paul never renounces his status as a "called apostle of Christ Jesus by the will of God" or his claim to be their "father in the Lord," but he reinscribes it with such rhetoric. Interestingly, Paul recognizes not only the right of local,

27. Martin refers to 1 Cor 9:4–6 and Paul's use of the word for "authority" (*exousia*) to make the point that Paul only required the "strong," or those with high status, to relinquish power, because those of lower status had no such *exousia* (121).

civil authorities to rule but characterizes their role as "ministers" (*dia-konoi*) of God to do "good."[28] He even asks the communities in Rome to obey them (Rom 13:1–4). It seems as though Paul's text here may suggest some knowledge and influence based on a "benevolent patriarch" model. It would have been problematic for Martin's "enslaved leader" to take such a tolerant position toward elitist authorities. But Paul was neither a strict kyriarchal elitist nor a proto-Robin Hood.

It should be noted here that Martin's "populist enslaved leader" model and my kyridoularchy model both differ from Gerd Theissen's "love-patriarchalism." Although Theissen advanced the discussion about the social conditions behind Paul's community formations significantly, "love-patriarchalism"—in similar fashion to Martin's "benevolent enslaved leader"—preserved kyriarchy and social hierarchy for those in power while requiring continued subordination and honor from the lower-class members. Love-patriarchalism would have simply made the old order more tolerable but never demanded an alternative model that stipulated kyridoularchal demands on those in power.

## Kyridoularchy in the Kyriarchal Households

The prevalent social institution for kyriarchy in the ancient Mediterranean world was the household: *oikos*. Here the father as "ruler of the house" (*oikodespotēs*) wielded his "paternal power" (*patria potestas*) with added support from the kyriarchal institutions of marriage, divorce, and remarriage.[29] White states that the term "lord" (Greek *kyrios*) was "probably the most common way of designating" the "father of the family" (Latin *paterfamilias*) (465). These kyriarchal terms indicate how the household functioned as a bastion for socializing members around obedient "loyalty" (Latin *pietas;* Greek *pistis*) to husband-father. This obligatory *filial piety* helped to construct and legitimize asymmetrical gender distinctions,

28. These local, city authorities generally were wealthy landowners and part of the aristocratic class. Such elitists felt both the right and obligation to look out for the interests of the city's order by ruling over subalterns and showing loyalty to Rome through festivals honoring patron gods and the emperor (see Malina and Pilch 279–80; Price 107–8).

29. White reminds us that "there is no exact Greek equivalent for *paterfamilias*, *oikodespotēs* was its most common Greek translation. Note also that the Greek *oikos*, *oikia* would have been translated into the Latin by *familia*" (464).

hierarchal patron-client relations, and honor-shame values. But to what degree could Paul have resocialized his Christ communities (staunchly ensconced in such a kyriarchal institution) toward kyridoularchy? And by what means could this have been done in light of the tenacity of ancient Mediterranean kyriarchy?

Stephan Joubert describes Paul's role among the Corinthian communities as *paterfamilias*. In other words, Joubert claims that as God's apostle, Paul "presented himself as broker on behalf of God, Jesus and the Holy Spirit (the heavenly patrons) to the Corinthians (the clients)" (216). Having been "ascribed with supernatural authority," Paul took the "highest rank for himself within the *ekklēsia*" and submitted to "nobody else" (216). God was the "heavenly *paterfamilias*" (1 Cor 8:4) and Jesus the *kyrios* of all (1 Cor 8:6; 12:3; Phil 2:11). "The kinship system thus provided the basic structure of Paul's symbolic universe, with images from the political sphere referring to but one aspect thereof, namely the present reign of Christ over the community of believers" (217). Joubert's interpretation of how all these kinship metaphors actually structured Paul's power relations with the Corinthians comes across as profoundly kyriarchal. Joubert says, "They were all metaphors which masked his apostolic superiority. Furthermore, Paul's use of egalitarian language images such as 'brothers' when addressing the Corinthians, to that of 'partners and fellow workers' (2 Cor 8:23) when referring to his helpers, also masked a relationship other than the one they implied, since these persons were in fact not his equals. They were socially inferior to him, because he had the authority to command their obedience" (217). Joubert's Paul acted according to a typical cultural script based on fathers and their households in order to control his communities—right down to their "sexual behavior" and "choice of marriage partners" (219). Those who challenged Paul's authority and threatened the communities' cohesion as a "new family" were disciplined to restore "subordination and obedience to himself" along with "harmony within the household" (222). When it came to Paul's use of power, based on Joubert's characterization, Paul did not equivocate or hesitate in the least.

From a similar social-scientific analysis that relies heavily on ancient kinship models with "patriarchal ideology" and honor-shame values, S. Scott Bartchy has found a very different Paul among the Corinthians. According to Bartchy, "Paul did not seek to exploit the managerial role of a father" (2003, 145). Paul should be compared to the Epicurean Philodemus, because both used a similar style of pedagogy in their "leadership of souls." Paul's critical language toward the Corinthians would have been valued as "therapeutic harshness" (2003, 145).[30] Bartchy understands Paul's use of power delimited by his "vision of a society of siblings in which only God is called 'father,'" and "each surrogate member used his or her strengths, whatever they were, to enrich the quality of life for the family rather than for themselves as individuals" (2003, 145, 146).

While Joubert downplays Paul's egalitarian rhetoric as a "mask" for kyriarchal authority to control the Corinthians, Bartchy mitigates Paul's "harsh" rhetoric by an idealized "non-patriarchal" "society of siblings" of mutual empowerment. Both approaches represent important social aspects of Paul's rhetoric and metaphors. But neither adequately accounts for Paul's paradoxical language. This undermines the import of both Joubert's and Bartchy's observations, leaving us with two very different perceptions of Paul's communities: one typically kyriarchal and the other nonkyriarchal. This remains a pivotal issue in Pauline scholarship, as noted in the previous chapter.

Bartchy's nonpatriarchal characterization of Paul can be viewed as already suggesting counterintuitive and paradoxical aspects in its kyriarchal cultural matrix. His nonpatriarchal model for Paul also fits well with different types of groups or associations in the ancient Mediterranean world. One must take precautions when labeling communities in the early Jesus movements because of their own social evolution and geographical locations. Both Bruce Malina and John Elliott have drawn attention to this with cross-cultural comparative analyses. Malina, using "small group formation theory," notes that the "Jesus group was an ephemeral social movement group. Subsequent Christian groups were not social movement groups at all, but rather Mediterranean voluntary associations" (1995, 110). Malina distinguishes between the "Jesus movement group" and the "Christian movement group" by identifying the former as a type of "political action group" that looked to God's intervention to change society, while the latter is a "fictive kinship group" shaped by the "norms of the prevailing kinship institution" (1995, 108). A distinctive feature of Malina's voluntary associations where Paul functioned as a "change

---

30. Sampley compares Paul's rhetoric with a type of "frank speech" appreciated by Greco-Roman authors in the maintenance of friendships (293, 304–12).

agent" was the fictive kinship "mutual loyalty" and "common interests and benefits for their primary kin group, not themselves alone" (1995, 108–9). I also see aspects of Malina's fictive kinship group during the ministry of Jesus of Nazareth, in communities that he established in addition to his traveling associates (see chapter 1). But Malina's "voluntary association" model does help us imagine how such communities would have understood and responded to Paul's rhetoric. For example, Paul's insistence on group solidarity and mutual support would resonate well with such groups that perceived themselves to be in conflict with the dominant culture.

John Elliott takes the social-scientific inquiry of group types in early Christianity one step further by discerning the transition of the early Jesus movements from "faction to sect" and then identifying early Christian features of sects found in the Second Testament (1995, 75–95). Paul's communities can be placed into Elliott's category of Jewish sect. I will only mention a few of Elliott's more salient characterizations of such sects, in order to bring Paul's fictive kinship communities into sharper focus.[31]

- The sect arises under "general conditions of stress and tension, instability, and social change" (80). This applies to Paul's communities, composed mostly of low-class members living in very diverse, sometimes hostile, segregated Greco-Roman urban centers.

- The sect protests or resists "conditions of perceived economic and societal disparity, deprivation, and repression"; along with a sense that the group's honor is being challenged (80–81).

- Such resistance takes the form of ideological teachings and political control, including ritual observance: "The sect is critical of and rejects the view of reality taken for granted by the establishment, thereby being labeled and treated as a group deviating from fundamental societal norms and values" (81).

- Paul's Christ communities are clearly defined communities, recognized as an identifiable social entity by outsiders (81).

- Paul's Christ communities include "all sectors of society" and

31. Elliott's excellent article covers the shift from faction to sect as well as several aspects of both types for different Second Testament texts.

"promotes equity or are egalitarian in their orientation," with the "deprived, marginalized, and socially depressed" especially drawn to them (81–82).

- As messianic sects, Paul's Christ communities excommunicate those who "disrupt the unity of the community," understand themselves as God's special people, and embrace an apocalyptic ("eschatological") view of the world (83, 85).

- Pauline Christ communities claim to be subject to "God's reversal of social status," are perceived to have inferior status by society at large, and claim God has given them "new honor"— honor from above (85).

The social frameworks that Malina and Elliott provide help one to imagine how such communities would have heard and responded to Paul's rhetorical kyridoularchy. Following Malina's and Elliott's general suggestions for "voluntary associations," "fictive kinship groups," and "Jewish, messianic sects," I find it quite feasible that the innovations and countercultural patterns associated with such small groups made kyridoularchy not only possible but an attractive option for Paul's communities in Corinth. But by what social mechanism could even groups disassociating themselves from their dominant culture actually have made kyridoularchy a social reality? Paul's vacillating rhetoric between kyriarchy and kyridoularchy indicates that his communities struggled to implement the latter. The power of rhetoric and metaphor to shape and change social reality is not questioned here.

Conceptual metaphor theorists like George Lakoff and Mark Johnson have helped us recognize the central role metaphors play in society, beyond mere forms of subjective expression and communication to the actual heart sustaining every aspect of social life. They speak of "a clear case of the power of metaphor to create a reality rather than simply to give us a new way of conceptualizing a preexisting reality" (1981, 144). Additionally, they claim that groups out of the mainstream of culture use metaphors to "radically redefine" mainstream culture's most central values (24). Conceptual metaphor theory postulates "metaphor as essential to human understanding and as a mechanism for creating new meaning and realities in our lives" (196).

But one final inquiry must be made to explore the likelihood that Paul's rhetoric and metaphors resulted in structural social changes toward kyridoularchy in the life of his communities. We have noted above that ancient rhetoric and metaphors were already embedded in some specific aspects of social structure—like households, religion, and rituals. Lakoff and Johnson state that "in actuality we feel that no metaphor can ever be comprehended or even adequately represented independently of its experiential basis" (19). For kyridoularchy to have moved from Paul's rhetoric into the communities' social life, it would had to have been reflected into their rituals. Lakoff and Johnson articulate this connection between metaphors and religious rituals. "In our terms, a ritual is one kind of experiential gestalt. It is a coherent sequence of actions, structured in terms of the natural dimensions of our experience. Religious rituals are typically metaphorical kinds of activities, which usually involve metonymies—real-world objects standing for entities in the world as defined by the conceptual system of the religion. The coherent structure of the ritual is commonly taken as paralleling some aspect of reality as it is seen through the religion" (234). "Cultural metaphors, and the values entailed in them, are propagated by ritual. Ritual forms an indispensable part of the experiential basis for our cultural metaphorical systems. *There can be no culture without ritual*" (234, italics added). Price, speaking from an anthropological perspective about religious rituals and the Roman imperial cult says, "Rituals are often felt to be 'mere' rituals, a 'symbolic' aspect of the 'real' state, a form of flummery which can safely be left in the care of certain specialists. Such a distinction between the 'real' and the 'symbolic' wrongly presupposes that the 'real' . . . is unproblematic" (1997, 67).

The early Christ communities regularly practiced three rituals, including their gathered worship in households, baptism, and a communal meal that Paul referred to as the "Lord's supper" (1 Cor 11:20; 12:13).[32] All three of these rituals represent significant social markers for those participating, indicating one's status in the communities. That is to say, any of the communities' public performances of these rituals would have carried social relevance for the communities collectively and the participants individually. The compound effect of all three together clearly

---

32. Paul mentions an offering to be brought on "the first day of the week" (1 Cor 16:2). He also suggests that whenever the communities "came together in the *ekklēsiai*" they also participated in their communal meal (1 Cor 11:20).

signified the communities' power relations in regard to gender and class for themselves and nonmembers.[33] Participating in these rituals left no doubt about either the person's inclusion as a member of the fictive kinship group or their relation to those with higher or lower status. As noted in chapter 3, rituals can function in one of two ways socially: either to confirm and legitimize reality by maintaining social boundaries or to transform and breach prior social boundaries based on status and gender. In chapter 3 I also noted that Dennis Smith's analysis of Hellenistic type meals reveals the meals' capacity to simultaneously indicate social stratification and equality (2003, 10–11).[34]

Hal Taussig notes that ancient Hellenistic type meals served to resist "Roman power over other Mediterranean cultures" (2009, 102, 115–43). In this vein, the Christ communities' rituals also served to resist and challenge the social status quo and deviated from strict observance of established boundaries with divine sanction to do so. God's "call" to "freedom" and the communities' ritual participation must have led to questions for some at Corinth about the need to maintain one's social status in order to serve Christ (7:17–24). As noted above, some of the Corinthians must have inferred from their divine calling and baptism that they either needed to or could now abandon their social status as married, single, Judean, non-Judean, or slave in order to better serve Christ.[35] Paul assured them that removing themselves from institutionalized social conditions was unnecessary in order to serve the Lord (7:2), even if it meant not being able to give the Lord one's undivided devotion (7:33–34). What mattered most was God's calling (7:24). Such advice made it clear that remaining in or becoming free from one's social condition was not equated with devotion to Christ (7:27, 28, 34). A dutiful wife's submitting to her husband was not tantamount to Paul's concept of devotion to Christ or to obeying

33. Jorunn Økland, addressing the relationship between ritual space and "gendered order," comments that "ritual space both reflects social reality and is a place where reality (in the sense 'view of reality,' cosmology) is produced" (36). Ritual functions both to confirm social reality and change it. The *ekklēsia* in households as the "space" where Christ communities worshiped and shared a common meal would have already served as a religious or sacred place throughout the ancient Mediterranean world.

34. Smith makes this a major part of his assessment of Hellenistic type meals.

35. Wire contends that "God's call reverses all peoples' desires and values but not their concrete social status" (31). This would mean an exception to the power of rhetoric and metaphors to transform social reality.

the commands of God. Instead, the institutions of kyriarchal marriage and slavery had been subordinated to serving Christ and his communities (3:23a; 12:7; 13:5). A slave could still serve God and his or her Christ community whether freed or not. Given that freedom meant a better option to carry out his or her calling, accordingly Paul encouraged slaves to make use of opportunity to gain freedom should it arise (1 Cor 7:21).[36]

The Christ communities' baptismal statements at Corinth and Galatia reveal that the persons being baptized were initiated into the communities' idealized social body defined by religious metaphors emphasizing unity ("one Spirit," "one body," all "in Christ," all "clothed in Christ," "all children of God," all "of Abraham's seed"; 1 Cor 12:12–13; Gal 3:26–29).[37] Unity in the new social body overcame traditional divisions based on the ethnic categories of "Judean" and "non-Judeans," the social classes between "slaves" and "free," and social division based on gender construction. The ritual context allowed for "diverse" and "marginalized voices" to be heard through Paul's paradoxical "body of Christ" metaphor in which a crucified lord serves others yet is raised in power (Kim 2008, 31). This rhetoric was symbolized in the ritual of baptism (Rom 6:3–6; 1 Cor 12:22–27; Gal 2:19b–20).

> Now [we are] many members but still one body. And the eye can not say to the hand, "I have no need for you," or again the head to the feet, "I have no need for you." But those members of the body seeming to be weaker are necessary, and those we deem having less honor, we clothe with greater honor. And our socially reprehensible members (*aschēmona*) we treat with greater respect. Our respectable members have no such need. But God has blended together the body giving greater honor to the one who lacks it. (1 Cor 12:22–24)[38]

36. See Bartchy 1973.

37. Malina and Pilch identify the "body" metaphor here as the "social body" (115). See Yung Suk Kim for an excellent and succinct summary on scholarship's interpretation of Paul's "body of Christ" metaphor in 1 Corinthians (23–31). Kim notes the paradoxical connotation of the metaphor to suggest unity yet express diversity through the "marginalized voices." The image of Christ's body crucified "gives hope to the weak and marginalized in the community," where they should be "empowered" because "they are also people of God" (31). See also below on the rhetorical tradition of Christ's "betrayal" at the Lord's Supper.

38. Theissen identified most of the Corinthians as from the "lower strata" in Corinth—a city on the economic upturn at the time. He also thinks that Paul only bap-

This ritually shrouded metaphorical rhetoric of kyridoularchy reflects an idealized world for the communities. It is only a question of to what extent the communities realized their symbolic world in actual, everyday practice.

Although Paul did not specifically mention "male and female" in the Corinthian baptismal creed as in Gal 3:28, he did use other unifying metaphorical expressions that would include men and women. For example, "In one Spirit we all have been baptized into one body" (1 Cor 12:13a), and "[we] all have been given one Spirit to drink" (12:13c), which is included in the "body of Christ" metaphor following this baptismal metaphor.[39] Notably, Paul also does not use the expression "baptized into Christ," found in the Galatians creedal formula. While these differences appear to have something to do with Paul's discourse on the operations of the spirit at Corinth, Paul's failure to explicitly mention "male and female" should not be taken here as his denial of gender social equality in the communities in Corinth.[40] The extant metaphorical expressions about unity of all in the "spirit" and "body" make a compelling case for gender equality without implying the end of sex differences (MacDonald 1987, 121, 126).[41] The fact that men and women experienced the same public baptism with the same inclusive metaphorical language was more important than either of these facts by itself.[42] Baptism for the early Christ

---

tized upper-strata folks (2004, 100, 102).

39. Wire thinks that the baptismal tradition that included "no male and female" was known by the Corinthians but reversed by Paul because of the Corinthian "interpretation of Christ as God's undifferentiated image who is not male and female (1 Cor 11:7) in favor of the male as God's image" (166–67).

40. See Orr and Walther for their note on the "operations of the spirit" in Corinth with reference to this text (1977, 284).

41. Økland, referring to ancient Greek philosophical conceptualizations of gender mentions the "one-sex-model." "This model constructs gender as two poles on one continuous axis . . . The male pole was the fully and perfectly human, while the female pole was lacking perfection. There was no fundamental difference between female bodies and male bodies" (46). This model may help explain the behavior of women in 1 Cor 11:5–6, 13–15.

42. Margaret MacDonald says with regard to "women's ritual performance" in Corinth, "their new status was visible to themselves, to other church members, and even to outsiders as it was reflected in their continence" (2004, 159). I do not necessarily disagree with MacDonald's explanation for the visible nature of the women's elevated status; but I would rather explain it by their public baptisms, participating in the worship service through spirit inspired speaking, and sharing the Lord's Supper.

communities was not gender specific or obsessed with purification.[43] And unlike those of us who comment on the omission of "male and female," the Corinthians did not have the text of Galatians in front of them to compare baptismal creeds. Thus, this baptismal rhetoric and ritual would have helped restructure traditional kyriarchal relations for the Corinthian Christ communities, and helped move them toward kyridoularchy. The synergistic effect was conferred to all who equally belonged to the same fictive kinship group as equal participants in God's call and "fellowship with his son Jesus Christ our Lord" (1 Cor 1:1–2, 9). Christ-community members now considered themselves "new creations in Christ," with the "former ways having passed away"; they were in the midst of a new order and commission (2 Cor 5:17–21). Unity, mutual care, and using one's power to benefit others were integral parts of God's calling, and when the communities appeared to deviate from this, Paul responded with kyriarchal rhetoric.

The communities' common meal or "Lord's supper" provides another example of social innovation among the Corinthians and can also be used to help explain how the shared meal itself cultivated an environment for their attempts at kyridoularchy. A substantial part of 1 Corinthians deals with food and meals (8:1—11:1). Paul did not simply give rules of etiquette for sharing food together in household meetings when they gathered as the *ekklēsiai* of Christ. Here again, Paul was responding to specific problems and concerns facing his communities: in this case, their divisive behavior at meals. Had the communities' social structure not already metamorphosed into some type of social ethic based on kyridoularchy, Paul would have had no reason to address concerns about those of lower social status being "injured" or "dishonored" regarding food and ceremonial eating (8:7, 9–12; 11:22b). In fact, since food and meals usually functioned to establish and protect social boundaries and status for those in power, might we not expect Paul to justify those entitled to eat meat offered to idols and to consume food and drink without waiting and sharing with the poor (8:10; 11:21)?[44] Furthermore, if the women were really the problem at Corinth for Paul (as Wire and others contend), did he not

43. Cf. Qumran's baptismal liturgy (4Q414); English translation, Wise, et al. 1996, 391.

44. Theissen says the conflict at the "Lord's supper" was between to social groups— "the rich and the poor" (2004, 151).

miss an excellent opportunity to put them in their customary subordinate and inferior place? Would not this have been an opportune occasion for Paul to gird his kyriarchal rhetoric with the ancient Mediterranean ritual protocol for women at meals? After all, the text about the communities' meal follows directly after a text about women's praying and prophesying with uncovered heads.[45] I suggest this meant that the communities' meals were not typical status-cementing and boundary-confirming ritual meals. Rather, women, slaves, and the poor became objects of mutual consideration, not of kyriarchal constraint. Not even Wire thinks that the women were restricted to traditional subordinate roles during the Corinthian meals. Quite to the contrary, Wire envisions that "the church functions as the primary family by sharing the day's meal in which hunger is satisfied and companionship shared. Although women probably cook, there is no effective caste system that separates women and the male slaves from the meal's participants by making them responsible for others. On the contrary, the early arrival of women may give them a certain prominence. Women prophets may give thanks and bless the bread as is expected before the meal in the tradition Paul assumes that they knew (11:24)" (108).

It appears the problem at Corinth with regard to food and their communities' meals stemmed from traditional kyriarchal practices reemerging during the "Lord's supper." Those with lower status among the women would have experienced devaluation of their status in the communities when the poor were excluded if a kyriarchal meal replaced the "Lord's supper." In this case, one can hear from the marginalized through Paul's

45. If the Corinthian women in 1 Cor 11:2–16 are examples of other women in antiquity "imitating the male appearance in an effort to become androgynous" (MacDonald 2004, 158), this no doubt would have posed several problems for the husbands of the women prophets and for traditional gender roles among other common women who lacked this spirit-filled community recognition and status. Paul does not silence them here or again use the communal meal to subordinate them. It appears that Paul may have been using traditional, hierarchal standards based on the Genesis creation stories and ancient androcentric Mediterranean honor-shame values to remind them of how the women prophets would have been understood by "outsiders" holding to such traditional, hierarchal values. Nonetheless, in v. 11 Paul essentially repudiated his previous gender order of hierarchy by commenting that man and women were dependent on one another reflecting their new alternative relationships "in the Lord." So with this theological metaphor Paul confirms the equal status of women in the community. He seems more concerned with outsider perceptions and harmony in the communities rather than with women exercising their gift of the spirit during worship.

voice: Generally "the system of hierarchy prevailed at meals" (Finger 2007, 181). One's gender, age, and social status predetermined how he or she would have been treated at meals (175). We recall Mary Douglas's now-famous dictum: food symbolizes social relations. "'The message is about different degrees of hierarchy, inclusion and exclusion, boundaries and transitions across the boundaries.'"[46] The standard function of meals in the ancient Mediterranean world protected the status of those who shared meals, and bound the participants together. Most of these meals denoted and humiliated those of lower status (if these were invited) by serving lesser-quality foods and wine as well as lesser quantities of these, by seating them in places of less honor than guests of higher rank, and perhaps by never speaking with them directly (Finger 2007, 173; Theissen 1975, 152–58). "As ceremonies, meals are expected to reinforce the roles and statuses of members of the group, thus confirming the map of persons which indicates rank and status" (Neyrey 1995, 378). We find such meals and typical social ranking at Qumran, in Philo, and in Pliny the Younger.

The community (*yahad*) at Qumran ate every meal with at least ten men gathered together in the same way that the coming eschatological meal with two messiahs was to take place. Notice in the following quotation that part of the instructions for their meals included each sitting "by rank" during the meal.

> When they gather at the communal table, having set out bread and wine so the communal table is set for eating and the wine poured for drinking, none may reach for the first potion of the bread or the wine before the Priest. For he shall bless the first potion of the bread or the wine, reaching for the bread first. Afterward the Messiah of Israel shall reach for the bread. Finally, each member of the whole congregation of the *Yahad* shall give a blessing, in descending order of rank. This procedure shall govern every meal" (Wise et al. 1996, 147).

The communal meal at Qumran seems to have included only full members in a hierarchal relation from the priest down. The *yahad*'s concern for purity was another central aspect of their meal. One could also be excluded from the meal at Qumran for challenging higher-ranking authorities. Here the Qumran texts show typical kyriarchal rhetoric toward

46. Quoted in Neyrey 1991, 362.

its rebellious members. Anyone "rebelling against the orders of his high-ranked comrade, has usurped authority; he is to be punished by reduced rations and exclusion from the pure meals for one year" (Wise et al. 1996, 135).

Philo describes the communal meal of the celibates at Alexandria as including women, most of them older virgins, but separated men on the right and women on the left. Philo also mentions their concern for a purified meal of unleavened bread (*Contempl. Life* 67–81). These types of status-specific meals were ubiquitous in Greco-Roman society as well. Pliny the Younger complains about attending a meal where the elegant food went to a few guests seated in the most honorable places around the table while smaller potions and cheap wine were distributed to those of lower rank. Pliny did not treat his guests this way, he claimed. But Pliny made it very clear that he only admitted to his table those he considered equal to himself (*Letters*, II,6). This adheres to Smith's observations of Hellenistic type meals. Smith maintains:

> Those who dined together were to be treated equally. This was a standard feature of ancient dining protocol. It functioned as an elaboration of the concept of social bonding at the meal and was a strong feature of banquet ideology at all levels of the data. The idea was that a meal that was shared in common and that created a sense of community among the participants should be one in which all could share equally and with full participation. In essence, then, a meal conceived in this way had the potential to break down social barriers and allow for a sense of social ordering internal to the group (2003, 11).

Paul's sharp rhetoric about abuses at the Corinthians' communal meal give no indication of seating by ranks, differences in the quality or quantity of food distributed, women's or servants' eating afterward with the poor, purity concerns, or excluding rebellious members. Paul's tone is authoritative (downright kyriarchal) about divisions in a meal that was supposed to unite the participants (11:19). He directs this kyriarchal rhetoric to the higher-status members, to those who have their own houses and can banquet with others of similar rank (11:21–22). He accuses the higher-status, wealthier members of "looking down on the *ekklēsia* of God and shaming the ones who have nothing" (11:22b). Such behavior was now considered deviant and shameful for the Christ

communities' communal meals. This represents a reversal of typical kyriarchal table-fellowship codes in ancient Mediterranean culture. Neyrey
suggests that "Jesus' selection of table companions is no mere lapse of
regard for the customs of his day but a formal strategy" that signals "God
extends an inclusive invitation to nonobservant and sinful outsiders for
covenant membership and for status as forgiven persons" (1996, 378).
The Corinthian meal appears to have been consciously modeled after the
tradition's memory of Jesus's table fellowship.

After criticizing the high-status and high-class Christ members for
deviating from a meal that appears to have been patterned after Jesus's
practice (11:20), Paul repeats the tradition he had received about the
"Lord's supper" (11:23–26). Christ communities were reminded of how
their meal continued to represent the "Lord Jesus," who gave his life "for
you" (11:24). Paul follows with a warning not to return to the "condemnation of the world" but to consider their "body," that is, the community, the
ekklēsia. Paul's warning amounts to waiting for the poor to eat. Again this
may sound trivial to modern readers. But based on the cultural metaphors
of the day and the social significance of participating in ritual meals, waiting for the poor amounted to demonstrating that they were of equal value
and honor (11:27–34). Paul centers on the example of the "Lord" Jesus's
kyridoularchy as part of his rhetoric against those in positions of power,
high status, and wealth for returning to a kyriarchal meal. As we have seen
above, this was typical of Paul's bifurcated approach to power relations in
Christ communities. It does reveal that Paul envisioned Christ communities in very different social terms than those of his kyriarchal culture. The
communities' socially diverse "Lord's Supper," hosted in certain wealthy
members' households, became an integral social strategy toward kyridoularchy. But, in an ironic set of circumstances, patrons with power and
resources could also become recipients of Paul's kyriarchal rhetoric if they
failed to submit to his apostolic vision for God's kingdom—that is, if they
failed to use their power and resources to benefit others and to unite the
communities.

## CONCLUSION

I have demonstrated from the ambivalent rhetoric in 1 Corinthians that
Paul's exercise of power was bifurcated. At times Paul's rhetoric is clas-

sically kyriarchal, and yet on other occasions it tends toward kyridou-larchy: the use of power to serve others made vulnerable by kyriarchal power structures. However, kyriarchy did not end in Paul's Christ communities. Paul relied on his apostolic authority and on kyriarchal rhetoric to shape his communities according to his understanding of what "God the Father and the Lord Jesus Christ" had called him to do. He directed his vituperate rhetoric toward anyone or any group that he thought challenged his vision or the communities' calling and unity. Those with power and resources who were initiated into Paul's Christ communities through baptism retained their power and resources as patrons, husbands, and as high-status and high-class men or women. Paul expected those with such kyriarchal status and monetary means to follow another model when it came to exercising their power in relations with other community members: Paul extolled the same model of service experienced at the "Lord's supper," metaphorically expressed by the "Lord Jesus's" death for them.

Paul also claimed that he himself imitated Christ's kyridoularchy. As discussed in the previous chapter, some have thought this was a mere kyriarchal device to reinscribe Paul's own authority over others and to demand "sameness" at the expense of diversity and other viable expressions of God's Spirit among his Christ communities. I have tried to illustrate, by examining parts of 1 Corinthians and the communities' rituals, that Paul's kyriarchal rhetoric was determined more by specific issues among certain members of high or low status, who either challenged Paul's vision of the communities' "calling" or deviated from kyridoularchy as an idealized model for his communities. Sameness, repression, and domination happened at times as a result, no doubt. Nevertheless, those who read Paul today as an authoritative voice that remains representative of any idealized Christian polity should not point to the inevitable presence of some kyriarchy in Paul's writings and communities to justify any form of kyriarchy. Recognizing Paul's kyriarchy (regardless of his intent) can advance the Christian tradition toward a much-needed kyridoularchy after years of colonialism and hegemonic politics. This work has identified two aspects of Paul's use of power in his writings and suggests that they must be held in tension. Since Paul continues to be viewed either as a source for modern abuses of power (kyriarchy) or as a paradigmatic liberator of the oppressed (kyridoularchy), the bifurcated Paul of antiquity may offer a solution.

# Conclusion: Comparing Jesus and Paul

## COMPARING WHAT, EXACTLY?

Analyzing Jesus and Paul in the context of power relations provides a theoretical framework to compare these ancient figures without using older comparisons based on theology. Beginning with such influential scholars like F. C. Baur (1831, 1845), William Wrede (1904), Albert Schweitzer (1906, 1930), and continuing with Rudolf Bultmann (1929, 1936), most early comparative works emphasized discontinuity between Jesus's teachings and Paul's theology.[1] These older, extensive theological comparisons appear to have run their course.[2] Not even the revived interest in the historical Jesus has been able to sustain interest in establishing and comparing the theologies of Jesus and Paul.[3] Additionally, social-scientific approaches have essentially eviscerated theological comparisons

1. Bultmann's pessimism concerning historical congruity between Jesus and Paul and its irrelevance did not deny the importance of similarities between the historical Jesus and the early church's kerygma. Some responded to the early Jesus and Paul debate by claiming Paul was familiar with some of Jesus's teaching and mission while also finding similarities between their respective theologies and ethics. The differences were attributed to Paul's personal experience, his rabbinic training, Gentile mission, and conflict with "Judaizers" (Barclay 1993, 493). Scholars felt Paul's Christology and concerns with his diaspora Christ communities either eclipsed most of the details about the historical Jesus or suggest little or no knowledge of Jesus's teachings, in much the same way as later Second Testament documents and gnostic Gospels remained virtually silent on the subject. Even the Synoptic Gospels exhibit more interest in Christology and their respective communities' own issues than a rote portrayal of Jesus's ministry.

2. For recent comparisons based on theological categories, see Still et al. 2007.

3. A few of Bultmann's students initiated what is called the "New Quest" for the historical Jesus with an emphasis on Jesus's and Paul's preaching, which was in turn deemed to be essentially compatible along ethical lines (see Käsemann 1964). Some have recently attempted to renew the historical debate of continuity and discontinuity between Jesus and Paul. It should be observed that such comparisons tend to suggest similarities between the two by returning to theological issues (Still et al. 2007).

and attempts at a Jesus–Paul synthesis. I do not wish to buck the current trend with my concluding remarks. But I do maintain that a comparison based on an analysis of power relations contributes important insights along with the more general contextual approaches to Jesus, Paul, and their respective communities.

This study set out to analyze power based on a complex set of intersecting social and cultural conditions by collaboratively applying various scholarly approaches. Comparisons based on such approaches do not depend on whether or not Paul had specific knowledge of Jesus's teachings or activities in Galilee.[4] Both similarities and differences must be understood as products of social phenomena and cultural scripts. Besides, the current scholarly discourse on both Jesus and Paul renders most attempts to make any direct or indirect connection between them inconclusive and problematic.

## ACCOUNTING FOR SIMILARITIES

The wide and pervasive swath Rome cut across the eastern Mediterranean world with its policies of taxation, urbanization, commercialization, and colonization produced various resistance movements in ancient Palestine (Horsley 1988; Carter 2002, 466–84). Jesus and Paul established and led similar resistance groups that have been analyzed according to conflict theory in this book. An approach based on conflict theory includes accounting for "tensions between social factions, institutions, and subcultures that are the product of power relations in which one group seeks to dominate, control, manipulate, or subdue the others for its own ad-

---

4. Yet despite the various differences between Jesus and Paul, Paul might have had some knowledge of the early tradition's memory of Jesus's practice of open commensality with his communities in Galilee. Paul told his Christ communities in Galatia that he did not confer with the apostles in Jerusalem immediately after his altered state of consciousness but rather went to Arabia and then back to Damascus. After spending three years with Christ communities in these regions, he eventually did make a short trip to Jerusalem and met with Cephas and James. From there, Paul spent time with Christ communities in Syria and Cilicia (Gal 1:15–21). The episode in Antioch involving Cephas and others at the community or communities' meal might reflect some knowledge of Jesus's practice of open table fellowship (Gal 2:11–14). So it is possible—especially in light of his relationship with early Christ's communities and contact with Peter and the Jerusalem Christ communit(ies)—that Paul had exposure to the early traditions' memory of Jesus's table fellowship (1 Cor 11:23).

vantage" (Hanson and Oakman 2008, 6).[5] This approach has revealed some rather typical and similar responses by Jesus and Paul to kyriarchal power brokers and their oppressive economic structures. Jesus and Paul provided alternative structures of power by establishing fictive kinship groups, essentially through the use of ancient Mediterranean rhetoric, rituals, and metaphors. These cultural artifacts offered standard social mechanisms to challenge and negotiate power relations for groups to resist the ubiquitous pressures and problems created by Roman policies. Ancient Israel's tradition—situated in the larger cultural matrix of the Mediterranean world—also availed Jesus and Paul a vital source of persuasive and transformative options for creating communities. Israel's apocalyptic motifs were part of the cultural amalgam that served both the rural, Galilean peasant Jesus and the urban, Hellenistic Israelite Paul. Both employed apocalyptic language and images to frame their rhetoric against Roman imperial domination and to persuade their respective communities. From their shared religious tradition, Jesus and Paul crafted political-theologies in which the God of Israel and his people were said to ultimately prevail without the need for political violence against Rome (Mark 12:13–17; Luke-Q 6:20b–23, 27–36; 22:25; Rom 11:25b–26a; 1 Cor 15:24–28; 1 Thess 4:17b—5:11).

Additionally, we noted that Jesus and Paul used households as social instruments of resistance and transformation. Here, they reclined with their communities around festive, Hellenistic type ritual meals that carried significant social meaning and formation, including the capacity for social innovations. The texts reveal the unconventional inclusion of women, low-status males, and—in the case of Paul—Jews reclining with Gentiles.[6] Both Jesus and Paul found themselves forced to adopt economic measures to address the needs of their poor through mutual sharing and the use of community patrons. Neither seems to have required those who served as patrons to relinquish their means and become poor as a standard requirement (Luke 19:1–9; 2 Cor 8:13). Jesus and Paul may be

5. Power relations are produced and manifested in "four primary social domains: kinship, politics, economics, and religion." Recall that "economics, religion, and education were all 'embedded' in kinship or politics" (Hanson and Oakman 2008, 6, 7).

6. Whether the meals reflected in the Second Testament Gospels and Paul's writings were more idealistic than actually mirroring social reality does not lessen Jesus's or Paul's challenge to traditional kyriarchal relationships by virtue of their participation in such meals (see Smith 2003).

considered ascetics in the more general sense that some are now using this term. That is, thinking of one aspect of asceticism as a challenge to the dominate culture by establishing an "alternate symbolic universe" (see Valantasis, 14–53). But I would not label Jesus or Paul sexual ascetics.[7] Furthermore, neither Jesus nor Paul adhered to the institution of traditional kyriarchal marriage—though not prohibiting marriage itself (Matt 19:3–12; 1 Cor 7:3–6, 10–15). Neither taught that renouncing marriage for celibacy elevated one's status in their communities. Both Jesus and Paul disrupted kyriarchal marriage and meals that led to changes in community relationships at large and the elevation all women in the process. This convergence of politics, economics, and religion in the context of Jesus's and Paul's fictive kinship groups reminds modern readers not simply to account for similarities based on theological constructs. It also serves to illustrate how powerful metaphorical language and ritual action actually shaped social reality.

## NOTING DIFFERENCES

### *Jesus*

Jesus's rebellious activities in Galilee began when he challenged kyriarchal authority at Nazareth that most likely included his own father, Joseph. Roman policies exacerbated tensions among Galilean village members over mounting debt, declining resources, and spiraling competition for honor among males, with concomitant economic ramifications. Jesus responded to this crisis by urging the village authorities in Nazareth to enforce the Mosaic release of indebtedness (Matt-Q 6:12), heed the prophetic call to justice and compassion for the poor (Luke 4:18–19; 6:20b), cease honor-shame antagonism against one another (Luke-Q 6:29a), and love the neighbor who had become one's enemy (Luke-Q 6:27–28). In this way, Jesus maintained God's anticipated rule among his people could

7. Because neither Jesus nor Paul required celibacy or renouncing marriage in order for one to be worthy of God's acceptance or to improve one's status in their communities. Sexual asceticism—as well as asceticism in general—serves as a means of personal power and elevated status. This would have been counterintuitive for Jesus's eunuchs for the Kingdom of Heaven and Paul's kyridoularchy. See also Colleen Conway who argues that sexual asceticism was a strategy for ancient Mediterranean men to become "hypermasculine" (122–24).

begin in the midst of Roman tyranny and a corrupt temple-state (Luke-Q 11:2b; 13:28–29, 31–35; 17:20b-21; Mark 11:15–24).

But it did not go well for Jesus in Nazareth (Luke 4:23–31a). Jesus's attempts at reform and mutual cooperation were staunchly rejected by his own village elders. After being labeled a rebellious son and ritually banned from Nazareth, Jesus took his kingdom-of-God message to Capernaum and other fishing villages around the northwest part of the Sea of Galilee, where he recruited followers and began communities (Matt 4:18–21). These Galilean communities became fictive kinship groups that evidenced the influence of Jesus's teachings and were structured after resistance to kyriarchal power, beginning with their own fathers (Matt 23:9).

Jesus's practice of inclusive table fellowship also helped set the pattern for his Galilean communities' resistance and repudiation of kyriarchy. The canonical gospels suggest the ameliorating social ramifications of such meals for women and low-status men. The communities' inclusive meals would have also functioned to further undermine kyriarchal marriage, divorce, and remarriage among members of the movement in Galilee. With the removal of this ancient kyriarchal institution, women found new freedom and equality (expressed metaphorically in the eunuch logion [Matt 19:10–12]) at the expense of traditional male power. Those who lost sanguine family bonds over Jesus's *basileia* of God movement found new families without kyriarchal roles for fathers, husbands, and men in general (Matt 20:25–27; 23:9). These new fictive kinship communities met economic challenges through the combination of two types of economic models found in advanced agrarian societies among peasant economies: generalized reciprocity and a modified patron-client model as in Luke's example of the wealthy Zacchaeus (Luke 19:1–9). Again noteworthy is that Jesus did not require Zacchaeus to give up all his wealth.

All this enables one to ask if Jesus can be thought of as kyriarchal in any sense, or as an advocate of kyridoularchy as Paul was? Jesus's rhetoric against village authorities and Jerusalem elites was very forceful (Matt 23:2–39). He also placed radical demands on his followers with an authoritative tone (Luke-Q 9:60; 14:12–14). Jesus, also like Paul, required those in positions of monetary means to help the poor (Mark 10:21a; Luke 14:12–14; 19:1–9; Matt 19:14). But Jesus's authoritative rhetoric and inclusive meals consistently attacked and challenged kyriarchal institutions like households and marriage—without using kyridoularchy as a central strategy (Mark 9:35; Matt 19:12, 14; 20:25–27; Luke 22:25–27). Jesus required that fathers, husbands, and all male followers refuse to exercise the power that culture had given them over others. Jesus did not use a model of kyridoularchy for himself or as paradigmatic for his communities. Husbands and fathers were not asked to use their power to empower their wives and children but to completely forsake it! Again, he used the metaphor of the eunuch for the *basileia* of heaven as paradigmatic for his movement. Although one of the movement's patrons, Zacchaeus, may be considered an example of kyridoularchy, Jesus did not pattern such patronage after himself so as to require others to imitate him. More important, Jesus did not attempt to reconfigure or modify kyriarchy into a more benevolent use of power modeled after "love patriarchalism," "the servant-ruler," or kyridoularchy. Zacchaeus's economic support for the Jesus's movement would not have entitled him to any privileged kyriarchal status. According to Jesus, Zacchaeus would have been honored by God as a "child of the Most High" because he honored the movement's poor based on his compassion (Luke-Q 6:33–36).

## Paul

The issue of Paul's use of power has become essential for Pauline studies. I have advocated that various scholarly paradigms on Paul's use of power can remain in an ambivalent relation to one another and yet stimulate further imaginative discussions. I have also suggested placing Paul's rhetoric of imitation and obedience in a contextual relationship to his communities' role as religious resistance movements against imperial ideology and to Paul's own struggles with his communities. This seems to mesh well with social-scientific approaches that address such movements. In chapter 4 I used both Bruce Lincoln's types of religions and James Scott's power relations in "hidden narratives" to characterize resistance movements such as Paul's communities. Cultural anthropology has also established general patterns for fictive kinship groups like Paul's *ekklēsiai* that emphasize "mutual loyalty and solidarity" in order to benefit their kinship group, in contrast to the modern value of individualism and self-enhancement (see Malina 1995, 108–10; and Scott 1985, 118). Although difficult for most modern Americans to grasp, the group came first because everyone's honor was embedded in the group—including God's!

Though similar to Jesus with regard to forming resistance communities that demonstrated mutual concern for one another, Paul was in certain aspects decisively different by virtue of using kyriarchal rhetoric to reinscribe his own authority (1 Cor 1:1; 4:14–21; 14:37). Paul's christological model of kyridoularchy was not the same as Jesus's eunuch model discussed in chapter 3. Paul did not attempt to completely remove kyriarchy but rather to modify it by requiring empowerment of others. Wives, women, and subaltern males may have achieved some semblance of mutual concern in Paul's Christ communities by virtue of their common meal and kyridoularchy. But kyridoularchy did not require the loss of power at the expense of male privilege. Paul's own kyriarchal rhetoric of submission and obedience appears at times to have actually eclipsed his claim to practice kyridoularchy (1 Cor 4:21; 14:37). No other dissenting voices were permitted to challenge Paul. Power could be used to empower others but never challenge Paul's authority even if others claimed their power came directly from above—like Paul's.

The analysis of Paul's use of power required a close examination of his texts that address submission, obedience, imitation, and kyridoularchy. In Paul's letters to the Corinthians, he reminded them of his apostleship and of their "calling," using the kyriarchal rhetoric of obedience and imitation (mimesis). Various texts reveal that Paul exercised power over his Christ communities, who, according to Paul, had already been empowered by the spirit of Christ (1 Cor 12:7).

Paul fluctuated between kyriarchy and kyridoularchy to control power relations in his communities and promote solidarity aligned with his own theological ideology. Jesus did not vacillate between kyriarchy and kyridoularchy since his eunuch model required everyone to repudiate the exercise of power over anyone (Luke-Q 22:25–27).[8] Paul's kyridoularchy still relied on aspects of kyriarchy. For example, Paul's kyridoularchy allowed him to refer to the Corinthians as his "beloved children" and himself as their "father" (1 Cor 4:14–15). This fact alone distinguishes Jesus and his Galilean movement from Paul and his urban Christ communities (Matt 23:9).

8. The reference of Jesus's disciples "seated on thrones" ruling over the "twelve tribes of Israel," is an apocalyptic metaphor of God's condemnation of the present kyriarchal powers—not a literal reversal of kyriarchal roles for the disciples in the future (Luke-Q 22:28–30).

I have coined *kyridoularchy* to characterize a central strategy of Paul to exercise power and control members of his communities. To justify Paul's use power because it served to empower others and unify his communities based on his understanding of the gospel and the communities' "calling" obscures the central and complex role power played (Rom 15:1–3; 1 Cor 12:7; Phil 2:1–7). Kyridoularchy was an idealized model for Paul that he required others to imitate as he himself did Christ (1 Cor 4:16; 11:1; Phil 2:3–11; 1 Thess 1:6). But again, Paul's demand for such obedient submission to kyridoularchy was ironically a form of kyriarchy itself. And Paul's mimesis ends up being an example of his ambivalent and bifurcated approaches to power relations. Members of his Christ communities in Corinth seem to have been confused by Paul's kyriarchy and kyridoularchy: "I myself, Paul, appeal to you through the meekness and gentleness of Christ—for when I am in your presence I am humble but act boldly towards you when away" (2 Cor 10:1; see also 1 Cor 14:34–35; 2 Cor 11:16–21).

Paul's kyriarchal episodes still fell far short of the juggernauts in fourth-century Christianity and beyond, whose master narratives transformed the antikyriarchal Jesus from rebellious son to Pantocrator, and eliminated Paul's kyridoularchy altogether for kyriarchy alone. Pauline texts were used to reinscribe kyriarchal authority and oppression in later Christendom. In effect, this often meant co-opting Jesus through the selective lens of Paul's kyriarchal rhetoric and deutero-Pauline texts. Similar abuses of power continue to prevail in modern American churches where Jews, women, gays, and peoples from non-European cultures are marginalized or even vilified with Paul's authority and in Jesus's name. It is hoped that this book will serve to challenge such uncritical and simplified readings of Jesus and Paul, based on its contextual analysis of their responses to and uses of power.

# Bibliography

Adas, Michael. 1979. *Prophets of Rebellion: Millenarian Protest Movements against the European Colonial Order.* Cambridge: Cambridge University Press.

Albright, W. F. and C. S. Mann. 1979. *Matthew.* AB 26. Garden City, NY: Doubleday.

Allison, Dale C. 1998. *Jesus of Nazareth: Millenarian Prophet.* Minneapolis: Fortress.

———. 2003. "The Eschatology of Jesus." In *The Continuum History of Apocalypticism,* edited by Bernard McGinn et al., 139–65. New York: Continuum.

Anderson, Janice Capel, and Stephen D. Moore. 2004. "Matthew and Masculinity." In *New Testament Masculinities,* edited by Stephen D. Moore and Janice Capel Anderson, 67–92. Semeia Studies 45. Atlanta: Society of Biblical Literature.

Arac, Jonathan. 1991. *After Foucault: Humanistic Knowledge, Postmodern Challenges.* New Brunswick, NJ: Rutgers University Press.

Arnal, William E. 2001. *Jesus and the Village Scribes: Galilean Conflicts and the Setting of Q.* Minneapolis, Fortress.

Ashton, John. 2000. *The Religion of Paul the Apostle.* New Haven: Yale University Press.

Austin, M. M., and P. Vidal-Naquet. 1980. *Economic and Social History of Ancient Greece: An Introduction.* Berkeley: University of California Press.

Bailie, Gil. 1995. *Violence Unveiled: Humanity at the Crossroads.* New York: Crossroad.

Balch, David L. 2003. "Paul, Families, and Households." In *Paul in the Greco-Roman World: A Handbook,* edited by J. Paul Sampley, 258–92. Harrisburg, PA: Trinity.

Banks, Robert. 1994. *Paul's Idea of Community.* Rev. ed. Peabody, MA: Hendrickson.

Barclay, John M. G. 1995. "Deviance and Apostasy: Some Applications of Deviance Theory to First-Century Judaism and Christianity." In *Modelling Early Christianity: Social-Scientific Studies of the New Testament in Its Context,* edited by Philip R. Esler, 114–27. London: Routledge.

———. "Jesus and Paul." 1993. In *Dictionary of Paul and His Letters,* edited by Gerald F. Hawthorne et al., 492–503. Downers Grove, IL: InterVarsity.

Bartchy, S. Scott. 1973. *Mallon Chrēsai: First-Century Slavery and the Interpretation of 1 Corinthians 7:21.* SBLDS 11. Reprinted, Eugene, OR: Wipf & Stock, 2003.

———. 1999. "Undermining Ancient Patriarchy: The Apostle Paul's Vision of a Society of Siblings." *BTB* 29:68–78.

———. 2002. "The Historical Jesus and Honor Reversal at the Table." In *The Social Setting of Jesus and the Gospels,* edited by Wolfgang Stegemann et al., 175–83. Minneapolis: Fortress.

———. 2003. "Who Should Be Called Father? Paul of Tarsus between the Jesus Tradition and *Patria Potestas.*" *BTB* 33:135–47.

Barton, S. C. 1993. "Social-Scientific Approaches to Paul." In *Dictionary of Paul and His Letters*, edited by Gerald F. Hawthorne et al., 892–900. Downers Grove, IL: InterVarsity.

Becker, J. Christiaan. 1982. *Paul's Apocalyptic Gospel: The Coming Triumph of God.* Philadelphia: Fortress.

————. 1990. *The Triumph of God: The Essence of Paul's Thought.* Minneapolis, Fortress.

Bell, Catherine M. 1992. *Ritual Theory, Ritual Practice.* New York: Oxford University Press.

————. 1997. *Ritual: Perspectives and Dimensions.* New York: Oxford University Press.

Betz, Hans Dieter, and Margaret Mitchell. 1992. "1 Corinthians." In *ABD* 1:1139–48.

Blasi, Anthony et al., editors. 2002. *Handbook of Early Christianity: Social Science Approaches.* Walnut Creek, CA: AltaMira.

Boer, Roland, and Gerald O. West, editors. 2001. *The Vanishing Mediator? The Presence/Absence of the Bible in Postcolonialism.* Semeia 88. Atlanta: Society of Biblical Literature.

Booth, Wayne C. 1979. "Metaphor as Rhetoric: The Problem of Evaluation." In *On Metaphor*, edited by Sheldon Sacks, 47–70. Chicago: University of Chicago Press.

Borg, Marcus J. 2006. *Jesus: Uncovering the Life, Teachings, and Relevance of a Religious Revolutionary.* San Francisco: HarperSanFrancisco.

Bolle, Kees W. 1968. *The Freedom of Man in Myth.* Nashville: Vanderbilt University Press.

Boyarin, Daniel. 1994. *A Radical Jew: Paul and the Politics of Identity.* Contraversions 1. Berkeley: University of California Press.

Brenner, Athalya, and Jan Willem van Henten, editors. 1999. *Food and Drink in the Biblical Worlds.* Special issue. *Semeia* 86.

Brown, Peter. 2008. *The Body and Society: Men, Women, and Sexual Renunciation in Early Christianity.* Twentieth anniversary ed. Classics in Religion. New York: Columbia University Press.

Butler, Christopher. 2002. *Postmodernism: A Very Short Introduction.* Very Short Introductions. Oxford: Oxford University Press.

Capes, Reeves et al. 2007. *Rediscovering Paul: An Introduction to His World, Letters and Theology.* Downers Grove, IL: IVP Academic.

Carter, Warren. 1994. *Households and Discipleship: A Study of Matthew 19–20.* JSNTS Series 103. Sheffield: JSOT Press.

————. 2001. *Matthew and Empire: Initial Explorations.* Harrisburg, PA: Trinity.

————. 2002. "Vulnerable Power: The Roman Empire Challenged by the Early Christians." In *Handbook of Early Christianity: Social Science Approaches*, edited by Anthony J. Blasi et al., 453–88. Walnut Creek, CA: AltaMira.

————. 2005. "Matthew's People." In *Christian Origins*, edited by Richard A. Horsley, 138–61. People's History of Christianity 1. Minneapolis: Fortress.

Castelli, Elizabeth A. 1991. *Imitating Paul: A Discourse of Power.* Literary Currents in Biblical Interpretation. Louisville: Westminster John Knox.

————. 2001. "Les Belles Infidèles/Fidelity or Feminism? The Meanings of Feminist Biblical Translations." In *Searching the Scriptures: A Feminist Introduction*, edited by Elisabeth Schüssler Fiorenza, 189–204. New York: Crossroad.

Chancey, Mark A. 2002. *The Myth of a Gentile Galilee.* SNTSMS 118. Cambridge: Cambridge University Press.

Chow, John K. 1997. "Patronage in Roman Corinth." In *Paul and Empire: Religion and Power in Roman Imperial Society,* edited by Richard A. Horsley, 104–25. Harrisburg, PA: Trinity.

Collins, Raymond F. 2008. *The Power of Images in Paul.* Collegeville, MN: Liturgical.

Conway, Colleen M. 2003. "Behold the Man! Masculine Christology and the Fourth Gospel." In *New Testament Masculinities,* edited by Stephen D. Moore and Janice Capel Anderson, 163–80. Semeia Studies 45. Atlanta: Society of Biblical Literature.

———. 2008. *Behold the Man: Jesus and Greco-Roman Masculinity.* New York: Oxford.

Corley, Kathleen E. 1993a. "Jesus' Table Practice: Dining with 'Tax Collectors and Prostitutes' Including Women." In *Society of Biblical Literature 1993 Seminar Papers,* edited by Eugene H. Lovering. 444–59. Atlanta: Scholars.

———. 1993b. *Private Women, Public Meals: Social Conflict and Women in the Synoptic Tradition.* Peabody, MA: Hendrickson.

———. 1996. "Feminist Myths of Christian Origins." In *Reimagining Christian Origins: A Colloquium Honoring Burton L. Mack,* edited by Elizabeth A Castelli and Hal Taussig, 51–67. Valley Forge, PA: Trinity.

———. 2002. *Women and the Historical Jesus: Feminist Myths of Christian Origins.* Santa Rosa, CA: Polebridge, 2002.

Craffert, Pieter F. 2007. *The Life of a Galilean Shaman: Jesus of Nazareth in Anthropological-Historical Perspective.* Matrix: The Bible in Mediterranean Context 3. Eugene, OR: Cascade Books.

Cromhout, Markus. 2007. *Jesus and Identity: Reconstructing Judean Ethnicity in Q.* Matrix: The Bible in Mediterranean Context 2. Eugene, OR: Cascade Books.

Crook, Zeba. 2009. "Honor, Shame, and Social Status Revisited." *JBL* 128:591–611.

Crossan, John Dominic. 1991. *The Historical Jesus: The Life of a Mediterranean Jewish Peasant.* San Francisco: HarperSanFrancisco.

———. 1998. *The Birth of Christianity: Discovering What Happened Immediately after the Execution of Jesus.* San Francisco: HarperSanFrancisco, 1998.

———. 2007. *God and Empire: Jesus against Rome, Then and Now.* San Francisco: HarperSanFrancisco.

Crossan, John Dominic, and Jonathan L. Reed. 2004. *In Search of Paul: How Jesus's Apostle Opposed Rome's Empire with God's Kingdom.* New York: HarperSanFrancisco.

Crossley, James G. 2006. *Why Christianity Happened: A Sociohistorical Account of Christian Origins (26–50 CE).* Louisville: Westminster John Knox.

Dahl, Nils Alstrup. 1977. *Studies in Paul: Theology for the Early Christian Mission.* Minneapolis: Augsburg.

De Boer, M. C. 2003. "Paul and Apocalyptic Eschatology." In *The Continuum History of Apocalypticism,* edited by Bernard McGinn et al., 139–66. New York: Continuum.

Deming, Will. 2004. *Paul on Marriage and Celibacy: The Hellenistic Background of 1 Corinthians 7.* 2nd ed. Grand Rapids: Eerdmans, 2004.

Deutsch, Celia. 2001. "Jesus as Wisdom: A Feminist Reading of Matthew's Wisdom Christology." In *A Feminist Companion to Matthew,* edited by Amy-Jill Levine, 88–113. Sheffield: Sheffield Academic.

Dickie, Matthew W. 2003. *Magic and Magicians in the Greco-Roman World.* London: Routledge.

Donaldson, Laura E. *Postcolonialism and Scriptural Reading.* Semeia 75. Atlanta: Scholars, 1996.

Douglas, Mary. 1966. *Purity and Danger: An Analysis of Concepts of Pollution and Taboo.* London: Routledge & Kegan Paul.

Downing, F. Gerald. 1998. *Cynics, Paul, and the Pauline Churches.* London: Routledge, 1998.

Downs, David J. 2009. "Is God Paul's Patron? The Economy of Patronage in Pauline Theology." In *Engaging Economics: New Testament Scenarios and Early Christian Reception,* edited by Bruce W. Longenecker and Kelly D. Liebengood, 129–56. Grand Rapids: Eerdmans.

Dube, Musa W. 2000. *Postcolonial Feminist Interpretation of the Bible.* St. Louis: Chalice.

———. 2006. "Reading for Decolonization (John 4.1–42)." In *Voices from the Margin: Interpreting the Bible in the Third World,* edited by R. S. Sugirtharajah, 297–318. Rev. and expanded 3rd ed. Maryknoll, NY: Orbis.

Duling, Dennis C. 1995. "The Matthean Brotherhood and Marginal Scribal Leadership." In *Modelling Early Christianity: Social-Scientific Studies of the New Testament in Its Context,* edited by Philip F. Esler, 159–82. London: Routledge.

———. 2003. *The New Testament: History, Literature, and Social Context.* 4th ed. Belmont, CA: Thompson/Wadsworth.

D'Angelo, Mary Rose. 1992. "'Abba' and 'Father': Imperial Theology and the Jesus Traditions." *JBL* 111:624–35.

Dunn, James D. G. 2005. *A New Perspective on Jesus: What the Quest for the Historical Jesus Missed.* Grand Rapids: Baker Academic.

Ehrensperger, Kathy. 2004. *That We May Be Mutually Encouraged: Feminism and the New Perspective in Pauline Studies.* New York: T. & T. Clark.

———. 2007. *Paul and the Dynamics of Power: Communication and Interaction in the Early Christ-Movement.* Library of New Testament Studies 325. London: T. & T. Clark.

Ehrman, Bart D. 2003. *Lost Christianities: The Battles for Scripture and the Faiths We Never Knew.* Oxford: Oxford University Press.

Eisenbaum, Pamela. 2004. "A Remedy for Having Been Born of Woman: Jesus, Gentiles, and Genealogy in Romans." *JBL* 123:681–92.

Elliott, John H. 1986. "More on Method and Models." *Semeia* 35:1–34.

———. 1991. "Temple versus Household in Luke-Acts: A Contrast in Social Institutions." In *The Social World of Luke-Acts,* edited by Jerome H. Neyrey, 211–40. Peabody: Hendrickson.

———. 1993. *What Is Social-Scientific Criticism?* Guides to Biblical Scholarship. Minneapolis: Fortress.

———. 1995. "The Jewish Messianic Movement: From Faction to Sect." In *Modelling Early Christianity: Social-Scientific Studies of the New Testament in Its Context,* edited by Philip R. Esler, 75–95. London: Routledge.

———. 2007. *Conflict, Community, and Honor: 1 Peter in Social-Scientific Perspective.* Cascade Companions. Eugene, OR: Cascade Books.

Elliott, Neil. 1997. "Romans 13:1–7 in the Context of Imperial Propaganda." In *Paul and Empire: Religion and Power in Roman Imperial Society,* edited by Richard A. Horsley, 184–204. Harrisburg, PA: Trinity.

———. 2008. *The Arrogance of Nations: Reading Romans in the Shadow of Empire.* Paul in Critical Contexts. Minneapolis: Fortress.

Ellwood, Robert S., and Barbara A. McGraw. 2009. *Many Peoples, Many Faiths: Women and Men in the World Religions*. Upper Saddle River, NJ: Prentice Hall.

Esler, Philip F. 1995a. "God's Honour and Rome's Triumph: Responses to the Fall of Jerusalem in 70 CE in Three Jewish Apocalypses." In *Modelling Early Christianity: Social-Scientific Studies of the New Testament in Its Context*, edited by Philip F. Esler, 239–58. London: Routledge.

———, editor. 1995b. *Modelling Early Christianity: Social-Scientific Studies of the New Testament in Its Context*. London: Routledge.

———. 2003. *Conflict and Identity in Romans: The Social Setting of Paul's Letter*. Minneapolis: Fortress.

Finger, Reta Halteman. 2007. *Of Widows and Meals: Communal Meals in the Book of Acts*. Grand Rapids: Eerdmans.

Fiore, Benjamin. 2003. "Paul, Exemplification, and Imitation." In *Paul in the Greco-Roman World: A Handbook*, edited by J. Paul Sampley, 228–57. Harrisburg, PA: Trinity.

Fitzgerald, John T. 2003. "Paul and Friendship" In *Paul in the Greco-Roman World: A Handbook*, edited by J. Paul Sampley, 319–43. Harrisburg, PA: Trinity.

Forbes, Christopher. 2003. "Paul and Rhetorical Comparison." In *Paul in the Greco-Roman World: A Handbook*, edited by J. Paul Sampley, 134–71. Harrisburg, PA: Trinity.

Foucault, Michel. 1977. *Language, Counter-Memory, Practice: Selected Essays and Interviews*. Edited by Donald Bouchard. Translated by Donald Bouchard and Sherry Simon. Ithaca: Cornell University Press.

———. 1980. *Power/Knowledge: Selected Interviews and Other Writings, 1972–1977*. Edited by Colin Gordon. New York: Pantheon.

———. 1994. *Power*. Edited by James D. Faubion. The Essential Works of Michel Foucault 3. New York: New Press, 2000.

Fowler, Robert. 2008. "Reader-Response Criticism: Figuring Mark's Reader." In *Mark & Method: New Approaches in Biblical Studies*, edited by Janice Capel Anderson and Stephen D. Moore, 59–94. 2nd ed. Minneapolis: Fortress.

Freyne, Sean. 1995. "Herodian Economics in Galilee: Searching for a Suitable Model." In *Modelling Early Christianity: Social-Scientific Studies of the New Testament in Its Context*, edited by Philip F. Esler, 23–46. London: Routledge.

———. 2004. *Jesus, a Jewish Galilean: A New Reading of the Jesus-Story*. London: T. & T. Clark.

Fuchs, Esther. 2003. "Men in Biblical Feminist Scholarship." *JFSR* 19:106–13.

Gans, Herbert. 2004. "Deconstructing the Underclass." In *Race, Class, and Gender in the United States: An Integrated Study*, edited by Paula S. Rothenberg, 103–9. 6th ed. New York: Worth.

Garnsey, Peter, and Richard Saller. 1997. "Patronal Power Relations." In *Paul and Empire: Religion and Power in Roman Imperial Society*, edited by Richard A. Horsley, 96–103. Harrisburg, PA: Trinity.

Gehring, Roger W. 2004. *House Church and Mission: The Importance of Household Structures in Early Christianity*. Peabody, MA: Hendrickson.

Gennep, Arnold van. 1961. *The Rites of Passage*. Translated by Monika B. Vizedom and Gabrielle L. Caffee. 1st Phoenix ed. Chicago: University of Chicago Press.

Georgi, Dieter. 1964. *Die Gegner des Paulus im 2. Korintherbrief: Studien zur religiösen Propaganda in der Spätantike*. WMANT 11. Neukirchen-Vluyn: Neukirchener.

————. 1986. *The Opponents of Paul in Second Corinthians: A Study of Religious Propaganda in Late Antiquity*. Philadelphia: Fortress, 1964.

————. 1992. *Remembering the Poor: The History of Paul's Collection for Jerusalem*. Nashville: Abingdon.

Giddens, Anthony. 1979. *Central Problems in Social Theory: Action, Structure and Contradiction in Social Analysis*. Berkeley: University of California Press.

Glad, Clarence E. 2003. "Paul and Adaptability." In *Paul in the Greco-Roman World: A Handbook*, edited by J. Paul Sampley, 17–41. Harrisburg, PA: Trinity.

Grubbs, Judith Evans. 2002. *Women and the Law in the Roman Empire: A Sourcebook on Marriage, Divorce and Widowhood*. London: Routledge.

Guggenheim, Scott Evan, and Robert P. Weller. 1989. "Introduction: Moral Economy, Capitalism, and State Power in Rural Protest." In *Power and Protest in the Countryside: Studies of Rural Unrest in Asia, Europe, and Latin America*, edited by Robert P. Weller and Scott E. Guggenheim, 3–12. Duke Press Policy Studies. Durham: Duke University Press.

Gutting, Gary. 2005. *Foucault: A Very Short Introduction*. Very Short Introductions 122. Oxford: Oxford University Press.

Hamerton-Kelly, Robert. 1985. "A Girardian Interpretation of Paul: Rivalry, Mimesis and Victimage in the Corinthian Correspondence." *Semeia* 33:65–82.

Hanks, Thomas D. 1992. "Poor, Poverty." In *ABD* 5: 404–24.

Hanson, K. C. 1988. "Servant/Slave (ANE and OT)." In *International Standard Bible Encyclopedia*, edited by Geoffrey W. Bromiley, vol. 4, 419–21. Grand Rapids: Eerdmans, 1988.

————. 1990. "The Herodians and Mediterranean Kingship, Part 3: Economics." *BTB* 20:10–21.

————. 1994. "'How Honorable!' 'How Shameful!' A Cultural Analysis of Matthew's Makarisms and Reproaches." *Semeia* 68:81–111.

————. 1997. "The Galilean Fishing Economy and the Jesus Tradition." *BTB* 27:99–111.

————. 2002. "Jesus and the Social Bandits." In *The Social Setting of Jesus and the Gospels*, edited by Wolfgang Stegemann et al., 283–300. Minneapolis: Fortress.

Hanson, K. C., and Douglas E. Oakman. 2008. *Palestine in the Time of Jesus: Social Structures and Social Conflicts*. 2nd ed. Minneapolis: Fortress.

Harland, Philip A. 2002. "The Economy of First-Century Palestine: State of the Scholarly Discussion." In *Handbook of Early Christianity: Social Science Approaches*, edited by Anthony J. Blaisi et al., 511–53. Walnut Creek, CA: AltaMira.

Harrill, J. Albert. 2003. "Paul and Slavery." In *Paul in the Greco-Roman World: A Handbook*, edited by J. Paul Sampley, 134–71. Harrisburg, PA: Trinity.

Hays, Richard B. 2005. *The Conversion of the Imagination: Paul as Interpreter of Israel's Scripture*. Grand Rapids: Eerdmans.

————. 1997. *First Corinthians*. Interpretation. Louisville: Westminster John Knox.

Hellerman, Joseph. 2009. "Brothers and Friends in Philippi: Family Honor in the Roman World and in Paul's Letter to the Philippians." *BTB* 39:15–25.

Herzog, William R. II. 2005. *Prophet and Teacher: Introduction to the Historical Jesus*. Louisville: Westminster John Knox.

Hock, Ronald F. 2003. "Paul and Greco-Roman Education." In *Paul in the Greco-Roman World: A Handbook*, edited by J. Paul Sampley, 198–227. Harrisburg, PA: Trinity.

Hollenback, Jess Byron. 1996. *Mysticism: Experience, Response, and Empowerment.* Hermeneutics, Studies in the History of Religions. University Park: Pennsylvania State University Press.

Horrell, David G. 1995. "The Development of Theological Ideology in Pauline Christianity: A Structuration Theory Perspective." In *Modelling Early Christianity: Social-Scientific Studies of the New Testament in Its Context*, edited by Philip F. Esler, 224–38. London: Routledge.

Horsley, Richard A. 1987. *Jesus and the Spiral of Violence: Popular Jewish Resistance in Roman Palestine.* San Francisco: Harper & Row, 1987.

———. 1995. *Galilee, History, Politics, People.* Valley Forge, PA: Trinity.

———. 1996. *Archaeology, History, and Society in Galilee: The Social Context of Jesus and the Rabbis.* Valley Forge, PA: Trinity.

———. 1997. "Corinthians: A Case Study of Paul's Assembly as an Alternative Society." In *Paul and Empire: Religion and Power in Roman Imperial Society*, edited by Richard A. Horsley, 242–52. Harrisburg, PA: Trinity.

———. 2000. "Rhetoric and Empire—and 1 Corinthians." In *Paul and Politics: Ekklesia, Israel, Imperium, Interpretation*, edited by Richard A. Horsley, 72–102. Harrisburg, PA: Trinity.

———. 2003a. *Jesus and Empire: The Kingdom of God and the New World Disorder.* Minneapolis: Fortress.

———. 2003b. *Religion and Empire: People, Power, and the Life of the Spirit.* Minneapolis: Fortress.

———. 2003c. "Subverting Disciplines: The Possibilities and Limitations of Postcolonial Theory for New Testament Studies." In *Toward a New Heaven and a New Earth: Essays in Honor of Elisabeth Schüssler Fiorenza*, edited by Fernando F. Segovia, 90–105. Maryknoll, NY: Orbis.

———. 2005. "Jesus Movements and the Renewal of Israel." In *Christian Origins*, edited by Richard A. Horsley et al., 23–46. A People's History of Christianity 1. Minneapolis: Fortress, 2005.

———. 2006. "A Prophet Like Moses and Elijah: Popular Memory and Cultural Patterns in Mark." In *Performing the Gospel: Orality, Memory, and Mark*, edited by Richard A. Horsley et al., 166–90. Minneapolis: Fortress.

———. 2008a. *Jesus in Context: Power, People & Performance.* Minneapolis: Fortress.

———. 2008b. *Wisdom and Spiritual Transcendence at Corinth: Studies in First Corinthians.* Eugene, OR: Cascade Books.

Horsley, Richard A., with Jonathan A. Draper. 1999. *Whoever Hears You Hears Me: Prophets, Performance, and Tradition in Q.* Harrisburg, PA: Trinity.

Horsley, Richard A., with John S. Hanson. 1985. *Bandits, Prophets, and Messiahs: Popular Movements at the Time of Jesus.* Minneapolis: Winston.

Ingraffia, Brian D. 1995. *Postmodern Theory and Biblical Theology: Vanquishing God's Shadow.* Cambridge: Cambridge University Press.

Jewett, Robert. 1979. *Jesus against the Rapture: Seven Unexpected Prophecies.* Philadelphia: Westminster.

———. 1997. "Honor and Shame in the Argument of Romans." In *Putting Body & Soul Together: Essays in Honor of Robin Scroggs*, edited by Virginia Wiles et al., 258–76. Valley Forge, PA: Trinity.

———. 2003. "Paul, Shame, and Honor." In *Paul in the Greco-Roman World*, edited by J. Paul Sampley, 551–74. Harrisburg, PA: Trinity.

Johnson, Mark. 1987. *The Body in the Mind: The Bodily Basis of Meaning, Imagination, and Reason*. Chicago: University of Chicago Press.

Joubert, Stephan J. 1995. "Managing the Household: Paul as Paterfamilias of the Christian Household Group in Corinth." In *Modelling Early Christianity: Social-Scientific Studies of the New Testament in Its Context*, edited by Philip F. Esler, 213–23. London: Routledge.

Käsemann, Ernst. 1964. *Essays on New Testament Themes*. Translated by W. J. Montague. Studies in Biblical Theology 41. Naperville, IL: Allenson, 1964.

———. 1980. *Commentary on Romans*. Translated and edited by G.W. Bromiley Grand Rapids: Eerdmans.

Keener, Craig S. 1992. *Paul, Women & Wives: Marriage and Women's Ministry in the Letters of Paul*. Peabody, MA: Hendrickson.

Kessler, Gwynn. 2005. "Let's Cross That Body When We Get to It: Gender and Ethnicity in Rabbinic Literature." *JAAR* 73:361–93.

Kim, Yung Suk. 2008. *Christ's Body in Corinth: The Politics of a Metaphor*. Paul in Critical Contexts. Minneapolis: Fortress.

King, Karen L. 2003. *What Is Gnosticism?* Cambridge, MA: Belknap.

Kittredge, Cynthia Briggs. 1998. *Community and Authority: The Rhetoric of Obedience in the Pauline Tradition*. HTS 45. Harrisburg, PA: Trinity.

———. 2000. "Corinthian Women Prophets and Paul's Argumentation in 1 Corinthians." In *Paul and Politics: Ekklesia, Israel, Imperium, Interpretation*, edited by Richard A. Horsley, 103–9. Harrisburg, PA: Trinity.

Klinghardt, Matthias. 1996. *Gemeinschaftsmahl und Mahlgemeinschaft: Soziologie und Liturgie frühchristlicher Mahlfeiern*. Texte und Arbeiten zum neutestamentlichen Zeitalter 13. Tübingen: Francke.

Kloppenborg Verbin, John S. 2000. *Excavating Q: The History and Setting of the Sayings Gospel*. Minneapolis: Fortress.

Koester, Helmut. 2007. *Paul & His World: Interpreting the New Testament in Its Context*. Minneapolis: Fortress.

Kövecses, Zoltán. 2002. *Metaphor: A Practical Introduction*. Oxford: Oxford University Press.

Kuefler, Mathew. 2001. *The Manly Eunuch: Masculinity, Gender Ambiguity, and Christian Ideology in Late Antiquity*. Chicago Series on Sexuality, History, and Society. Chicago: University of Chicago Press.

Kwok, Pui-lan. "Engendering Christ." In *Toward a New Heaven and a New Earth: Essays in Honor of Elisabeth Schüssler Fiorenza*, edited by Fernando F. Segovia, 300–313. Maryknoll, NY: Orbis, 2003.

———. 2005. *Postcolonial Imagination & Feminist Theology*. Louisville: Westminster John Knox.

———. 2009. "Elisabeth Schüssler Fiorenza and Postcolonial Studies." *JFSR* 25:191–96.

Lakoff, Goerge, and Mark Johnson. 1981. *Metaphors We Live By*. Chicago: University of Chicago Press.

Lampe, Peter. 2003a. *From Paul to Valentinus: Christians at Rome in the First Two Centuries*. Translated by Michael Steinhauser. Edited by Marshall Johnson. Minneapolis: Fortress.

———. 2003b. "Paul, Patrons, and Clients." In *Paul in the Greco-Roman World: A Handbook*, edited by J. Paul Sampley, 488–523. Harrisburg, PA: Trinity.

Lenski, Gerhard E. 1984. *Power and Privilege: A Theory of Social Stratification*. McGraw-Hill Series in Sociology. Chapel Hill: University of North Carolina Press.

Levine, Amy-Jill. 1988. *The Social and Ethnic Dimensions of Matthean Salvation History*. SBEC 14. Lewiston, NY: Mellen, 1988.

———. 1999. "Women in the Q Communities and Traditions." In *Women & Christian Origins*, edited by Ross Shepard Kraemer and Mary Rose D'Angelo, 150–70. New York: Oxford University Press.

———. 2006. *The Misunderstood Jew: The Church and the Scandal of the Jewish Jesus*. San Francisco: HarperSanFrancisco, 2006.

Levine, Amy-Jill, with Marianne Blickenstaff. 2004. *A Feminist Companion to Paul*. Cleveland: Pilgrim.

LiDonnici, Lynn R. 1999. "Women's Religions and Religious Lives in the Greco-Roman City." In *Women & Christian Origins*, edited by Ross Shepard Kraemer and Mary Rose D'Angelo, 80–149. New York: Oxford University Press.

Liew, Tat-Siong Benny. 2008. "Postcolonial Criticism: Echoes of a Subaltern's Contribution and Exclusion." In *Mark & Method: New Approaches in Biblical Studies*, edited by Janice Capel Andersen and Stephen D. Moore, 211–32. 2nd ed. Philadelphia: Fortress.

Lincoln, Bruce. 2006. *Holy Terrors: Thinking about Religion after September 11*. 2nd ed. Chicago: University of Chicago Press.

Loader, William. 2005. *Sexuality and the Jesus Tradition*. Grand Rapids: Eerdmans.

Lukes, Steven. 1986. *Power*. Readings in Social and Political Theory. Washington Square, NY: New York University Press.

MacDonald, Dennis R. 1987. *There Is No Male and Female: The Fate of a Dominical Saying in Paul and Gnosticism*. Harvard Dissertations in Religion 20. Philadelphia: Fortress.

———. 2000. *The Homeric Epics and the Gospel of Mark*. New Haven: Yale University Press.

MacDonald, Margaret Y. 2004. "Virgins, Widows, and Wives: The Women of I Corinthians 7." In *A Feminist Companion to Paul*, edited by Amy-Jill Levine, 148–68. Cleveland: Pilgrim.

Mack, Burton L. 1993. *The Lost Gospel: The Book of Q & Christian Origins*. San Francisco: HarperSanFrancisco.

———. 2001. *The Christian Myth: Origins, Logic, and Legacy*. New York: Continuum.

Malina, Bruce J. 1982. "The Social Sciences and Biblical Interpretation." *Interpretation* 37:229–42.

———. 1986a. *Christian Origins and Cultural Anthropology: Practical Models for Biblical Interpretation*. Atlanta: John Knox.

———. 1986b. "Normative Dissonance and Christian Origins." *Semeia* 35:35–59.

———. 1993. *Windows on the World of Jesus: Time Travels to Ancient Judea*. Louisville: Westminster John Knox.

———. 1995. "Early Christian Groups: Using Small Group Formation Theory to Explain Christian Organizations." In *Modelling Early Christianity: Social Scientific Studies of the New Testament in Its Context*, edited by Philip F. Esler, 96–113. London: Routledge.

———. 2001. *The New Testament World: Insights from Cultural Anthropology.* 3rd ed. Louisville: Westminster John Knox.

———. 2002. "Social-Scientific Methods in Historical Jesus Research." In *The Social Setting of Jesus and the Gospels,* edited by Wolfgang Stegemann et al. 3–26. Minneapolis: Fortress.

Malina, Bruce J., and Jerome H. Neyrey. 1988. *Calling Jesus Names: The Social Value of Labels in Matthew.* Foundations & Facets. Social Facets. Sonoma, CA: Polebridge.

———. 1991. "Conflict in Luke-Acts: Labelling and Deviance Theory." In *The Social World of Luke-Acts,* edited by Jerome H. Neyrey, 97–124. Peabody, MA: Hendrickson.

———. 1996. *Portraits of Paul: An Archaeology of Ancient Personality.* Louisville: Westminster John Knox.

Malina, Bruce J., and John J. Pilch. 2006. *Social-Science Commentary on the Letters of Paul.* Minneapolis: Fortress.

Malina, Bruce J., and Richard L. Rohrbaugh. 1992. *Social-Science Commentary on the Synoptic Gospels.* Minneapolis: Fortress.

Marchal, Joseph A. 2008. *The Politics of Heaven: Women, Gender, and Empire in the Study of Paul.* Paul in Critical Contexts. Minneapolis: Fortress.

Martin, Dale B. 1990. *Slavery as Salvation: The Metaphor of Slavery in Pauline Christianity.* New Haven: Yale University Press.

McClintock, Anne. 1992. "The Angel of Progress: Pitfalls of the Term 'Post-Colonialism.'" *Social Text* 31/32:84–98.

McKnight, Edgar V. 1988. *Postmodern Use of the Bible: The Emergence of Reader-Oriented Criticism.* Nashville: Abingdon.

Meeks, Wayne A. 1982. "The Social Context of Pauline Theology." *Interpretation* 3:266–77.

———. 1983. *The First Urban Christians: The Social World of the Apostle Paul.* New Haven: Yale University Press.

Meier, John P. 1991. *A Marginal Jew: Rethinking the Historical Jesus,* Vol. 1, *The Roots of the Problem and the Person.* Anchor Bible Reference Library. New York: Doubleday.

Moore, Stephen D., and Fernando F. Segovia, editors. 2005. *Postcolonial Biblical Criticism: Interdisciplinary Intersections.* The Bible and Postcolonialism. London: T. & T. Clark.

Moxnes, Havlor. 1988. *The Economy of the Kingdom: Social Conflict and in Economic Relations in Luke's Gospel.* Reprinted, Eugene, OR: Wipf & Stock, 2004.

———. 1991. "Patron-Client Relations and the New Community in Luke-Acts." In *The Social World of Luke-Acts: Models for Interpretation,* edited by Jerome H. Neyrey, 241–68. Peabody, MA: Hendrickson.

———, editor. 1997. *Constructing Early Christian Families: Family as Social Reality and Metaphor.* London: Routledge.

———. 2003. *Putting Jesus in His Place: A Radical Vision of Household and Kingdom.* Louisville: Westminster John Knox.

Murphy-O'Connor, Jerome. 1992. "Corinth." In *ABD* 1:1134–39.

Nanos, Mark D. 2000. "The Inter- and Intra-Jewish Political Context of Paul's Letter to the Galatians." *Paul and Politics: Ekklesia, Israel, Imperium, Interpretation,* edited by Richard A. Horsley, 146–59. Harrisburg, PA: Trinity.

———. 2002a. *The Galatians Debate: Contemporary Issues in Rhetorical and Historical Interpretation.* Peabody, MA: Hendrickson.

———. 2002b. *The Irony of Galatians: Paul's Letter in First-Century Context*. Minneapolis: Fortress.

Neufeld, Dietmar, editor. 2008. *The Social Sciences and Biblical Translation*. SBLSS 41. Atlanta: Society of Biblical Literature.

Neyrey, Jerome H. 1986. "Body Language in 1 Corinthians: The Use of Anthropological Models for Understanding Paul and His Opponents." *Semeia* 35:129–70.

———. 1991. "Ceremonies in Luke-Acts: The Case of Meals and Table-Fellowship." In *The Social World of Luke-Acts: Models for Interpretation*, edited by Jerome H. Neyrey, 361–88. Peabody, MA: Hendrickson.

———. 2007. "Encomium versus Vituperation: Contrasting Portraits of Jesus in the Fourth Gospel." *JBL* 126:529–77.

———. 1995. "Loss of Wealth, Loss of Family and Loss of Honour." In *Modelling Early Christianity: Social-Scientific Studies of the New Testament in Its Context*, edited by Philip F. Esler, 139–58. New York: Routledge.

———. 1996. "Meals, Food, and Table Fellowship." In *The Social Sciences and New Testament Interpretation*, edited by Richard L. Rohrbaugh, 159–82. Peabody, MA: Hendrickson.

———, editor. 1991. *The Social World of Luke-Acts: Models for Interpretation*. Peabody, MA: Hendrickson.

Oakman, Douglas E. 1985. "Jesus and Agrarian Palestine: The Factor of Debt." In *SBL 1985 Seminar Papers*, 57–73. Chico, CA: Scholars.

———. 1986. *Jesus and the Economic Questions of His Day*. SBEC 8. Lewiston, NY: Mellen.

———. 1991. "The Ancient Economy in the Bible: *BTB* Readers Guide." *BTB* 21:34–39.

———. 1992. "Was Jesus a Peasant? Implications for Reading the Samaritan Story (Luke 10:30–35)." *BTB* 20:117–25.

———. 1996. "The Ancient Economy." In *The Social Sciences and New Testament Interpretation*, edited by Richard L. Rohrbaugh, 126–43. Peabody, MA: Hendrickson.

———. 2002. "Money in the Moral Universe of the New Testament." In *The Social Setting of Jesus and the Gospels,* edited by Wolfgang Stegemann et al., 335–48. Minneapolis: Fortress.

———. 2008. *Jesus and the Peasants*. Matrix: The Bible in Mediterranean Context 4. Eugene, OR: Cascade Books.

Oakes, Peter. 2009. "Methodological Issues in Using Economic Evidence in Interpretation of Early Christian Text." In *Engaging Economics: New Testament Scenarios and Early Christian Reception,* edited by Bruce W. Longenecker and Kelly D. Liebengood, 9–34. Grand Rapids: Eerdmans.

Økland, Jorunn. 2004. *Women in Their Place: Paul and the Corinthian Discourse of Gender and Sanctuary Space*. JSNTSup 269. London: T. & T. Clark.

Orr, William F., and James A. Walther. 1977. *First Corinthians: A New Translation*. AB 32. Garden City, NY: Doubleday.

Ortony, Andrew, editor. 1998. *Metaphor and Thought*. 2nd ed. Cambridge: Cambridge University Press.

Osiek, Carolyn, and David L. Balch. 1997. *Families in the New Testament World: Households and House Churches*. The Family, Religion, and Culture. Louisville: Westminster John Knox.

Osiek, Carolyn, and Margaret Y. MacDonald, with Janet H. Tulloch. 2005. *A Woman's Place: Houses Churches in Earliest Christianity*. Minneapolis: Fortress.

Petersen, Norman R. 1985. *Rediscovering Paul: Philemon and the Sociology of Paul's Narrative World*. Reprinted, Eugene, OR: Wipf & Stock, 2008.

Pickett, Ray. 2005. "Conflicts at Corinth." In *Christian Origins,* edited by Richard A. Horsley, 113–37. A People's History of Christianity 1. Minneapolis: Fortress.

Pilch, John J. 2002. "Altered States of Consciousness in the Synoptics." In *The Social Setting of Jesus and the Gospels,* edited by Wolfgang Stegemann et al., 103–16. Minneapolis: Fortress.

Pilch, John J., and Bruce J. Malina, editors. 2000. *Handbook of Biblical Social Values*. Peabody, MA: Hendrickson.

Polaski, Sandra Hack. 1999. *Paul and the Discourse of Power*. Biblical Seminar 62. Sheffield: Sheffield Academic.

Price, S. R. F. 1997. "Rituals and Power." In *Paul and Empire: Religion and Power in Roman Imperial Society*, edited by Richard A. Horsley, 47–71. Harrisburg, PA: Trinity.

———. 2002. *Rituals and Power: The Roman Imperial Cult in Asia Minor*. Cambridge: Cambridge University Press.

Rabinow, Paul, editor. 1984. *The Foucault Reader*. New York: Pantheon.

Reed, Jonathan L. 2000. *Archaeology and the Galilean Jesus: A Re-Examination of the Evidence*. Harrisburg, PA: Trinity.

Reese, James M. 1998. "Obedience." In *Handbook of Biblical Social Values*, edited by John J. Pilch and Bruce J. Malina, 142–43. Peabody, MA: Hendrickson.

Richardson, Peter, and Douglas Edwards. 2002. "Jesus and Palestinian Social Protest: Archaeological and Literary Perspectives." In *Handbook of Early Christianity: Social Science Approaches,* edited by Anthony J. Blasi et al., 247–66. Walnut Creek, CA: AltaMira.

Roetzel, Calvin J. 2000. "Response: How Anti-Imperial Was the Collection and How Emancipatory Was Paul's Project?" In *Paul and Politics: Ekklesia, Israel, Imperium, Interpretation*, edited by Richard A. Horsley, 227–30. Harrisburg, PA: Trinity.

Rohrbaugh, Richard L., editor. 1996. *The Social Sciences and New Testament Interpretation*. Peabody, MA: Hendrickson.

———. 2007. *The New Testament in Cross-Cultural Perspective*. Matrix: The Bible in Mediterranean Context 1. Eugene, OR: Cascade Books.

Sacon, Kiyoshi K. 1974. "Isaiah 40:1–11: A Rhetorical-Critical Study." In *Rhetorical Criticism: Essays in Honor of James Muilenburg*, edited by Jared J. Jackson and Martin Kessler, 96–116. PittTMS 1. Pittsburgh: Pickwick Publications.

Sahlins, Marshall. 1968. *Tribesmen*. Foundations of Modern Anthropology Series. Englewood Cliffs, NJ: Prentice-Hall.

Said, Edward W. 1985. *Orientalism*. Hammondsworth, UK: Penguin.

Saldarini, Anthony. 2004. "Absent Women in Matthew's Households." In *A Feminist Companion to Matthew,* edited by Amy-Jill Levine, 152–63. Sheffield: Sheffield Academic.

———. 1999. "Asceticism and the Gospel of Matthew." In *Asceticism and the New Testament*, edited by Leif E. Vaage and Vincent L. Wimbush, 11–28. New York: Routledge.

Sampley, J. Paul, editor. 2003. *Paul in the Greco-Roman World: A Handbook*. Harrisburg, PA: Trinity.

Sánchez, David A. 2008. *From Patmos to the Barrio: Subverting Imperial Myths.* Minneapolis: Fortress.

Satlow, Michael L. 2001. *Jewish Marriage in Antiquity.* Princeton: Princeton University Press.

Sawicki, Marianne. 2000. *Crossing Galilee: Architectures of Contact in the Occupied Land of Jesus.* Harrisburg: Trinity.

Schmithals, Walter. 1971. *Gnosticism in Corinth: An Investigation of the Letters to the Corinthians.* Translated by John E. Steely. Nashville: Abingdon.

Schüssler Fiorenza, Elisabeth. 1983. *In Memory of Her: A Feminist Theological Reconstruction of Christian Origins.* New York: Crossroad.

———. 1987. "Rhetorical Situation in I Corinthians." *NTS* 33 386–403.

———. 1992. *But She Said: Feminist Practices of Biblical Interpretation.* Boston: Beacon.

———. 1994. *Jesus: Miriam's Child, Sophia's Prophet.* New York: Continuum.

———. 1995. *Bread Not Stone: The Challenge of Feminist Biblical Interpretation.* 10th anniversary ed. Boston: Beacon.

———. 1999. *Rhetoric and Ethic: The Politics of Biblical Studies.* Minneapolis: Fortress.

———. 2001. *Jesus and the Politics of Interpretation.* New York: Continuum.

———. 2005. "Feminist Studies in Religion and Theology: In-Between Nationalism and Globalization," *JFSR* 21:113–22.

———. 2007. *The Power of the Word: Scripture and the Rhetoric of Empire.* Minneapolis: Fortress.

Scott, Bernard Brandon. 1989. *Hear Then the Parable: A Commentary on the Parables of Jesus.* Minneapolis: Fortress.

Scott, James C. 1976. *The Moral Economy of the Peasant: Rebellion and Subsistence in Southeast Asia.* New Haven: Yale University Press.

———. 1985. *Weapons of the Weak: Everyday Forms of Peasant Resistance.* New Haven: Yale University Press.

———. 1990. *Domination and the Arts of Resistance: Hidden Transcripts.* New Haven: Yale University Press.

Smith, Dennis E. 2003. *From Symposium to Eucharist: The Banquet in the Early Christian World.* Minneapolis: Fortress.

Smith, Jonathan Z. 1987. *To Take Place: Toward Theory in Ritual.* Chicago Studies in the History of Judaism. Chicago: University of Chicago Press.

Spivak, Gayarti Chakravorty. 2009. *Outside in the Teaching Machine.* Routledge Classics. New York: Routledge,

Stark, Rodney, and Roger Finke. 2000. *Acts of Faith: Explaining the Human Side of Religion.* Berkeley: University of California Press.

Stegemann, Ekkehard W., and Wolfgang Stegemann. 1999. *The Jesus Movement: A Social History of Its First Century.* Translated by O. C. Dean Jr. Philadelphia: Fortress.

Stegemann, Wolfgang. 1984. *The Gospel and the Poor.* Translated by Dietlinde Elliott. Minneapolis: Fortress.

Stegemann, Wolfgang, Bruce J. Malina, and Gerd Theissen, editors. 2002. *The Social Setting of Jesus and the Gospels.* Minneapolis: Fortress.

Stendahl, Krister. 1976. *Paul among Jews and Gentiles, and Other Essays.* Philadelphia: Fortress.

Still, Todd D., editor. 2007. *Jesus and Paul Reconnected: Fresh Pathways into an Old Debate.* Grand Rapids: Eerdmans.

Stowers, Stanley K. 1994. *A Rereading of Romans: Justice, Jews, and Gentiles*. New Haven: Yale University Press.

———. 2003. "Paul and Self-Mastery." In *Paul in the Greco-Roman World: A Handbook*, edited by J. Paul Sampley, 524–50. Harrisburg, PA: Trinity.

Strenski, Ivan. 2006. *Thinking about Religion: An Historical Introduction to Theories of Religion*. Malden, MA: Blackwell.

Sugirtharajah, R. S. 1996. "From Orientalist to Post Colonial: Notes on Reading Practices." *Asia Journal of Theology* 10:20–27.

———. 2003. "The End of Biblical Studies?" In *Toward a New Heaven and a New Earth: Essays in Honor of Elisabeth Schüssler Fiorenza*, edited by Fernando F. Segovia, 133–40. Maryknoll, NY: Orbis.

———. 2006a "Postcolonial Biblical Interpretation." In *Voices from the Margin: Interpreting the Bible in the Third World*, edited by R. S. Sugirtharajah, 64–84. Rev. and expanded 3rd ed. Maryknoll, NY: Orbis.

———, editor. 2006b. *Voices from the Margin: Interpreting the Bible in the Third World*. Rev. and expanded 3rd ed. Maryknoll, NY: Orbis.

Talbott, Rick F. 2006. "Imagining the Matthean Eunuch Community: Kyriarchy on the Chopping Block." *JFSR* 22:22–43.

———. 2008. "Nazareth's Rebellious Son: Deviance and Downward Mobility in the Galilean Jesus Movement." *BTB* 38:99–113.

Taubes, Jacob. 2004. *The Political Theology of Paul*. Translated by Dana Hollander. Cultural Memory in the Present. Stanford: Stanford University Press.

Taussig, Hal. 2009. *In the Beginning Was the Meal: Social Experimentation & Early Christian Identity*. Minneapolis: Fortress.

Theissen, Gerd. 1976. "Itinerant Radicalism: The Tradition of Jesus Sayings from the Perspective of the Sociology of Literature." In *The Bible and Liberation: Political and Social Hermeneutics; A Radical Religion Reader*, edited by Norman K. Gottwald and Antoinette Clark Wire, 84–93. Berkeley: Community for Religious Research and Education.

———. 1978. *Sociology of Early Palestinian Christianity*. Translated by John Bowden. Philadelphia: Fortress.

———. 1982. *The Social Setting of Pauline Christianity: Essays on Corinth*, edited and translated by John H. Schütz. Reprinted, Eugene, OR: Wipf & Stock, 2004.

———. 1992. *Social Reality and the Early Christians: Theology, Ethics, and the World of the New Testament*. Translated by Margaret Kohl. Minneapolis: Fortress.

Thomas, Garth. 1984. "Magna Mater and Atis." In *Aufstieg und Niedergang der römischen Welt* II.17.3, 1500–35. Berlin: de Gruyter.

Tolbert, Mary Ann. 2001. "Social, Sociological, and Anthropological Methods." In *Searching the Scriptures*. Vol. 1, *A Feminist Introduction*, edited by Elisabeth Schüssler Fiorenza, 255–71. New York: Crossroad.

Tuckett, Christopher M. 1996. *Q and the History of Early Christianity: Studies on Q*. Peabody, MA: Hendrickson.

Turcotte, Paul-André. 2002. "Major Social Scientific Theories: Origins, Development, and Contributions." In *Handbook of Early Christianity: Social Science Approaches*, edited by Anthony J. Blasi et al., 29–60. Walnut Creek, CA: AltaMira.

Turner, Victor W. 1967. *The Forest of Symbols: Aspects of Ndembu Ritual*. Ithaca: Cornell University Press.

———. 1969. *The Ritual Process: Structure and Anti-Structure.* The Lewis Henry Morgan Lectures 1966. London: Routledge & Kegan Paul.

Valantasis, Richard. 2008. *The Making of Self: Ancient and Modern Asceticism.* Eugene, OR: Cascade Books.

Vermasern, Maarten J. 1977. *Cybele and Attis: The Myth and the Cult.* Translated by A. M. H. Lemmers. London: Thames & Hudson.

Wainwright, Elaine M. 1998. *Shall We Look for Another? A Feminist Rereading of the Matthean Jesus.* Bible and Liberation Series. Maryknoll, NY: Orbis.

Wan, Sze-kar. 2000. "Collection for the Saints as Anticolonial Act: Implications of Paul's Ethnic Reconstruction." In *Paul and Politics: Ekklesia, Israel, Imperium, Interpretation,* edited by Richard A. Horsley, 191–215. Harrisburg, PA: Trinity.

Ward, William A. 1992. "Temples and Sanctuaries." In *ABD* 6:369–72.

Wegner, Judith Romney. 1991. "Philo's Portrayal of Women—Hebraic or Hellenic?" In *"Women Like This": New Perspectives on Jewish Women in the Greco-Roman World,* edited by Amy-Jill Levine, 41–66. Early Judaism and Its Literature 1. Atlanta: Scholars.

Weidmann, Frederick W. 1997. "An (Un)Accomplished Model: Paul and the Rhetorical Strategy of Philippians 3:3–17." In *Putting Body and Soul Together: Essays in Honor of Robin Scroggs,* edited by Virginia Wiles et al., 245–57. Valley Forge, PA: Trinity.

Wendland, Ernst R. *Analyzing the Psalms: With Exercises for Bible Students and Translators.* Dallas: Summer Institute of Linguistics, 1998.

———. 2002. "Aspects of Rhetorical Analysis Applied to New Testament Texts." In *Handbook of Early Christianity: Social Science Approaches,* edited by Anthony J. Blasi et al. 169–96. Walnut Creek, CA: AltaMira.

Wenham, Gordon J., and William E. Heth. 2002. *Jesus and Divorce.* Carlisle, UK: Paternoster.

White, L. Michael. 2003. "Paul and Paterfamilias." In *Paul in the Greco-Roman World: A Handbook,* edited by J. Paul Sampley, 457–87. Harrisburg, PA: Trinity.

Wicker, Kathleen O'Brien. 2001. "Teaching Feminist Biblical Studies in a Postcolonial Context." In *Searching the Scriptures.* Volume 1, *A Feminist Introduction,* edited by Elisabeth Schüssler Fiorenza, 367–80. New York: Crossroad.

Wiley, Tatha. 2005. *Paul and the Gentile Women: Reframing Galatians.* New York: Continuum.

Williams, David J. 1999. *Paul's Metaphors: Their Context and Character.* Peabody, MA: Hendrickson.

Wimbush, Vincent L. 1987. *Paul, The Worldly Ascetic: Response to the World and Self-Understanding according to 1 Corinthians 7.* Macon, GA: Mercer University Press.

Wire, Antoinette Clark. 1990. *The Corinthian Women Prophets: A Reconstruction through Paul's Rhetoric.* Reprinted, Eugene, OR: Wipf & Stock, 2003.

Wise, Michael et al. 1996. *The Dead Sea Scrolls: A New Translation.* San Francisco: HarperSanFrancisco.

Witherington, Ben III. 1995. *Conflict & Community in Corinth: A Socio-Rhetorical Commentary on 1 and 2 Corinthians.* Grand Rapids: Eerdmans.

Worsley, Peter. 1974. *The Trumpet Shall Sound: A Study of "Cargo" Cults in Melanesia.* New York: Schocken.

Wright, N. T. 2005. *Paul: In Fresh Perspective.* Minneapolis: Fortress.

Yarbrough, O. Larry. 2003. "Paul, Marriage, and Divorce." In *Paul in the Greco-Roman World: A Handbook*, edited by J. Paul Sampley, 404–28. Harrisburg: Trinity.

Zaidman, Louise Bruit, and Pauline Schmitt Pantel. 1992. *Religion in the Ancient Greek City*. Translated by Paul Cartledge. Cambridge: Cambridge University Press.

Zanker, Paul. 1997. "The Power of Images." In *Paul and Empire: Religion and Power in Roman Imperial Society*, edited by Richard A. Horsley, 72–86. Harrisburg, PA: Trinity.

Zetterholm, Magnus. 2009. *Approaches to Paul: A Student's Guide to Recent Scholarship*. Minneapolis: Fortress.

# Index of Ancient Sources